MEKONG
DREAMING

MEKONG DREAMING

LIFE AND DEATH ALONG A CHANGING RIVER

ANDREW ALAN JOHNSON

Duke University Press   Durham and London   2020

Designed by Drew Sisk
Typeset in Portrait Text, ITC Century Book, and Univers by
Westchester Publishing Services
Library of Congress Cataloging-in-Publication Data
Names: Johnson, Andrew Alan, author [date].
Title: Mekong dreaming : life and death along a changing river /
    Andrew Alan Johnson.
Description: Durham : Duke University Press, 2020. | Includes
    bibliographical references and index.
Identifiers: LCCN 2019054747 (print) | LCCN 2019054748 (ebook)
ISBN 9781478009771 (hardcover)
ISBN 9781478010821 (paperback)
ISBN 9781478012351 (ebook)
Subjects: LCSH: Economic development projects—Environmental
    aspects—Mekong River Watershed. | Economic development
    projects—Social aspects—Mekong River Watershed. |
    Dams—Environmental aspects—Mekong River Watershed. |
    Dams—Social aspects—Mekong River Watershed. | Ethnology—
    Mekong River Watershed. | Rivers—Religious aspects.
Classification: LCC HC441.Z9 E444 2020 (print) |
    LCC HC441.Z9 (ebook) | DDC 959.4—dc23
LC record available at https://lccn.loc.gov/2019054747
LC ebook record available at https://lccn.loc.gov/2019054748

Cover art: The sun rises over Bird Island. Photograph by Andrew
Alan Johnson.

For Dad

CONTENTS

ACKNOWLEDGMENTS

This book was written across multiple places, and within multiple academic and nonacademic appointments. I first turned toward working with fishermen when fishing on the Nansemond River with David Racicot, my parents' neighbor, where I found that two men who didn't know each other well could have long conversations so long as they were looking together at a river, or a fish, rather than at each other. I began my fieldwork the next year, in 2014, while I was a faculty member at Yale-NUS College in Singapore. I conducted additional research and most of the writing during my appointment at Princeton University and, later, at Stockholm University and the University of California, Berkeley. This latter period was also an extremely difficult time in my life, and I am grateful for those people and those institutions that helped me through.

First, I wish to thank Ken Wissoker and Josh Tranen at Duke University Press. Duke UP has been a fantastic group to work with, and I am humbled and honored to have this book as a part of their collection. I also thank my anonymous reviewers for their suggestions and comments. Work for this project has been funded by Yale-NUS College, Princeton University, and a joint Princeton University–Humboldt Universität zu Berlin grant (with Benjamin Baumann).

This project would not have been possible without the generosity and support of my interlocutors and collaborators in Thailand, with whom I have developed close personal and professional relationships. This book has been a personal journey as well as an academic one, and finding common ground with fishermen, activists, and migrants, and sharing stories of marriages and divorces, births and deaths with them has been a life-changing process. While promises of anonymity prohibit me from naming my key interlocutors, I would like to acknowledge the assistance of Orbmun Thipsuna, Siwakorn Muangkote, Rungnapa Kitiarsa, Saman Kaewphuang, Winai Kaewphuang, Cinnakon Kaewphuang, and others. In Bangkok, the monks of Wat Mahabut and Auntie Lek have been helpful in allowing me access to the Ya Nak shrine, a place that continues to fascinate.

I have also found the Thai scholarly community an invaluable help. Jakkrit Sanghamanee at Chulalongkorn University has supported and assisted me, especially in the final year of writing. Visisya Pinthongvijayakul and Soimart

Rung are inspirational scholars working on Isan issues, and Samak Kosem is a close friend. This book is deeply indebted to the work of the late Pattana Kitiarsa, whose dedication to Isan I have always admired. Thai studies scholars based outside of Thailand also provided commentary, assistance, and inspiration, especially Claudio Sopranzetti, Benjamin Baumann, Edoardo Siani, Eli Elinoff, Greg Green, Christine Gray, and Rachel Harrison. Ian Baird and Philip Hirsch do important work on Mekong issues, and I wish that I could have collaborated with them more than I have.

Elsewhere, a number of other scholars contributed to this work. In Singapore, I would like to acknowledge the friendship and help of Claudine Ang and Taran Kang, as well as Barney Bate. Anne Rademacher and Kalyanakrishnan Shivaramakrishnan's workshops in Yale and Hong Kong were instrumental in writing this book. I also wish to acknowledge Becky Butler and Leedom Lefferts at the University of North Carolina, Anne Kreps at the University of Oregon, Guido Sprenger at Heidelberg University, and Stuart McLean at the University of Minnesota. Jerome Whitington and Gökçe Günel were terrific interlocutors on issues of infrastructure. Hoon Song and David Rojas provided support of another, indirect, kind, and I am grateful to them for it.

At Princeton, the "Anthropology of Ruins" seminar and its students provided a fantastic theoretical background to much of this work, as did the Princeton Mellon Initiative in Architecture, Urbanism & the Humanities. Within the Department of Anthropology, I wish to note Serguei Oushakine, Carol Greenhouse, Carol Zanca, and Mo Lin Yee, as well as Grace Carey, Karolina Koziol, Veronica Sousa, E. B. Saldaña, and Brandon Hunter.

In the year since Princeton, several colleagues have gone out of their way to support my scholarship, and I am eternally grateful to them. Significantly, Johan Lindquist sponsored a semester at Stockholm University and was a friend in a time of need. Erik Harms remains a source of advice, both anthropological and personal. Aihwa Ong sponsored an affiliation at UC Berkeley's Center for Southeast Asian Studies, and Andrew Willford supported my work with an affiliation with Cornell University's Southeast Asia Program (SEAP). Additionally, outside of the academy, Zach Bush and Arne Schmidt of Firaxis Games offered me a position when I had none.

Several names deserve particular mention. Dominic Boyer remains a source of advice and guidance. Andrew Willford, in addition to his sponsorship at SEAP, was a pillar of support when I needed it. Justin McDaniel, too, was also a friend in a time of need and I am grateful for him both in that and in his tireless work for Southeast Asian studies and, of course, for making the best cocktails in Philly.

I particularly wish to point out Michael Herzfeld's support. Between gigantic and fiery Thai dinners, Michael helped me to find my way through troubles personal and academic; I will never forget his mentorship and will never be able to repay it. Daena Aki Funahashi deserves particular praise here, for never giving up on my scholarship, for being an endless source of inspiration and critique, and for being understanding and forgiving of my many errors.

Finally, I wish to thank my parents, Bob and Jean Johnson. Without their love and support I would not be present to complete this manuscript. A parent's love is endless.

THROUGH A GLASS, DARKLY

"At night, I close my eyes and all I can see is the dam."

Lert told me this as he lay back in the hammock underneath his house, as we both waited for the afternoon heat to fade and the time to come for the evening's fishing. Lert's house was on the bank of the Mekong River, where it forms the border between central Laos and northeastern Thailand. He and I had been talking about the decline in his fish catches in recent years. The troubles began with the construction of the Jinghong Dam in southern China, a dam that cut across the main stream of the Mekong just north of the Lao-Chinese border, about 500 kilometers upstream from Lert. But it wasn't just the numbers of fish that the dam affected. Lert described how, after construction began, the water in the Mekong began to act "against nature" (*phit thammasat*).[1] This disruption started in the middle of the dry season in 2006, when the river rose and tore through Lert's house without a drop of rain having fallen. After this, problems continued. The steady, constant torrent of 2015 starved riverbanks of sediment and smothered dry-season plants. The drought of 2016 dropped the river to record lows.

And the dam sent Lert dreams.

[The dam's Chinese engineers] promise that they built it solidly, but I don't believe [them]. When I see the dam [behind my closed eyelids], I see a crack. It is long and black, running from the base to the top. Dark water is spilling out from the crack. I see that one day the dam will break open. And when it does, everyone here will die. Everything here will disappear, fallen into the water.

I wish to be clear here: Lert did not see his dream as arising from his anxiety about the dam. He did not dream about the dam (*fan kiaw kap khuean*). Rather, he saw the dam (*fan hen khuean*), although whether he saw the dam in the future or in the present, in a physical or figurative sense, was not clear to him.

Lert's apocalyptic tone is shared across the community. Others in "Ban Beuk," Lert's town, spoke in such a register about the impact of the Jinghong Dam and the potential impacts of the new Sayaburi Dam under construction in Laos.[2]

These dams were only the latest environmental and economic interventions in what planners term the Greater Mekong Subregion, including new Special Economic Zones and high-speed rail projects, each received with pronouncements of both ecological and economic transformation: a diversion project was to take water straight from the Mekong and pipe it to farmers in the Chao Phraya (Central Thai) basin, starving the northeast to save Bangkok; China's Belt and Road Initiative was to include a high-speed rail line running straight through Nong Khai, not far from Ban Beuk.

The dam here emerges as a new figure in the ecology, economy, and cosmology of Ban Beuk. Here, I see infrastructure as more than material; rather, as in my previous work (Johnson 2014) as well as in new scholarship on infrastructure (Anand, Gupta, and Appel 2018; Larkin 2013; Schwenkel 2017), I ask: what is the relationship between infrastructure and a form of dwelling that includes dreams? Objects like the Jinghong Dam interpose themselves between fishermen and their fish, between riverbank farmers and their crops, and insinuate themselves into fishermen's dreams. With changes in the hydrology of the river—with the, in Heidegger's terms, challenging-forth of the dam and the loss of lived worlds— comes a sense of menace, a shadow that affects ecology, economy, love, and cosmology downstream. It is a shadow that provokes Lert and others to think about the nature of their relationships with other sources of potency—human, animal, ecological, and supernatural—and it signals that these relationships are in flux.

—————————

Juxtaposed with Lert's vision of the breaking dam is another, similar vision, another dream of water flowing from a distant source. This is the revelation of new sources of potential, of a utopic reshaping of the world as opposed to the apocalyptic. One night, like Lert, I too dreamed of the river. In my case, I dreamed of an island. I had been sleeping in a hut at the edge of the river, facing east across the flow into the Lao People's Democratic Republic (PDR). The first thing that I saw each morning was the sun, reddened by the smoke hanging in the morning air, rising over an island midstream. This island, Bird Island (*don nok*), was a hill about half a kilometer long and a hundred meters wide, covered in dense vegetation. Standing up from the center of the island, just where the sun rose, was the stump of a *takhian* tree (*Hopea odorata*).

In my dream, I saw this island clearly (figure I.1). Each leaf on each tree was fully illuminated from all directions, making the colors stand out as if drawn in crayon. Near the base of the takhian tree, crystal-clear water was gushing from a spring, but the water seemed viscous and thick. Thick globs of transparent fluid rolled off the tree's leaves and plopped down, disappearing into the reddish-brown Mekong. They left football-sized chunks of perfectly clear water in the otherwise opaque stream.

Over breakfast, Thip, a woman in her early forties and the sister of the man in whose compound I was living, asked me about my dreams. She had started asking me to describe them in detail each morning some weeks before, after I had given her and her sister, Yai, lottery tickets as gifts, one of which turned out to be a winner (Thip and Yai won about $200 each—not a small amount). But my dreams always disappointed her—she hoped to hear about a prominent animal that would "really" be a code for a particular number, or perhaps a lottery number given to me by a woman wearing ancient Lao dress, and the litany of anxieties infesting my junior academic's subconscious frankly bored her.

This dream, however, did not. She listened with interest to my description, a description that, I should note, might paint a different picture in Lao than it does in English (compare terms like *nam yot khon-khon, sii sai, meuan kaew* [viscous drops of water, clear like crystal] instead of "thick globs of transparent fluid"). The takhian tree, too, was significant. It was a kind that often was host to dangerous but potentially powerful spirits known to give good fortune to people—especially men—that they fancied. Thip asked me for more and more details, and I filled them in as best as I could. At last, she was quiet. "So, what do you think it means?" I asked.

She shrugged. "I don't know. The island's king [*jao don*] was talking to you," she said succinctly. "But sometimes it's hard to understand him when he speaks. The water is coming from him. It is his *barami* [charismatic power]." She thought it might indicate the potential for *sok lab* (sudden, unexplained fortune). She thought for a moment. "Or maybe it was the tree [that sent dreams]."

I asked her to elaborate on what she knew about that island. Was Bird Island, like an island a bit farther upstream, the center of a cult of a jao don, an island lord? Thip was adamant that she did not know. In her experience, Bird Island was just an island, one where she had grown up and that she had lived next to for her entire life. Sometimes her brothers would go there to hunt birds or gather fruits—indeed, that was why they had given it the name. Others might call it something else. Sometimes a Lao man would come from the opposite bank to

Figure I.1: The sun rises over Bird Island

plant a banana orchard (*suan*). While sometimes islands had jao, "kings," divine lords that would occasionally possess mediums and show their favor to those who made them offerings, she wasn't aware that this island had one until my dream. The dream, too, was merely suggestive: it meant that this island could have a king, perhaps one that had been hiding and was only coming out now as it was interested in talking with a foreigner. But you could never tell.

These two dreams tell us particular things. Just as the hydrology and ecology of Ban Beuk have altered, and just as new biological species enter this disrupted realm, new sources of potency (spirits, among others) also emerge. After the day of my dream, Thip asked me each morning (and continues to ask, when I am in Ban Beuk) if I have dreamed again about the island and, of course, if I should like to choose any lottery tickets for her. While she remains uncertain as to the exact identity of what spoke to me in my dream, she is convinced that something did. And it is this uncertainty, this sense of coinhabiting a space with things that, like both the dam and the island, carry the potential of an alien agency, something distant from us epistemologically or spatially, but under whose influence we exist.

These two dreams—Lert's dream of the wounded dam leaking dark water and threatening to destroy everything along the river, and Thip's interpretation of my dream of a heretofore unremarkable island gushing prosperity and fortune to those on its banks—share much. In each, there is the perception of a powerful controller sitting astride the river, deciding when to release and when to hold back fortune. They also reflect two potentialities in the Mekong and its apocalyptic/messianic futures. On one hand, environmental, economic, and political catastrophe has damaged the lives of those living on its banks and threatens to do so in the future, and on the other hand, forces of prosperity reemerge in new ways to those who can perceive them. Both potentials emerge from present-day disruption.

In each, dreams reveal something. Lert is specific—he is not dreaming of the dam because he is worried about the dam. Instead, in his dream, he sees the actual dam. Mine, in Thip's interpretation, is also a communication. Dreams here are not a subjective interpretation of one's inner life, but intersubjective. They are connections with something outside, not a turning inward, but a perception outward that goes beyond waking life.

This communication is with something distant and only partially known, something occult, in Cornelius Agrippa's (1486–1535) sense of a thing possessing a hidden cause but perceivable effects (Agrippa 2018). Occult worlds, involving fortune, magic, or river gods, or at the same time a foreign spouse or a dam controller in China, are only partially accessible to humans. From the vantage point of Ban Beuk, dams and spirits are both occult forces in that their power stems from an unseen place. What these forces say (in dreams and otherwise) and how they operate is unclear. One possesses only fragmentary awareness of their experience. Here is a world-making project that entangles people, animals, water, and spirits in its nets, but the resultant world is graspable only in parts, such that complete knowledge is always elsewhere.[3] Other people—especially unusual people such as mediums, the disabled, or foreigners—may perceive the world better (see also Sprenger 2015). The (possible) island king, who sees things more clearly than Thip does, sends incomprehensible dream messages not to her or to her brother, Mon, but to a foreigner. In other examples that I address in this volume, the actions and intentions of a far-off dam controller are only guessed at via changes in the water level and clarity. The divine king of the catfish draws his subjects away from the world of fishermen because of a breach of trust over fishing practices in the river. Migrant laborers attempt to understand cryptic messages sent to them via spontaneously appearing shapes and images on a tree trunk. Something in the experience of Mekong lives has changed.

Such a world revealed in fragments, where each individual can see only a shard, holds utopic as well as apocalyptic potential. Spirit messages were often winning lottery numbers, and, for development agents and those in Ban Beuk following them, the Mekong dams would control (not cause) floods. As a related part of national and international projects involved in developing the Mekong, Special Economic Zones connected to high-speed rail corridors would lead to the region's ascendance. Mirroring state promises of coming fortune were other utopic promises spread by more local interests: entrepreneurs would drive around Ban Beuk in shiny new cars selling miraculous new seeds that they claimed would revitalize the flagging rubber industry. Elsewhere, new democratic political movements promised to remove Bangkok from its privileged position in Thailand and give power to the marginalized northeast. In short, in the dreams that those in Ban Beuk revealed to me, utopia and disaster both lurked just over the horizon.

This world also speaks to the entanglements that we have with other beings. In a recent collection, Anna Tsing, Elaine Gan, Heather Swanson, and Nils Bubandt (2017) take up the idea of the ghosts and monsters of the present era. But these are not ghosts in the sense of the island king; rather, they are those plants whose pollinating partners have gone extinct, introduced species that wreak havoc on local ecologies, the futures that haunt the landscape. The ghosts and monsters of the Anthropocene[4]—that climatic moment in which we find ourselves—are similar to what I seek to explore here: the nonhuman, the material, but also what I call the *in*human, those other beings whose subject position is uninhabitable or unlocatable.

These beings include a host of materials, spirits, humans, and nonhumans. First, there is the river itself, newly made unpredictable and unreadable. Then the dam that blocks it and its controller, upstream in China, have a profound effect, but are practically unreachable (except in dreams or rituals I describe elsewhere in this volume). There is also the large Mekong fish, desired and sought but no longer appearing in nets except as a hybrid species. Within families, too, the problem of opacity emerges with family members who have migrated to foreign places and send remittances back, but who in their absence have grown strange. There are spirits of the water: nagas, island kings, and divine catfish whose messages grow obscure as the river changes around them. And, finally, there are those divine beings that look after migrant workers, threatening them with accident and promising fortune in equal measure.

With this emphasis on distant, opaque sources of potential, I turn also to the fantastic and messianic qualities of such beings. Their presence in the world reminds us that we do not wholly know the world in which we live, and that reality is fundamentally unfamiliar and uncertain. Such beings and forces that I discuss here can never be entirely understood, but they can be lived with.

Indeed, as I show here, not only can they be lived with, but they must be in order for a world to take shape. Heidegger (1977) argues that modern technology—in his case, also involving a river—leads to the destruction of worlds. But via *techné*, we can reforge those links and learn to dwell, to live in a way that preserves and exists in harmony with a world. In Heidegger's famous example, a silversmith allows a silver chalice to take form (*eidos*) via anticipating its function (in a Christian ceremony of communion), considering the potential of the material and the idea of the chalice. Through this craft, the silversmith opens a space for Being, for something larger. It is a nice expression of how things come into being, but it does not work on the Mekong. A fisherman might imagine his catch, work with his net, and engage with the water, but without result. Instead, on the Mekong another power is needed, something from outside both the fisherman and the material: an excess. A potency. And what has changed in the shadow of Jinghong is the source of this potency.

This book explores the idea and allure of distant potency and present moment on the Mekong as one of estrangement from (but immersion in) an opaque world. I do so via looking at the entanglements between human, nonhuman, and inhuman entities. It is via engagement with the potential in distant beings and objects that the possibility for radical change—in the self, in the world—emerges.

This is not the first study of uncertainty upon the Mekong. While scholars have focused intensively upon the entanglements of expert knowledge and development ideology along this and other Southeast Asian rivers (see Goldman 2005; Jakkrit 2018), Jerome Whitington (2018) provocatively takes up the link between hydropower and uncertainty. Whitington notes how hydropower projects create uncertain ecological and economic environments, environments that in turn create new managerial needs, but needs that arise from the very ecological unpredictability that the dam has created. In a similar vein, the nonhuman turn in anthropology (Grusin 2015) has addressed how people manage the emergent and often unpredictable worlds that arise out of the wake of human destruction. Indeed, the term Anthropocene or, in Whitington's case, Anthropogenic points to a clear cause and a clear break—the present moment is separated from the past.

But I am deliberate in my invocation of spells and spirits in the same breath as hydropower and fish—these are things that cocompose "divine worlds" (Ishii 2012) or composite objects (Jakkrit 2018). I do this because this is precisely what my interlocutors in Ban Beuk do: I (and they) see the present moment as a transformative time, one that alters both the material and immaterial— indeed, I deal with spirits as no less material than absent lovers, migrant workers, distant dams, or missing fish. It is a transformation enabled by Ban Beuk's entanglements with and dependence upon the sources of power elsewhere: migrant remittances, dead nagas, and genetically modified organisms, to name a few. The foundations of the earth change and new beings arise. This time, sources of potency in Ban Beuk become distant, be they human (fishermen who disappear for hours at a time turn into migrants who leave for years) or nonhuman (hybrid catfish whose qualities are uncertain), or inhuman (nagas who no longer sun themselves on the bank nor intermarry into the village but which send lottery numbers from afar). The price of rubber, the attention of a foreign spouse, international migrant labor, one's livestock, and now, after the construction of the Jinghong Dam, the river itself all come to be operated by distant but potent sources of power.

Distance here is important. It implies both physical and epistemological distance. When I sat across from Thip, relating to her my dream, I did so as a person whose subject position is difficult to inhabit—she often cobbled together ideas about the "outer lands" (*meuang nok*), from which I come, from things she had seen on television, most of which seemed to be related to India. Similarly, as I sit on Mon's porch and look across at Bird Island, I am physically close to the island king, but cannot imagine what his thoughts or perceptions might be. He is elsewhere metaphysically, even if physically he is present. It might be easy to imagine distance as a kind of failure, as something that weakens. But here, I show how distance acts as a kind of potency. Power accrues as it rolls to us over distance, and the mark of the foreign is a mark of this power.

But distance in this sense is not just external—we also find a sense of distance within ourselves—namely, the unconscious. Here, I do not necessarily mean the unconscious in a strictly Freudian sense of a world repressed that emerges in unexpected ways, but rather an unconscious that reflects the way that we open ourselves toward the world outside of our cognition. As we live with other beings and landscapes, the material qualities of this world, the ways that we interact with these material qualities, and the actions of other-than-human actors shape us. As such, the unconscious here is a Deleuzean unconscious, an openness to the world, and the target of schizoanalysis, not psychoanalysis (Deleuze and Guattari 1980, 18).

Consider the dream of the island king. It is my dream, and my own interpretation and memory of my dream. But it arises out of my openness to the island king, from sleeping in his shadow each night. A psychoanalyst attentive to the influence of the material world, Gaston Bachelard (1999), might also mention the ludic qualities of the water that runs between the island king and myself, a materiality that impinges upon me in ways that I only partially know. In short, just like the Mekong, just like the realm of foreigners, we also contain distances within us or hidden depths that are intertwined with the world around us in ways of which we may not be immediately aware. And these distances—present, but absent from our conscious consideration—can be powerful.

The distant dam—a thing that Lert has never seen—is likewise absent-present in the water's flow. Water rises and falls owing to distant action, exerting power that no proximate source could ever have done. At the same time, spirits and other forces are integrated into villagers' networks not as explanations for (mis)fortune, but as adaptable (but distant) partners that also contend with such forces. Imperfectly known beings—naga, dam, and migrant—become the sources of potency in the world, and those at risk of losing their own ability to act seek out these new sources of potency.

My perspective, then, is to approach networks of human, nonhuman, and inhuman actors from the viewpoint of my interlocutors. Other than drawing in things that are not always present in the world (such as nagas), this perspective also gives weight to things that might be there, or that are sometimes there (like island kings). I find that I am speaking of potency rather than action, of presences that are often absent, usually distant, and sometimes unknowable. I use this term—*potency*—to mean the potential for action, even if action is not taken. A focus on hidden and distant sources of potential should not be surprising to scholars of Southeast Asia. *Potency* is my own word—in Thai and in Lao it might correspond to aspects of "force" (*phon*), "sacred power" (*sak*), "royal charisma" (*barami*), or "existence" (*khwam pen*).[5] Elsewhere in Southeast Asia, Benedict Anderson (1990) writes in the case of Java, and Geertz (1980) in his model of the Balinese "theater-state," of potency at the still center, in the figure of a ruler who draws upon hidden sources. The Javanese king who retains a *halus* (placid, calm) composure despite the frenetic flailings of demons, or the Buddha seated slightly smiling in the face of tumult—these are the signs of potency in the world. Similarly, for Margaret Wiener (1995), it is not actions taken and resources controlled in the physical realm that generate power, but rather the occult links—sources of secret knowledge, favors of holy sites and gods, and the keeping of magical objects and texts—that give rulers their charismatic draw. Thai and Lao speakers might immediately think of the distinction between barami and *amnaj*, between the gravitational pull of a charismatic king versus the rough hand of a military general. Thus, potency is the capacity to effect change in the world, but it does not necessarily imply action upon that capacity. It is, like the Javanese *sekti* (Anderson 1990; Thai *sak*), something that causes ripples downstream without having to be physically present.

In the present tumultuous moment, the focus of what is potent changes. As in other such moments, potency changes as infrastructure alters the fabric of the world. New beings become potent in new ways as what was previously potent fails, and new sources of potency are identified, unreachable but nonetheless present. Thus, unknown or partially known things act upon us from an occult distance—their sources hidden by physical or metaphysical distance, but with a power nonetheless.

THE PROMISE OF "MAYBE"

This notion of Ban Beuk as caught in the gravitational pull of such distant but nonetheless powerful forces is something that pervaded my fieldwork. Indeed, my own presence in Ban Beuk was often given as an example of distant potency coming to bear, and the links that brought me to Ban Beuk were continually explored by many of my interlocutors. Thip's sister, Yai, used the Mekong as an example of just such a link: "If I were to take a boat and go upstream," she asked me, "would I get to your home?" She continued, recounting her imagined journey: "I would pass Laos, pass China, go through mountains with snow on top, and then to the land of Westerners [*meuang farang*]."[6] Yai imagined here a line extending out from her home that draws a physical link between us, one separated by foreigners similar to herself (Laos), less-similar foreigners (Chinese), different biomes (snow), and finally the land of entirely different foreigners (farang)—distant, but linked by the Mekong.

This connection is more than just geography. At the same time as she posited this geographic link, she also posited a kin and temporal one: "Your name is An," Yai told me, dropping off the last syllable of Andrew. "My [deceased] son's name was Man.[7] You call me *mae* [mother]." She flatly stated, "You are him, returned in a new body." We are linked.

Here is something like what Thip sought (unsuccessfully) to do with my dream. A few months after meeting me, Yai draws me to her in terms of geography ("we are linked via this river"), kinship ("you are my son"), and temporally ("you were here [as Man], then left and returned [as An]"). But, of course, unlike Man (but like his ghost), I retain my foreignness. Indeed, this is my appeal—Yai constantly asked to be taught English or, like her sister, for winning lottery numbers. In other words, I am not rendered "known" to Yai even though we share this geographical, lineal, and temporal link: I am not identical to Man, nor is my home in "meuang farang" rendered the same as Ban Beuk. This would be to give Yai a perspectival outlook upon the world, where all places are knowable in a similar cultural configuration. Rather, I am for Yai a thread linking her to some unknown quantity, toward a new realm of possibility.

For many others, too, links in the networks of humans and nonhumans often point toward distant or nonlocatable points. For Lert, the dam controller is just such a distant figure with whom communication is difficult, as is the island king. While one may argue that the former, being a human in an office in China, is fundamentally different from the latter, a possessing spirit, I see these figures from Thip's perspective. Thip might be able to communicate with a spirit; she cannot communicate with the controller of the Jinghong Dam. While the dam controller is a human, Thip could never travel to meet him. Even were she to do so, they could not communicate, and he is a foreigner. Spirits at least speak Lao.

Each distant point, too, is a potential source of power and knowledge and a new perspective upon the world, something necessary, as no one entity has complete knowledge of what is "out there"—there is no hermetically sealed world that encapsulates all the beings in the world and their relationship with each other outside of the Buddha (who has departed the world) and the dharma (the world as it is and should be). Instead, unenlightened beings (i.e., everyone but the Buddha) gaze only upon a small part of the world, and even then what they see gives conflicting and contested images. Distant forces, magic, and radical change in the world are rolled into one another.

This would come as little surprise to anthropologists of magic. For Marcel Mauss ([1950] 2001), whereas religion occupies the role of collective effervescence and social unity, magic exists on the sidelines, associated with marginal individuals and foreign influences and thriving exactly because of the patina of the exotic and the unknown. Marginal groups—Roma ("gypsies"), Saami ("Lapps")—were seen to have special access to power.[8] Such association holds today in tropes such as the "magical Negro" (Glenn 2009) in Hollywood film, the mystical indigenous person in New Age spiritualism (see Castaneda [1968] for a classic example), or the exotic East in the lives of bourgeois white Americans (see Gilbert 2006). But the trend persists in many places: Vinay Kamat (2008) notes how Tanzanians seeking magical healing consistently preferred healers from a distant village to healers from their own precisely because of the imaginary that such distance provided, or in Kamat's terms "the allure of the culturally distant."

The distant and the partially known, then, have power. But what is this power? Jean and John Comaroff explore how distant forces—neoliberal capitalism, in their example—become locally understood as the workings of sinister magic (Comaroff and Comaroff 1999; 2001). As the Comaroffs argue, in the wake of South African liberation, certain individuals became rich while others did not. Saturated in the narrative that the end of white supremacy in South Africa would raise all fortunes, those who found their situation unchanged began to suspect that others had mystically stolen it from them, or had discovered secret, magical means to fortune. Pyramid schemes, rumors of magical get-rich-quick techniques, and hidden monsters proliferated. These were, the Comaroffs argue, the mysterious workings of capital translated via the logics of magic. Commodity fetishism (in its neoliberal, more abstracted guise) becomes mystical fetishism.

I have argued along the Comaroffs' lines in an analysis of the cults of nature spirits among migrant workers in Bangkok (Johnson 2012). Faced with the chaos pervading their precarious lives, workers seek out sources of that very chaos—spirits associated with traffic deaths, for instance—as ways to ameliorate and engage directly with that precarity. Making friends with death in the form of a spirit means making friends with it in the form of the potential fatal accident.

But perhaps this conclusion is too simplistic. The "occult economies" approach is one that Bruce Kapferer (2003), among others, has criticized for overemphasizing the role of mystification. In short, Kapferer's critique is that the idea of occult economies assumes that people who don't know the real reason (economic exploitation from afar) that they remain poor and others become rich mistakenly attribute their loss and others' gain to the occult. Neoliberalism is the man behind the curtain, and monsters and magic are simply the face of Oz, the great and terrible.

This is really a question about symbols versus content, and whether one can neatly separate the two. A critique of this divide is what drives the "ontological turn" today (Holbraad and Pedersen 2016). Ontological anthropologists, criticizing the turn toward representation, correctly argue that the proposition that ontological objects encountered in the field (e.g., ghosts) are really other objects native to the ethnographer's world (e.g., the market) fails to do adequate justice to peoples' lived worlds and wastes the opportunity to present novel forms of philosophical analysis. If, as Freud is supposed to have said, a cigar is sometimes just a cigar, maybe we should start from the basis that a ghost is sometimes just a ghost.

But, as any ethnographer knows, ontology is messy, and a ghost is a ghost for some and not others. The island king of whom Thip speaks might not actually be there. The medium might just be a crazy old lady (as Lert asserts). My dream might just be a dream. While Thip and Lert (and anyone with whom I spoke in Ban Beuk) accept that island kings as a rule exist, their ontological status in any one instance is far from certain. Some element of representation—that word *belief*—comes into play here. Do island kings exist? Do nagas—those subterranean and aquatic serpents that spit fire into the sky on the full moon—exist? Does it matter?

The answer that my interlocutors in Ban Beuk give is a forceful "maybe." Maybe they're real at some times and not at others. Maybe the island king isn't there, but another ghost is. Maybe someone else knows better than we do. As with numinal objects, their actual existence lies hidden behind an opaque screen, through a glass darkly, and one must find other ways—dreams, for instance—to see past it.[9] If ontology determines the possibility that a particular kind of entity exists, here I show how we do not actually know what kinds of things can manifest—rather, we know that there is a potential for novelty, for our understanding of the world to be broken.

The question of opacity is one that Nils Bubandt (2014) also addresses in his analysis of Buli witchcraft. For Bubandt, Buli witchcraft is a problem of doubt. Rejecting accounts of witchcraft that seek its cognitive, social, or symbolic function, Bubandt (2014, 6) focuses on witchcraft as a Derridean aporia, "an impassable situation, where understanding and the will to knowledge fail." And, like aporia, cannibal witches are the dragons that haunt the blank spaces on the map, spaces that persist despite (and, Bubandt further argues, because of) new technologies, religions, and epistemologies.

Similarly, Lisa Stevenson (2014), working in the Canadian Arctic, is also concerned with such "maybe" beings that mark an outside to knowledge. One of her interlocutors mentions that a raven in his backyard might be an ancestor, or might just be a raven. He's not sure. Then, he adds, "It's still there." The raven, the uncle, the potential, in other words, is still there. Even if its ontological status as ancestor or bird (or both) is unknown, something certainly exists.

Returning to Lert, Thip, and Yai, and anticipating others in and from Ban Beuk that I mention here, what is the importance, then, of this opacity, the screen between how the world is and how we can perceive it? Good ethnography, and really listening to what our interlocutors say, requires us to reject the idea that the dragons in the blank spaces on the map (or beneath the surface of the river) are either stand-ins for our beasts (of the neoliberal market, for instance) or defined entities fully real within a particular worldview or ontology (and not within others). But in our analysis, can we build upon what our interlocutors say about such problematic spaces—spaces where things might be—in human/nonhuman networks as sources of potential? And, why are, for my interlocutors, such blank spaces all the more attractive for their uncertainty, their otherness?

My focus here is on the productive potential of "maybe." I see "maybe" as a space of possibility. By announcing that a thing may exist, or by asserting that its essential qualities are uncertain, one allows for the possibility that the present order of things might be overthrown. "Maybe" points to the existence of things beyond apprehension, and to their potential ability to overturn the mundane. The uncertainty opened by "maybe" allows for new things to enter into the world.

This attraction comes at a moment of catastrophic change. Here, rather than seeing alterations in the nonhuman world as imaginative responses to the environmental and social disruptions that I describe here, changing spiritual and other worlds on the Mekong are one part of the larger changes in the material, animal, and social worlds brought about by the Mekong dams, military crackdowns, and new free trade corridors in the area. I argue that these alterations amount to a fluttering of an opaque curtain: just as old situated knowledge fails, new knowledge can suddenly work. And dreams occasioned by an unconscious opened to networks only partially known are not the curtain's removal: just as new insights (new sources of potency) are revealed, old ones have their power stripped away. Power requires engagement with this unknown place.

WEIRD PHENOMENOLOGY

A perspective that is concerned with the unknowable state of reality and people's limited perspective upon it invokes phenomenology. But here I wish to depart from a tradition entirely rooted in Western epistemology. In other words, this is not an issue of simply Kant's numina (things as they are) and *phenomena* (what we can perceive of them); instead, it is informed by the Theravada Buddhist/Thai-Lao animist worlds of my interlocutors.[10]

In *Ghosts of the New City* (Johnson 2014), I describe "progress" in the Thai idiom of *jaroen* as a great ladder.[11] On this ladder are all things—spirits, gods, monks, humans, animals, and ghosts. In *Ghosts*, I was concerned with movement up or down this ladder (i.e., progress and ruination) and anxieties about something that might appear to have jaroen but which in fact was a ruin-in-waiting. But here I am interested in the vantage points that various rungs supply. A being higher up sees more of the world than a being lower down—something true of both humans and other-than-humans (e.g., a spirit sees more than a person; a person sees more than an animal; a malevolent ghost might be somewhere more complicated). Upon reaching the top of this imaginary ladder, one exits (*nibbana*—what in Sanskrit is *nirvana*). Only one being, the Buddha, has done so, and because of the knowledge gained from achieving this top rung, he is now no more.[12] He exists only in the path he has left with his teachings. Knowledge annihilates.

This is an idea of knowledge that sits oddly alongside phenomenology. Essences are unknowable, and the only being to truly know them has vanished— indeed, he has vanished because of this very knowledge! Thus, all knowledge (that non-Buddhas have) must be partial. So with all perspectives partial and impermanent (*anitjang* in Thai, *anicca* in Pali), one must guess at these essences. But we are not alone in this search—others assist us: those above us on the ladder, who see things (and, indeed, who see us) more clearly than we do.[13]

But because of our human status, the glimpses that we receive are often strange. Thip reads my dream as a message, but a confusing one. "It's hard to understand him when he speaks," she says of the island king. As Lert examines the Mekong in the evening for signs that it will rise in the night (thus threatening his house and livestock), he looks for water clarity or evidence of a recent surge, and finds instead a strange foam floating in a long trail downstream—a foam trail no one in town has seen before, nor can anyone attribute it to a distinct source. When a medium becomes possessed by a naga, he at first jabbers in a high-pitched voice, "angelic language" (*phasa thaewada*), before lowering himself to speak in Lao. Even the foreign professor is hard to understand, when he mispronounces things or badly mangles an attempt to explain his writing in Lao.

How to think about such moments when a glimpse into a higher plane reveals a garbled, incomprehensible message? I have mentioned Agrippa's notion of the occult—a force that one sees in its results but cannot perceive its cause. But there are other, more recent attempts to deal with such uncertainty. Structuralist literary critic Tzvetan Todorov argues that, in literary works, the fantastic is just such a moment. The fantastic emerges when "an event [occurs] which cannot be explained by the laws of this same familiar world. The person who experiences the event must opt for one of two possible solutions: either he is the victim of an illusion of the senses, of a product of the imagination—and the laws of the world then remain what they are; or else the event has indeed taken place, it is an integral part of reality—but then *this reality is controlled by laws unknown to us*" (Todorov 1975, 25, emphasis added). Todorov (1975, 35) argues that the fantastic is unstable—one either asserts that the irruption of the unusual into the everyday is explainable by the laws of the everyday (and thus is uncanny), or one learns the new laws of the new world (the marvelous). One thinks of Harry Potter's initial wonderment when he sees the wizards' school Hogwarts later turning to a banal inhabitation once he learns the rules. But on the Mekong, this state of the fantastic is maintained: the everyday world is dependent on other, deeper forces, but these are forces whose contours remain opaque. There is no such revelation of the laws of the world—there is no Dumbledore who knows and can guide us in our knowledge—instead, the world is revealed to be always already unknowable and unknown.

"Object-oriented ontology" philosopher Graham Harman (2012), in looking at the fiction of early twentieth-century "weird fiction" writer H. P. Lovecraft, argues for a "weird realism" in which there is "a 'cubist' tension" (34) between objects and their sensual qualities, especially when these qualities each give very different perspectives. But where a cubist perspective presents different angles upon a coherent object, a "weird" object has contours that suggest a tension that is fundamentally unresolvable (Harman 2012, 258). That is to say, two different vantage points upon a weird object do not give a better image of a thing, but rather suggest that the thing can never be fully perceived, at least by a subject similar to the observer.

The distinction between cubist and weird is important. Most ethnography has been positivist in the sense that we assume that we are describing a very different take upon a shared world—a cubist perspective. You see this face in this way, whereas I see it, from my vantage point, like so. By comparing our perspectives, we can agree on how the face really is. But whereas new ontological anthropology posits worlds not shared (de la Cadena and Blaser 2018), what of the weird dimensions within a subject? That is to say, what of those moments when I (or Thip) see the contours of a thing (e.g., Bird Island) in ways that do not line up?

Thinking of the ladder of jaroen, one sees the difference between a Buddha or a spirit, who can—more or less—see things as they are (but whose position is uninhabitable), and a human, who sees that s/he does not see clearly.

Thus, perceiving an object and recognizing that one is unable to resolve the properties of the object into a whole reveals, for Harman (2012), the "separateness" between observer and reality. Reality is revealed to be more than can be comprehended by the observer, at least without radically transforming the observer himself (as in the case of the Buddha as much as in Lovecraft's protagonists). Reality is weird, at least when seen from human eyes.

Moving from Todorov's fantastic to Harman's weird, then, we see a reality that eludes capture. It is that state of unknowing that is, here, sought out not to reconcile its weirdness (as in the detective novels or horror literature that Todorov or Harman analyze) and convert it to a branch of the everyday (e.g., Todorov's uncanny or marvelous), but to embrace it because of its alterity. One might call this an "instrumental weirdism."[14] This book is inspired by this notion of the weird, and it is for this reason that its title, *Mekong Dreaming*, refers simultaneously to the distant specter of the dam in Lert's dream, to the dreams of national development of which the dam is a manifestation, but also to this body of "weird fiction" from which Harman draws (cf. Lovecraft's [1933] "The Dreams in the Witch House").

As Lovecraft (1926) himself writes, "the most merciful thing in the world, I think, is the inability of the human mind to correlate all its contents." Lovecraft's stories revolve around encounters between humans and something truly alter—beings, objects, or even a color from a different time and place, a world that Lovecraft suggests is more important or more vital than the human realm. In most of his stories, his protagonists go mad in struggling to make sense of this alterity—seeing things as they really are breaks the mind.

Lovecraft's critics have focused on his racism—he was certainly a racist. His supporters (Harman) in turn argue for its irrelevance. I see things differently. Lovecraft's xenophobia is integral to his writing, as the frightful alienness of the other is precisely his concern, whether that be the other to humanity or the other to Lovecraft's own New England white society. As with Heidegger's Nazi politics, we must surely be repulsed by Lovecraft's racism. But, just as with Heidegger, we must see these repugnant politics as integral to his ideas. Lovecraft's xenophobia is not that of the white supremacist who argues for a war against "impure" peoples—a fear of the outside that manifests in a call to close oneself off from the world. Rather, Lovecraft's racism is one that finds the struggle already lost; the other is simply too great, too powerful, or too *prior*. Further, Lovecraft's characters often find themselves already entangled with these outside forces: the narrator of "Shadow over Innsmouth" discovers that he himself is one of the monsters that so repulse him. Unlike Bram Stoker's Victorian heroes in *Dracula* (1897), there is no pure English blood that can be transfused into the tainted victim. For Lovecraft, one cannot fight the foreign, as the foreign is too powerful, and at the same time one cannot shut it out, as the foreign is already inside us.

Early twentieth-century American horror writing may seem to be a long distance from the Mekong, giant aquatic beasts notwithstanding. But the link here lies in the revelation of a world that is unknown and unknowable, but one more powerful and vital, more real even as it is inhuman. But, unlike Lovecraft's haunted New England, there is little horror in Ban Beuk, at least as concerns river beings. Thip reacts to the island king not with fear, but with interest. Mon (as I detail elsewhere in this book) responds to sightings of naga (water dragons) in the river not with avoidance, but with offerings of coffee and Fanta soda. Absolute knowledge will not break the mind, as it does for Lovecraft's protagonists, but is accepted as fundamentally unknowable. In these, and also with Thip, the world is revealed to be incomplete from a human perspective. Thip tells me that humans cannot see the world as the island does, and so she does not try to see like an island. Devotees of tree spirits in eastern Bangkok understand that their karmic power is not visible to themselves but is known to a ghostly observer (see also Johnson 2012). In short, like a character in a Lovecraftian story, we do not and cannot fully understand the world and its contents—including ourselves—and must rely upon partial signals and indications from fundamentally Other intelligences.

Lovecraft's idea of being always already interpenetrated by foreign forces has been taken up in lectures by Donna Haraway (2016). Modifying the term *Anthropocene* to *capitalocene*, to indicate that it is not necessarily humans but capitalism that has engendered the wide-scale changes normally associated with the former term, Haraway also introduces the term *Chthulucene*, taking both the name of one of Lovecraft's (1926) hostile entities, Cthulhu, and also playing upon the meanings of "primal, earthy" in the term *chthonic*. For Haraway, the *Chthulucene* is a time when we find ourselves living in aggregate with nonhuman forces, already dependent upon other powers that move through us and without which we are incapable of life.[15] We are physically alien to ourselves. We must be, or we die.

I take this long detour through contemporary ecophilosophy and early twentieth-century horror to highlight the contribution that a Mekong phenomenology makes in establishing an open-ended network of beings, only some of which are captured by human perception, but also to point out where such a perspective can contribute to current scholarship on such worlds. The unknown and unassimilable for each of these authors discussed above—Bubandt, the Comaroffs, and Lovecraft—is a place where the uncertain is unquestionably negative. Buli aporia become cannibal witches in Bubandt's (2014) *Empty Seashell*. Capitalist networks become zombie-making sorcerers in the Comaroffs' "occult economies" (Comaroff and Comaroff 1999). A glimpse into a reality inaccessible to humans induces madness in Lovecraft's (1926) stories.

Here is a common theme—ontological uncertainty is a problem. But I argue that it is not always so. Returning to Ban Beuk, in the Hindu- and Theravada Buddhist–influenced orbits of Southeast Asia, we see something else. In Bali and Java, for instance, potency rests in invisible—and here I would say "opaque"—sources of power. I argue that these sources of power are not simply known sources rendered invisible to the uninitiated (as I believe Anderson [1990] intends), but rather areas with entirely open signifieds. It is not that one knows that a god exists but the ways of getting at him are complicated; rather, there is a great unknown that exists (and, additionally, ways of getting at it are complicated). The unknown is limitless, and gods are limited.

Elsewhere (Johnson 2012) I have written about the act of naming sources of danger and thereby entering into a relationship with them. But, as James Siegel notes, naming does not bring a thing entirely into domestication. For Siegel (2005), naming allows for individuals to temporarily address and resolve "death" (what Siegel terms that which lies outside of culture or comprehension) in ways that eventually demand another naming when death persists. Something dangerous and unknowable is abroad in East Java, as Siegel writes, and the identification and killing of someone labeled a witch temporarily convinces people that this thing has been dealt with, at least until it recurs. Here, I argue that, on the contrary, there is power in keeping one end of this relationship open, in acknowledging that the named being or object is still fundamentally unknown and thus has additional potential.

It is my argument here that the ecological, economic, and cultural shifts that confront my interlocutors present moments where new vistas onto reality present themselves. New realms of the unknown and unnamed present themselves, and there is potency—apocalyptic and messianic—in the distant, fantastic, and weird. Rather than a bounded worldview (which places meaning and essences at the center of things), and rather than a rhizome (which places relation and action at the center), I present a middle ground: a hauntological alternative, where meaning exists and influences, but is only partially accessible.

METHODOLOGY

I deliberately chose the example of my own dream in this introductory chapter to make a particular point about the boundaries of fieldwork—or lack thereof. If my interlocutors in Ban Beuk struggled with the questions of reality, opacity, and the attempt to resolve the two, I was not the dispassionate observer watching them squirm. Nor was I asking questions and seeking elucidation of what they believe. Rather, my interlocutors and I were in a similar situation—each possessing the knowledge that truths are inherently partial, and holding the idea that the paths toward that truth run through empirical exploration, the key difference between myself and Thip being the kinds of questions asked of dreams and mediums, and the sorts of information desired.

Fieldwork pushes boundaries. Such was the crux of anthropology's "reflexive turn," a turn that is largely relegated to anthropology's recent past. But in Thai-language anthropology, this notion of "boundary" (*chai-daen*) has found new relevance. Expanding upon the notion of "border" and "boundary," Jakkrit Sangkhamanee (2017b) argues that ethnographic fieldwork is a process of pushing the boundaries not of knowledge, but of what falls under the gaze of knowledge in ways that also complicate the divide between the personal and the academic. One recalls the disbelief in an undergraduate student's voice when reading ethnography for the first time—"This isn't *data*! This is *personal anecdote*!" Contributors Samak Kosem (2017) and Soimart Rungmanee (2017) each in different ways expand upon the personal nature of ethnographic fieldwork— separations and boundaries between informant and researcher are as extensive as the other kinds of boundaries that I complicate here. As coresearchers, my interlocutors and I speculated about things as varied as the affection of a distant romantic partner, the nature of reality, or the quality of data, and in our talks we attempted to understand (but not resolve) the incommensurate glimpses that we each gleaned. It is this mutual entanglement of ideas about the mutual entanglement of human, nonhuman, and inhuman worlds that I seek to elucidate here.

The research that I conducted took two phases: one based in Bangkok among migrant workers, and another in the town of Ban Beuk, a municipality (*tambol*) in Thailand's northeast. Within tambol Ban Beuk are three subunits: Ban Beuk village, Ban Thong village, and Ban Kham village—all within fifteen minutes' drive from each other. While I lived in Ban Beuk, many of my interlocutors (Lert, for instance) came from these nearby towns.

Bangkok and Ban Beuk are linked: the majority of my interlocutors in Ban Beuk had worked as migrant laborers in Bangkok. Indeed, it was partially through meeting the latter that I initially became interested in working in Ban

Beuk. The flow back and forth between a remote rural fishing village, the Thai capital, and international chains of labor demonstrates the impossibility—if it was ever possible—of conceiving of small-scale, village-based fieldwork; the villagers of Ban Beuk are certainly cosmopolitans "from below," in Breckenridge's sense (Breckenridge et al. 2002).

All of my interlocutors were northeasterners, a label with heavy significance in Thailand, something into which I delve in more detail in chapter 1. Thailand's northeast, or Isan (I use the terms interchangeably), is its poorest region and one known for political divisions with Bangkok. It was and is still occasionally referred to as a Lao region, as its people before the twentieth century leaned closer to Vientiane than Bangkok (or Bangkok's predecessor, Ayutthaya). Indeed, the label *Lao* before the twentieth century indicated not a specific language or ethnicity as it does now, but a pejorative term referring to anyone from the lands north or northeast of Bangkok—*Siam* being the older term for the Central Thai heartland. Under the heavily centralized Thai state, Isan languished in relative poverty, poverty that bred resentment toward Bangkok and occasionally flared into various revolts (from millenarian to communist to democratic) during the twentieth and early twenty-first centuries (see Pattana 2015).

Today, Isan is still largely Lao-speaking, although the label *Lao* covers a multitude of different dialects. Lao is close to, but not mutually intelligible with, Thai, and the similarities and differences between the two languages (and local dialects) lead to an intricate array of code switches in everyday conversation, with local terms played up to emphasize difference from Bangkok or, occasionally, Central Thai features (e.g., a rolled *r*) when people wanted to adopt an official, authoritative stance. Occasionally, this latter drops into satire, with heavy Bangkok *rs* dropped into the middle of words where they do not ordinarily go (e.g., "Nong Khrrrai" instead of the province name Nong Khai). With me, most used Vientiane Lao or Bangkok Thai, two languages in which I am fluent, although local dialects varied from village to village (villagers in Ban Thong, for instance, spoke a dialect more similar to that of Loei province in Thailand or Luang Prabang, in Laos).

Ban Beuk is a town of approximately three hundred households. In turn, Ban Kham has eighty and Ban Thong, 110. I chose the site for a number of related reasons: some of the interlocutors that I got to know working on spirit shrines in Bangkok were from the district; an environmental nongovernment organization (NGO) leader whom I knew from Nong Khai had a friend in the village headman; and Ban Beuk sits close to where the Mekong emerges from Lao PDR to form the Thai-Lao border, thus making it one of the first sites in Thailand to be downstream of the Sayaburi dam project.[16]

During my fieldwork, I lived in a room that Mon, a fisherman of around my age, let out during the winter months to passing tourists (indeed, he often let out his own room and slept in a tent on the riverbank during the high season). In 2015–2016, and for periods in 2017 and 2019, I stayed close with him and his family, fishing with his brothers, attending temple services with his sisters, and interviewing (and fishing with) men in the town. Later, Pla and Kai, two local activists, moved into town, and together we arranged for a group of local high school and college-aged students to conduct a formal survey of fishermen in the area (for most of these, this involved interviewing their parents, aunts, uncles, and grandparents).

Ban Beuk is a pseudonym, as are Ban Kham and Ban Thong. The names are the most generic that I could come up with—although "Beuk" is named after the giant catfish that forms a central part of this book (not to mention the pun on *book*), "Kham" and "Thong" are words for "gold."[17] In addition to the standard ethical practice of granting anonymity to research interlocutors, the current Thai political climate raises the stakes for all involved. The Ban Beuk section of my research was done in the wake of the 2014 coup d'état and subsequent political repression of prodemocratic Red Shirt activists.[18] My informants who self-identified as former Red Shirts (and even some of their rival Yellow Shirts) now report fear over political repression and harassment by police.

This threat extended to me as well. At the International Conference of Thai Studies in 2017, where I presented this work, five Thai studies scholars were charged with unlawful assembly (Pratchatai 2017). Based upon my support of these scholars, I am detained and questioned by immigration police each time that I enter and leave Thailand. At another presentation of this work at Chiang Mai University, soldiers lined the back of the room and photographed my talk and others. While this book does not deal directly with the coup and the subsequent repression and crackdown, the simple topic of Isan evoked political divisiveness. Former Red Shirts were deliberately targeted by the military following the coup, and environmental issues and activism of any kind were—are—sensitive topics.

With that in mind, I trust the reader can forgive the omission of an exact location for Ban Beuk. But I can give a general introduction.

BAN BEUK

Ban Beuk is three parallel lines running southeast.

The first of these is the ridgeline of a low series of hills, covered in alternating forest and small-scale plantations of rubber, papaya, and banana. The ridge marks an important geographic distinction, separating the central Isan plateau from the Mekong valley proper, and dividing realms dominated by farmers from those dominated by fishermen. Except where rural roads cut through passes, this ridge is sharp enough that farmers must come and go on foot, up red-orange dirt tracks.

An hour farther south, past the district seat, enterprising temple administrations have built platforms from which one can look out over the Mekong River, especially in the winter, where morning fog makes a "sea of clouds" (*thale mohk*) over the valley.[19] In Ban Beuk itself, a shrine to the lord of nagas— river dragons that play an important role in this book—sits atop one such viewpoint, and a medium for this spirit makes his practice here in a cave that was, thousands of years ago, a copper mine.

From these viewpoints, one looks out across the Mekong River into the Lao PDR. Excepting slightly fewer electric lights on the Lao side, the view toward either bank is much the same: secondary-growth forest alternating with plantations and small towns. In the dry seasons, fires planted by farmers often run out of control, and plumes of smoke dot the horizon during the day, changing to low red flames at night. But these fires burn on the Thai side as well.

The next line is the highway. It is a narrow road with a single lane running in each direction, built in the 1980s with the assistance of the military. It is not a major traffic artery—to get between provincial capitals in the region, such as Loei, Nong Khai, or Udon Thani, one should take Highway 210, much farther inland. But there is some traffic heading between district seats, stocking markets or transporting livestock. Occasionally this combination of narrow road and traffic can be deadly: in 2016 in Ban Beuk, an eighteen-wheeler went off the road and destroyed a villager's house, killing the woman inside—an aunt of my key interlocutor, Mon.

Mostly, one takes this road just to take it. It makes for a pretty drive, when it comes across broad vistas over the river. In the cold season, domestic tourists—mostly Thais from Bangkok or Khon Kaen—descend upon the district seat, looking for Mekong River fish and cold lemonade in the afternoon, but these tourists usually pass by Ban Beuk in a blur on their way to the trendier town of Chiang Khan.

Alongside the highway run Ban Beuk's houses. Most stick close to the main road, but in the centers of Ban Beuk, Ban Kham, and Ban Thong, side roads branch off for two or three blocks. These houses are made partially of cinderblock and partially of wood and follow the pattern typical to Thai-Lao homes: two floors, with the upper story for sleeping, and the lower used for housing animals, fishing nets, and motorcycles. This lower level is where people rest during the heat of the day, sleeping in hammocks, doing laundry, mending nets, or chatting with neighbors. It is where most of my fieldwork took place.

On the side of the road, bamboo platforms create other ubiquitous spaces. These are spaces of waiting. One waits on the platforms for the bus or for fishermen to return, or one just waits there for the day to pass. In the middle of the day, older women sit watching people come and go. On other platforms, women lay out the day's catch, the fish often still gasping in the air. A big fish—a large goonch catfish (*pa khae*), for instance—will draw people from across the street to ask about it: where it was caught, by whom, how much it will sell for, what techniques brought it in. This last question is a loaded one; it means, "Did the fisherman use an electric shock or dynamite to get the fish?," techniques that are extremely common but also universally frowned upon. Alternately, it might suggest a particular magical spell (*khatha*) that particular fishermen were known to use (but never divulge). At night on these platforms, men gather and drink Sangsom rum, industrially produced rice wine (*sii-sip degree*), or large bottles of Leo beer, and talk about migrant work, the river, women, and ghosts, if not always in that order.

The third line is the riverbank.

At Ban Beuk, the Mekong River forms the border between Thailand and the Lao PDR. The word *Mekong* is a simplification of the Thai *mae nam khong* (Lao: *nam khong*). While foreign travelogues have pointed to the evocative "mother of waters," which is the literal translation of *mae nam*, in practice the name is not so poetic. It is just "Khong River," or simply, in local parlance, "Khong water."

The river flows from its headwaters in Tibet, through China, where it is the "Turbulent River" (*lancang jiang*).[20] Then, as it emerges from Yunnan Province, it weaves between the Southeast Asian countries, first creating the border between Laos and Burma near the infamous Golden Triangle, then demarcating the border between Thailand and Laos at Chiang Khong. Disappearing back into Laos, the river reaches the old Lao royal capital of Luang Prabang, flows through the Sayaburi Dam site, then reemerges to create the border again at Chiang Khan. For a great stretch, the Mekong divides Thailand and Laos before it disappears back into Laos near the old city of Champassak. At the Lao-Cambodian border, it enters a dramatic series of waterfalls at Khone and flows into Cambodia. There, in Cambodia, where the river simply becomes "the great river," the Mekong becomes the environmental, ecological, and agricultural heart of the country. As it flows past the Cambodian capital, Phnom Penh, the Mekong performs a stunning hydrological feat: during the rainy season, the river flows backward, filling up the Tonle Sap lake in the center of the country, the place where Angkor Wat is located, which was the heart of the Khmer Empire. Finally, the river flows into Vietnam, becoming known as the Seven Dragons as it divides and forms the massive Mekong Delta.

Ban Beuk has also been undergoing rapid change. From incorporation into the Siamese polity in the past century (detailed in chapter 1) to the building of infrastructure, to the communist insurgency that tore apart the village in the 1980s, the area has been in flux for years.

In broad sketches, Ban Beuk looks like many other towns in the northeast. There is a clear class division, with local administrators and teachers on top. Women in Ban Beuk on average make more than men, given the fact that girls are more likely to complete their education than boys, and thus women dominate within middle-range bureaucratic jobs, although the town's mayor, headmen, and district head are men. Among these male officials, most also own a host of fishing and agricultural pursuits, including private fishing grounds (*luang mong*) in the river, riverbank gardens for flood-retreat agriculture, and cash crop orchards stretching up the side of the hill. Beneath this stratum are those who rely solely upon fishing, and beneath them again are those who do so without a dedicated fishing ground. Finally, there are those that own no land and get by doing odd jobs for other villagers or perhaps fishing with a hand net on a public spot.

Nearly everyone, male and female, excepting the very poor, had gone elsewhere for several years to work as migrant labor.[21] Some of these—men of a certain age and women of a younger generation—worked in factories in Bangkok, Taiwan, Israel, South Korea, or a host of other sites. Some women had also been sex workers in Bangkok or abroad, and some married foreigners and sent money back home (see Johnson 2018). All families with whom I spoke had some member located abroad, and all relied upon their own or other family members' remittances to get by.

The road through the town was completed roughly thirty years ago, and most of the wealthier residents travel on occasion to nearby centers in Nong Khai, Loei, Udon Thani, or, more rarely, Chiang Mai or Bangkok. Children grow up quickly, and it is not uncommon to marry and have children instead of going to the final years of high school (*mathayom*). Traditionally, Lao villages are uxorilocal, with men coming from outside into the village. While this is generally the case for those born in the 1970s, younger people might be patrilocal. Indeed, there is a recent trend (expressed more in desire than in practice) for men in Ban Beuk to marry Laotian women from across the river, often in response to an outflow of women from Ban Beuk who are marrying men from regional capitals, Bangkok, or abroad.

And soon to come is another disruption. Ban Beuk exists in the path of China's Belt and Road Initiative, a proposition that will remake the Mekong River and run high-speed rail from China to Singapore near the town. Another Chinese measure is the blasting of rapids in the Mekong, in order to render the river navigable to container ships, at least from Jinghong past Luang Prabang to Vientiane.

What was always a cosmopolitan town, sending out locals abroad, will suddenly have the world not just at its doorstep, but rushing by at high velocity.

OUTLINE OF CHAPTERS

This book is divided into six chapters. This chapter, the introduction, has described the central ideas of the text and key arguments in the literature as well as Ban Beuk itself. Then, in chapter 1, "Naga and Garuda," I look at Ban Beuk as a border town, between Thailand and Laos. Drawing upon theories of the border (cf. Nail 2016), I see the town's marginality as enabling certain flows and distributions of power. Additionally, I situate Ban Beuk in regional history, especially in light of moments of economic, political, and religious revolution in Thailand's northeast, beginning with the millenarian *phi bun* (Holy Man) revolts around the turn of the twentieth century. These revolutions proclaimed a coming radical change in reality, both political and in the natural world (cf. Keyes 1977; Murdoch 1974; Toem 1987). They coincided with the incorporation of Isan into the Thai polity, and the attempt by Bangkok to create an absolute monarchy where once were tributary states with their own dynasties. This I relate to later revolutions, including that of the Communist Party of Thailand, which had its base near Ban Beuk and whose actions in turn triggered the direct military rule of the town. And, more recently, the Red Shirt movement, which called for, among other things, increased political power in the provinces, had Isan at its core. Revolution seems integral to the soil of Isan, and, accordingly, I discuss the region as Bangkok's "skeptical frontier," where the hegemony of the center-oriented Thai state dwindles.

Now is no different. In the current revolution in the natural world, when nature itself is becoming altered, these latent apocalyptic and messianic futures suddenly seem about to manifest, especially as the Thai monarchy under Rama X has seemed to reach a low point. Here, then, I ask: How are the collapse of political, economic, and environmental futures linked? How is the erosion of royal sovereignty (in a sense of *khwam pen jao*) linked with the decline of the river? What life is imagined to persist (and how) in the "blasted landscape" (Tsing 2015) after the revolution? How does hydropower play into such moments of revolt?

In my second chapter, "River Beings," I turn to an analysis of the Mekong, those within its waters, and those on its banks. Here, too, I deal with the dam. Unlike previous work on hydropower on the Mekong (Goldman 2005; Whitington 2018), my focus is not on those creating it, but rather on how it affects those downstream. The dam, in this volume, is a distant source—an absent thing that has very real consequences upon the networks of living and nonliving, material and spirit, downstream.

Water, fish, and humans are intertwined in intimate ways, both biological and social, extending even to the incorporation of river flukes into human and fish bodies, changing immune systems in ways that can be both beneficial and catastrophic (Echaubard et al. 2016). As the title of the chapter suggests, playing upon Marisol de la Cadena's "earth beings," I draw here upon new work on new materialism (Hastrup and Hastrup 2016), the "nonhuman turn" in anthropology (Grusin 2015), and the interplay between geography, ecology, and local knowledge (Cruikshank 2005; de la Cadena 2015).

But what I discovered was that, in the wake of the dams, the ways in which one dwells with the river fail—water in the new river comes in the dry season without, or with different kinds of, fish. And as previously known qualities of the river cease to be, water reemerges as something unreadable, something under the sway of a distant force. In short, the whole appears to be more than the sum of its parts—something additional, something occult, is acting along with the material qualities of the river. While new materialist literature stresses the productive power of material actors (Bennett 2010), here I choose to look at those actors that are not directly present.

People, too, are absent-present. I continue in chapter 3, "Dwelling under Distant Suns," to look at the relationship between Ban Beuk and migrant labor. The figure of the migrant, like that of the dam, becomes a lens through which to see how power and potency are experienced in Ban Buek. Via engagement with worlds elsewhere—via learning to live in and be a part of a foreign world, be that world Bangkok, Seoul, or Sweden—these migrants access new sources of distant potential and promise to bring it back home. But as the anxieties of my interlocutors suggest, such a return might not happen. If migrant workers are a sort of shaman, sent abroad to return with power, they, like the shaman, return changed, if at all.

My metaphor of a more cosmological, animist way of seeing power in connection with migration is intentional. Other-than-humans migrate, too. Mon and others discussed nagas who "died" but returned in a ghostly form to give gifts to those on the riverbank. New spirits arrived, and old spirits either transformed or lost their power in the landscape of the new Mekong. In chapter 4, "The River Grew Tired of Us," I look at this transformation. I ask, how does the movement of gods and spirits, water serpents and ghosts, fit into the larger moment of migrants and dams, changes in the water and in the political fortunes of Isan?

Finally, in chapter 5, "Human and Inhuman Worlds," I return to the theoretical ideas with which I began: potency, dwelling, and opacity. I look at the speculative aspect of the future promised (or threatened) by revenants such as the naga, the island king, the phi bun of the 1920s, the migrant, the dam, or the many others that I describe here. This speculative time becomes intertwined with notions of hope (Miyazaki 2004) and doubt (Bubandt 2014), as it is in the fragmentation of worlds in which one dwells that new possibilities come into being. Here I argue that the search for efficacy along the Mekong reveals the unknown and opaque not as an ontological problem to be resolved, but as a means of productively breaking apart the world in order to open the space for new possibilities. Thus, changes arising from the new Mekong point not to a re-formation around an ontological proposition, an assimilation and dispelling of doubt and risk, but instead a way of living with a new, weird existence, one in which opacity is fundamentally embedded. Out of this configuration emerges the figure of the inhuman—a being who is a subject, but whose subject position is unimaginable. One cannot—and does not try—to think like the naga's ghost, but one must engage with it nonetheless. I argue that this perspective sheds new light on what it means to live with things beyond our ken without reducing them to that which emerges from human worlds.

1

NAGA AND GARUDA

Ban Beuk is a border town. Depending on whom one asks, the Lao-Thai border is crossed either when one sets foot in the Mekong, or when one passes by a line of concrete pyramids built by the Laotian military midstream. When I spoke with Lao fishermen, they claimed the entire river and maintained that Thais were only permitted out of their generosity. Thais largely pointed to the channel markers, but crossed this invisible line daily, without comment. Regardless of where the border lies, as a border town, Ban Beuk has been home to all the conflicts that label implies: border skirmishes, smuggling and trafficking, increased scrutiny, and migration.

So what does it mean to be a border town? What do borders enable? In his novel *The City and the City*, China Miéville (2010) describes a fictional city split in half. The residents of either city live alongside each other, but harbor mutual mistrust and antipathy and are continually vigilant for signs that the border between the cities has been breached. But his Besźel/Ul Qoma is no East and West Berlin, divided by a physical wall into separate zones. Instead, the residents of Miéville's city share the same physical space, brushing past one another in the street while remaining socially, symbolically, practically in different cities. Their division is learned, one that comes from seeing styles of dress, language, architecture, or even colors used in one city versus the other. They learn to see their own city, and unsee that which belongs to the other.

But to insist, as foreign visitors to this divided city do, that the division is somehow "not real"—to deliberately see across this boundary—is to miss the point. The border enables certain ways of being: languages, artistry, and means of control. Seeing Besźel allows for a certain way of being that seeing Ul Qoma, or seeing both cities, does not. A border here is not a line on the map—it is a state of being, a deliberate seeing and unseeing. Seeing the border here is a recognition of the border as both arbitrary and also productive of potential because of the difference that it provides.

Borders are not lines on a map, Franck Billé (2017) argues, but "skin-worlds," regions that enable particular forms of movement and circulation (see Nail 2016), and potential libidinal zones.[1] The border at Ban Beuk enables and impedes particular flows and kinds of authority, produces and limits certain potentialities. When we discuss power and potency on the Mekong, the temporal, political, and ontological question of the border is inescapable.

Borders here are especially significant given that the Mekong runs through six countries over the course of its flow. Its fish do not carry passports when they migrate, and the harnessing of its flow for hydropower involves national and international parties. As such, the river-as-border presents a contradiction. The border enables claims to authority and power by various actors (both local and state), while the flow of the river violates these very claims.

WARS WITHOUT BORDERS

The Buddhist heavens consist of five sacred peaks rising out of an ocean. In this ocean are giant serpents, naga, which, despite their fearsome aspect, are intelligent creatures possessing the capacity for noble thought and a devotion to Buddhism, but who choose to dwell in oceans and subterranean depths. But clinging to the rocky seaside cliffs are the birdlike *garuda*, other intelligent and powerful beings, ones used by the divine Vishnu as a steed. Between the naga and garuda is an endless hatred. The garuda dive into the depths of the sea, drawing naga up, while naga in turn swallow stones to make their bodies too heavy to lift. For epochs, naga have been killed by talons and beaks, and garuda overburdened and drowned in the sea.

Here on Earth, there are naga and garuda as well. Naga patrol the Mekong outside of Vientiane, and across Isan—the term for the northeastern, Lao-speaking part of Thailand—villagers often see naga and their tracks winding up out of holes in the ground toward spirit shrines. The garuda, in contrast, graces the official seals of the kingdom of Thailand. Indeed, this symbol shows the implicit hierarchy of Thai politics: with Thai kings of the Chakri dynasty naming themselves after Vishnu's avatar Rama, the nation (the garuda) becomes the vehicle upon which the king (the god) rides. Contra Derrida (2009), the beast in this case *is* the law, which the divine sovereign—literally referred to as having power "above the Constitution" (*amnat neua ratchathamanoon*)—rides. Lao iconography is not so specific with respect to the monarch, but in much political iconography the naga becomes a metaphor for the Lao nation and the protector of Vientiane. Thus, in popular depictions (such as the poem "San Seupsoon"), the hatred between the naga and garuda becomes the conflict between Laos and Thailand. From the lens of divine beasts, Thailand becomes the Brahmanic hegemon, appealing to Indic forms of kingship, whereas Laos draws from more local chthonic and riparian powers.[2]

But we should not simply accept that *Lao* and *Thai* reflect two ageless kingdoms in the region—projecting the present-day nation-state back into the past (as Anderson [2016] cautions against). As many scholars have pointed out (Wolters 1999, 16–17), the notion of a bounded polity in the past simply does not apply to Southeast Asia. Thongchai Winichakul (1994), in his classic *Siam Mapped*, describes how the notion of a nation-state built around borders, rather than on its capital, was alien to most of mainland Southeast Asia until the arrival of the Europeans. Instead, the premodern polity, that is, before the mid-nineteenth century, when colonial powers in the region aggressively implemented technologies of control over their subjects, was something different. It was built around an idea of space that was infused with sources of potency: kings, primarily, but also temples, Buddha footprints, the inhabitation of spirits, and so on. Scholars of premodern Southeast Asia point to the mandala (circle) model, a Theravada Buddhist state that draws upon the legitimacy of the capital and its ruler and extends that out to the countryside. Thus, these polities built their appeal and their ability to mobilize the power of potential tribute and subjects upon the symbolic power of the capital, the power of its religious objects, and the power of its king. This, in turn, can be summed up in one word—*barami*, a term for charismatic power that derives from morally righteous sources. In theory, a wise and pious ruler would ensure, through his barami, the success of his nation.[3]

At times, the influence of one mandala would overlap with another—for instance, Thongchai cites the Vietnamese emperor, Gia Long, in 1811 explaining to the Siamese Rama II that "the Thai king is like [the Cambodian king's] father, and the Vietnamese one like his mother" (1994, 85). Land-based vassalage, sovereignty, and conceptions of absolute authority familiar to European or Japanese politics simply do not apply here.

The premodern mandalas were occasionally loosely integrated empires, and occasionally independent constellations of city-states. Such was the case with the semi-independent northern Thai kingdom of Lanna (Chiang Mai), the city of Nan, the Luang Prabang–based kingdom of Lan Xang, the Shan *möng* in what is now Myanmar, and the Tai Lue kingdoms of Sipsong Panna (in present-day Yunnan). But as Indian Ocean trade increased in importance, polities with links to the coast (e.g., Siam) waxed, and landlocked ones waned. As such, the mandala steadily centralized at major river mouths over the course of the second millennium, so that the late eighteenth century found powerful Burmese, Vietnamese, and Siamese states battling over lordship of lesser mandalas, such as the three states that currently make up Laos: Luang Prabang, Vientiane, and Champasak (Pakse).

Clifford Geertz (1980, 9), in order to understand these mandala states, turns to nineteenth-century Bali for an analogy. Bali, before the Dutch tightened control in the early twentieth century, was a series of kingdoms clustered in river valleys, each centered on the figure of a charismatic king. Management of resources or other mundane tasks was left to organizations such as the irrigation society (*subak*), independent of kingship. Instead, the state in Bali was oriented "toward spectacle, toward ceremony, toward the public dramatization of the ruling obsessions of Balinese culture: social inequality and status pride" (Geertz 1980, 13). Warfare, counter to the assumptions of political scientists, was not a struggle over resources but rather a dramatic demonstration of prestige and mystical might (see also Weiner 1995).

Geertz intends for his model of Bali to stand in for the premodern states of Southeast Asia, and we can productively see pre-nineteenth-century Thai/Lao conflicts in this light. Indeed, like a macrocosm of Bali's river valley–centered polities, in mainland Southeast Asia polities were similarly based around different river systems: the Siamese on the Chao Phraya, the Burmese on the Irawaddy, the Lao on the middle Mekong, and irrigation was central to these. It is no surprise that, even today, the most significant rituals of Thai kingship surround rainmaking (supplemented in the case of Rama IX by a—dubiously scientific—royal rain-making project). And, similarly, prestige in the form of claims to barami—the potency of the center—were significant reasons for war. This barami could be contained in a reputation of martial prowess, or in an object: Buddha images, for example. Or both—one could easily capture the latter via the former.

If Geertz focuses too much on the symbolic, charismatic use of power in pre-colonial Southeast Asia as opposed to its political economy, James Scott, another theorist of the Southeast Asian state, fixates overly on coercion. But why not have both? Kings were both world conqueror and world renouncer (Tambiah 1977), possessing both noble *phra-khun* and violent *phra-dej*. Both of these came to bear in a terrible way upon Vientiane and the Isan and Laotian countryside in 1828, a moment that shaped Lao-Thai relations and the identity of Isan.

The Emerald Buddha

The Temple of the Emerald Buddha sits in the center of the Grand Palace at Bangkok. As the seat of the ruler from the city's founding in 1782 until 1925, for a long period the complex held the center of Siamese barami. As temple and palace both, it was the center of the Siamese mandala—uniting ruler and religion. And, as if to rule the region in miniature, the palace features statues of Chinese guards alongside garuda, and even a large-scale model of the Cambodian ruins at Angkor Wat as a way to stake a claim to that symbolic center. The Emerald Buddha itself—mystically discovered after a lightning strike—is the heart of this palace and acts as the palladium of the Thai kingdom. Art historian Melody Rod-Ari characterizes the Emerald Buddha's presence as making Thailand "the symbolic center of the Theravada Buddhist world" (2009, 55).

But, much like an outsider king, the Emerald Buddha is not originally Thai. In the wake of the destruction of the previous Thai capital at Ayutthaya in 1767, the Siamese state and monarchy had to reconfigure itself. It did so under Taksin, a military leader who claimed to be a bodhisattva, an incipient Buddha, and professed supernatural powers.[4] He established a new capital (Thonburi, part of present-day Bangkok) and undertook a campaign of expansion in search of new vassals, new territory, and new artifacts—the Emerald Buddha among them. When Taksin's forces sacked Vientiane in 1779, they plundered the Emerald Buddha from its remains and brought it back to Bangkok.[5]

Following the capture of the Emerald Buddha, Laos was a vassal kingdom under the Siamese crown, but the Lao royalty chafed under Siamese rule, turning the loss of the Emerald Buddha into a point of obsession (Ngaosivat and Ngaosyvathn 1998, 56). Eventually, in 1826, one rebelled: *jao* Anuvong, who sought to reclaim what had been lost from Laos, even to the point of building multiple replicas of the Emerald Buddha as an attempt to harness its power in facsimile (see Sujane 2012). A brief war raged in Isan, but in 1828 Anuvong's rebellion was cut down, and in its wake Vientiane was destroyed.

The population of Vientiane was not destroyed along with the city. Instead, large numbers of formerly Lao subjects were resettled in Isan, a practice that one northern Thai lord claimed was like "picking vegetables and putting them in baskets, picking serfs and putting them in cities" (Johnson 2014, 35). Thus, while Isan had always been in the overlapping spheres of influence between Thailand and Laos and Cambodia, in this one stroke, Isan became ethnically Lao even as the possibility of it being nationally Lao was foreclosed.

But despite these wars and movements, nineteenth-century Southeast Asia was still a world without borders as lines on a map, or even as skinworlds.

Along with the process of moving from a mandala state to a state configured around Westphalian lines (i.e., with borders) came an idea of joining a "replicable series" (see Anderson 2016) of nations, states with notions of spatial and demographic boundedness and a sense of permanence and inevitability, however false. In this, the idea of nation-space as centered on sacred artifacts and locations shifted to one centered on historical sites and narrative. With this in mind, Siam began to discover or manufacture ancient polities (e.g., Sukhothai) that would suggest a Siamese claim to land (Mukhom 2003; Strate 2015).[6] This process continued into the early twentieth century, when city-states that had retained their own monarchies, script, and Buddhist practices were required (often violently) to replicate the speech and religion of the center, and to follow its crown alone. Thus, what had originally been a part of a loosely related continuum of Tai or Lao groups joined a nation.[7] Chiang Mai became Thai (see Johnson 2014); Luang Prabang became Lao (a French colony); and Sipsong Panna became Xishuangpanna, a part of China. Thus, Ban Beuk became Thai, and the modern border came down like a wall, separating it completely from Laos.

Of course, "Laos" after 1893 meant "French." In the late nineteenth century, Siam had laid claim to Laos, ostensibly to protect it from Chinese invaders (the misnamed "Haw") but also to beat Europeans to the claim.[8] The French, in response, sailed a gunboat just opposite the Grand Palace. As a result, they forced the Siamese to relinquish claims to most of present-day Laos (Luang Prabang, the ruins of Vientiane, and Champassak). While Siamese sources present the takeover as a loss of territory (Strate 2015), Lao sources are more complicated—the French were outsiders, true, but domination by outsiders was nothing unusual. Rather, the French presence was an opportunity—rule by a distant other meant that the more proximate Siamese powers were curtailed in the region, and disinterested French rule presented an opportunity for local lords to renew old claims both within Laos and across the border in Isan (see Baird 2017) in ways that were shielded from the centralization and consolidation happening in Siam.

During the final part of the nineteenth century and the early twentieth century, European powers in the region (especially the British and the Dutch) sought to incorporate formerly independent regions (Siegel 1969; Weiner 1995) and extend biopolitical control over areas that were already occupied by military forces (Stoler 1996). In this, Siam carefully followed European powers, but did so in its own way, incorporating European norms while at the same time stridently proclaiming the state's uniqueness—a model of governance that Michael Herzfeld (2002) terms "crypto-colonialism." Building upon models of Victorian England and imperial Germany, the Siamese established an administrative bureaucracy appointed by Bangkok, but they also reformed the Buddhist *sangha* (monastic community) in order to bring local temples more directly under Bangkok's control.

From a Bangkokian perspective, this was a relatively straightforward process of integrating half of a former vassal and modernizing a feudal infrastructure along the lines of what was being put in place in the European colonies. But these changes dramatically altered Isan society in unforeseen ways. New systems of taxation that bypassed traditional lords not only alienated the local elite and disrupted patronage systems (see Anan [1984] for a northern Thai example) but also gave rise to new forms of exploitation, as impostors were too eager to collect taxes on behalf of the Siamese government only to disappear once the real tax collectors came around (Keyes 1977, 295).

In northern Thailand, similar processes were also underway in a region on the borders of British Burma and Siam. But unlike Isan, which consisted of the resettled serfs of Vientiane foisted upon a local population, the north was an intact kingdom prior to incorporation. There, too, the reaction to Siamese centralization led to an armed revolt framed along ethnic lines (Sarasawadee 2005; Walker 2014) as well as cosmic ones—a local monk, Sriwichai, became a rallying figure and was often cited as holding magical powers (see Bowie 2014). As a case in point, a list of charges against Sriwichai distributed in the north included accusations that he floated above his supposed Bangkokian superior and would not come down, and that he caused the rain to fall upon the monk from Bangkok whereas Sriwichai remained dry. Here was a clear challenge to the barami of the center in ways that would have been legible to Taksin, but which were in the twentieth century no longer effective enough as rebellion.

In the northeast, a hinterland without a center, a more fundamental change was promised. In 1902, rumors swept the region that a transformation in the state of affairs was coming. The rumors varied from place to place (Keyes 1977, 295) but involved a transformation in the ontic. Rocks would become gold; buffaloes would become demons; silkworms would become carnivorous mermaids. A wind would blow through the land, and only holding onto clumps of lemongrass could one keep rooted to the ground (Toem 1987, 446). Here was not a rally to an alternate flag, as in Chiang Mai; here was a statement that the era of flags was over, to be replaced by something new. And this "new" was a return to a notion of land that rested upon the presence of divine power.

In several of these Holy Man (*phi bun*) revolts, this "new" was given an old name—Vientiane (Chatthip 1984). But this was not a call to reoccupy the site on the left bank of the Mekong where the capital once stood eighty years prior. Rather, Chattip Nartsupha (1984) argues that Vientiane in Isan occupied the status of a "new Jerusalem." It was a call to a half-remembered place, which one's grandparents or great-grandparents called home, and which would be made manifest at the place of the revolt.

This was no organized movement, at least not at first. Rather, to be a part of it, one had to prepare—and to wait. In the wake of the rumor, fields went unharvested. Animals—potential demons—were slaughtered, and villagers who followed the rumor, or those "holy men" who claimed to be the heralds of the change, awaited the coming of a new hero—not the Buddhist Maitreya, but an alternative holy king (see Keyes 1977; Murdoch 1974; Toem 1987).[9] Instead of collecting cash, villagers collected gravel (Lao: *hin hae*; Toem 1987, 445). Productive activity that would articulate with Bangkok's new regime of taxation and regulation ceased, to be replaced with activity that seemed, from a bureaucrat's standpoint, irrational or self-defeating.

Accounts of the revolt (e.g., Keyes 1977; Murdoch 1974; Tej 1987; Toem 1987) discuss efforts to force Isan residents back to work, the resultant discontent, and the eventual armed uprising. These classic analyses of the uprising describe it as a reaction to Isan's incorporation into Bangkok, a last attempt to preserve a feudal order in the face of a new, modern reality. More recently, Walker (2014) and Baird (2013) situate the uprising in regional context and frame the rebellions of 1901 as seizing an opportunity provided by a new border with neighboring French Indochina (Walker 2014), including recently dispossessed Laotian royals (Baird 2013).[10]

Unmentioned by many of these accounts is that the Holy Man revolts were no special moment occasioned by the political and economic changes at the time. Chatthip Nartsupha, pulling from oral history as well as Bangkok's archives, documents a number of uprisings taking place from the nineteenth century up until the 1960s. Each of these revolts has a common theme: a holy man appears, makes a claim that a new order is imminent, establishes a new holy site (often associated with a new Vientiane), and is then struck down.

For Chatthip (1999), these commonalities speak to a timeless peasant consciousness against Bangkok. I agree that something lingers in Isan, but I diverge from his community-oriented Marxist approach. In my analysis, activities that seem nonsensical are not just the "weapons of the weak" (Scott 2005) used to opt out of productive aspects of the state (see also Scott 2009). There are more resistant, more antistate things that one could do than amass gravel, slaughter buffalo, and plant lemongrass at one's doorstep. Instead, these are attempts at preparation for a world to come, preparations for a new ontic. They are motions to dwelling in a way that is profoundly changed—it makes sense to operate in ways that are nonsensical, if the future that one anticipates is one with radically different ways of being.

Chatthip's (1999) account of Holy Man revolts ends in the mid-twentieth century. But this does not mean that revolutions end. Isan remains to this day a place where central authority is routinely contested, and often those contesting Bangkok's rule draw clear links back to earlier revolts (Saowanee 2016). During the 1980s, Isan (and specifically the northern section of Isan, where Ban Beuk lies) was the heart of the Communist Party of Thailand (CPT), and during the 2000s and 2010s, this same region formed the backbone of the Red Shirt movement (see Sopranzetti 2017b). Thus, while many have come to speak of a newly awakened rural Thailand (Walker 2011; Keyes 2014) in recent years, I argue here that the potentiality was always there, from the Holy Man revolts, to the communist insurgency of the 1980s, to the present day.

From Anuvong to the present, Isan has held a skepticism of the centers of power. It is this that Chatthip (1999) wants to idealize in his "community culture" model, and it is this that provoked CIA-linked American investigations into potential (and actual) communist activity in Isan (Wakin 2008).

At the same time, Isan has always been peripheral. *Lao* in its use in late nineteenth- and early twentieth-century Thai referred to any northern or northeastern peasant, from Chiang Mai to Khorat to Vientiane. In Thongchai Winichakul's (2000) study of the hierarchies that late nineteenth-century Siamese elites made of the residents of Siam, *Lao* clearly fits within the *chao bannok*, the term for "out-country people." For elites of the time (and of today), villagers from rural regions were uninteresting as curiosities and assumed to be largely unsophisticated versions of elites, in need of the guiding hand of a Thai elder brother. King Chulalongkorn (r. 1868–1910) likened the role of Bangkok vis-à-vis Lao populations to the role of Western missionaries toward the populations they sought to convert: as a *mission civiliatrice* (Sarasawadee 1982, 33).

Such a sense of marginality continues today. The phrase *na lao* (Lao face) is an insult for an unattractive person with dark skin. It is often delivered disparagingly and with no sense of irony to Southeast Asian–appearing Thais by Bangkokians of Chinese descent (Hesse-Swain 2006). It was a phrase that I often heard used by Bangkok-based Thais against those with whom I worked, and a term that blended ethnic discrimination with class-based hierarchies. This hierarchy extends to language as well. For instance, when speaking with a young woman in Ban Beuk, she complimented me on my Isan dialect. I replied that I'd studied Vientiane Lao for a year, and her smile faded. "They're not the same [Isan and Lao]. They're very different. For instance, [for noodle soup] Isan people say *kwaitiaw* [a Teochieu loanword] and Lao people say *feu* [a Vietnamese loanword]." I fumbled for a moment before replying, "Yes, there are some differences. But Lao and Isan are closer to each other than Isan is to [Central] Thai, isn't that right [*maen boh*]?," to which she readily agreed. Here, she readily accepted difference from Bangkok; it is the label of "Lao" that is problematic.

Today, the "Lao-ness" of Isan Thais is invoked, at different times, as an insult (as in "na lao"), a joke, a flatly stated fact, an embarrassing label to be denied heartily, and a marker of cultural intimacy (Herzfeld 2005). Michael Herzfeld describes "cultural intimacy" as "the recognition of those aspects of a cultural identity that are considered a source of external embarrassment but that nevertheless provide insiders with their assurance of common sociality" (2005, 3). When I was introduced to people in Ban Beuk, their friends might mockingly introduce them as being ethnically or nationally Lao, as in, "Andrew! Here is Ngoen! He's Lao, from the other bank!" It was only much later that I confirmed that Ngoen was in fact a native of Ban Beuk, and was as Lao as the others in town—but here the embarrassment afforded by an outsider "misrecognizing" an Isan person as Lao provided a space for Ngoen's mockery, even though every resident could him- or herself become the target of such a joke.

In a larger context, even as Thai claims to ethnic homogeneity and the superiority of Siamese (and Sino-Siamese) predominates in Thai media, a skeptical voice emerges on the periphery. In the mandala system, the authority of the center fades as one reaches the periphery. In contrast, in the nation-state, borders are absolute up until the point where one crosses them. The Thai-Lao border at Ban Beuk is caught between these two models. Just as in the mandala state, where control is strongest at the center, claims to "Thai-ness" (*khwampenthai*; see Thongchai 1994) are at their height in Bangkok. On the edge are those that could go either way—potential subjects (*kha*) who might join Bangkok or might join Laos, or might simply break away and join the regional center. They are, in this light, quite far from the caricature of ignorant peasants that one finds in the Thai media (see Funahashi 2016), but are, as I show throughout this volume, actively considering and contesting truth claims, from communist to capitalist to Buddhist to monarchist. The frontier between mandalas, then, is a skeptical frontier.

Here, I mean the term *skeptical frontier* as a counterpart to the depictions of the radiant center of the mandala. Indeed, the mandala that relies upon claims to righteous power and magical potency would seem to require such a frontier—those who are most exposed to competing claims and for whose loyalty one strives.

The border at Ban Beuk is just such a skeptical frontier. In 2016, when the Thai king Bhumibol Adulyadej died, the country was gripped by mourning. Websites went dark, lavish ceremonies were held at the Grand Palace, and Thailand sought to portray a country stricken with grief by the death of a leader, a father, and a divinity (*samuttithep*; see Jackson 2010). Some in Ban Beuk took photos of themselves wearing black on Facebook, or sharing royalist slogans online. But these digital displays rarely bled into public displays of monarchical piety. And Mon summed up the attitude toward what Bangkok was considering the most significant event of a lifetime by simply saying to me: "Krung thep . . . man klai."

"Bangkok is far away."

It has been my argument here and elsewhere (Johnson 2014) that the magico-religious logic of the mandala state runs through the present-day nation-state. At its margins, we should expect the frontier to be taking claims of the center's authority skeptically. But, of course, the border is not simply the petering out of the mandala into the skeptical frontier. The Thai-Lao border exists also in the sense of the skinworld—the edge of the nation-state. Here, the existence of the border allows for particular kinds of exploitation, for navigation, fishing, irrigation—and hydropower.

HYDROPOWER ON THE MEKONG

In July 2018, a dam under construction finally broke in Laos. The Xepian-Xe Nam Noy, after showing signs of strain for hours, finally gave way to monsoon floods, and a torrent of water swept through parts of Attapeu district. The floods continued across the Cambodian border, leading to mass evacuations.

The fallout from the collapse has, at the time of writing, not been resolved. Thousands are displaced, and likely hundreds are dead in Laos and Cambodia. SK Construction, the South Korean company involved in the construction, is facing harsh criticism from human rights groups outside of Laos, and the viability of Laotian hydropower has suddenly been thrown into question (BBC News 2018; Erickson 2018). Lert's dark dream of Jinghong breaking seems to, in a day, be made more real.

But with Xepian-Xe Nam Noy, as with Jinghong, hydropower is inseparable from the issue of borders. The Xepian-Xe Nam Noy dam was Korean-built, financed by the Electricity Generating Authority of Thailand, and sent nearly all of its electricity to Thailand via yet another Thai company. Power and capital, in other words, flow across borders toward bright centers—to Bangkok's royally owned shopping malls, for instance. But the water, and the destruction that it caused, flowed elsewhere.

Those killed in its collapse were Lao, and, for the victims of the disaster, its provenance was unclear. The Lao authorities restricted information about the collapse. Further, the runoff flooded into Cambodia. Dislodged and redistributed during the flood were unexploded ordinance left over from the American bombing campaign against Vietnam, making a return to flooded villages dangerous. In one disaster, we have Thailand, Laos, South Korea, the United States, and Cambodia all at once.

Against the Flow

Borders, to return to Nail (2016), enable particular flows. This is especially literal when borders are themselves in motion—rivers, for instance, physically move material from one nation to the next. Even as rivers are often used to define borders (just think of the Rubicon), they in their very materiality violate borders.

Krista Harper (2005), describes how, in Hungary, in the years just prior to the end of state socialism, plans to dam the Danube had unexpected consequences. Hydropower projects that had recently been the iconic symbols of socialist planning, progress, and development suddenly provoked not only a critique of the government but linkages with environmental movements also concerned with the Danube, upstream, in Slovakia and Austria.

What, then, of the parallels with Laos, where a similar state socialist hydropower project runs into cross-border environmentalism? How does the issue of hydropower span and contest the notion of border as skinworld? Here, then, I survey the issue of hydropower on the Mekong and trace the entanglements that the river creates across (and because of) borders.

The Mekong, compared to other rivers in Asia, has been underexploited for hydropower. In the People's Republic of China, the regions through which the Mekong (Lancang) runs are distant from centers of Han ethnicity and power and thus were largely ignored through most of the twentieth century. In Laos, the Mekong formed a tense—often violent—border between opposing sides in the Cold War, and, farther downstream in Cambodia, tragedies like the genocide under the Khmer Rouge preempted other kinds of development.

But during the 1980s, a shift occurred. Cambodia, emerging from UN control after the fall of the Khmer Rouge, began to set its sights on national development. Laos, following the lead of Vietnam, opened some aspects of its economy and state up to outside actors. And China's economic boom meant that every corner of the country was now a candidate for large-scale projects.

Fantastic books have been written on Lao hydropower projects, including in-depth accounts of how funding agencies plan them (Goldman 2005), how teams on the ground work through (and, indeed, create) uncertainty (Whitington 2018), and the often devastating environmental and social impacts of these projects (Shoemaker and Robichaud 2018). This book does not seek to do what these previous projects have done. Go and read them if you want to understand planners.

But I am indebted to two scholars on dams in Southeast Asia: Jakkrit Sangkhamanee (2017b) and Jerome Whitington (2018). Both of these scholars approach hydropower from a science and technology studies (STS) perspective, one that I do not share, but their perspectives yield fruitful insights.

Jakkrit pulls from the Latourean idea of a "parliament of things" in order to understand the heterogeneous factors that play into Thai hydropower projects. In Jakkrit's approach, objects speak through their "representatives"—climate, for instance, is a "quasi-object" that emerges from atmosphere "represented" by climate science, farmers' observations on crops, and so on. Similarly, Thai hydropower incorporates influences as diverse as naga vehicles, bureaucracies, and engineers. For Jakkrit, hydropower reveals "a blurring of nature, society and divinity occurring at the very heart of the Thai engineered state" (2017b, 276).

Whitington, also writing on (Lao) hydropower via the lens of STS, takes an analysis a step further. Hydropower creates uncertain environments. One can see that clearly in Mon's and Lert's experience—the river is no longer predictable. Similarly (I go into more detail in subsequent chapters) the biota of the river are also uncertain. But for Whitington's interlocutors in hydropower development, this uncertainty is the point. The very kinds of knowledge valorized and produced by Lao hydropower are entrepreneurial, oriented toward, not away from, uncertainty. Thus, managing these uncertain realms and playing different interest groups off each other becomes itself a skill mastered by individuals involved in these projects.

Dams are, in this light, not carefully arranged puzzle pieces, but rather a distracted child's LEGO tower, built without a clear vision of what will come and made up of things from entirely different sets. They are amalgams of disparate objects that stem from very different ontological worlds—offerings to nagas and community interests cohabit with engineering efforts and international electricity trade agreements, and their effects and impact are unclear. Here, then, I go into a history of these interventions on the Mekong with an eye toward the uncertainty that they engender.

So let us start where the river starts, in China.

Jinghong

The dam that features in Lert's dream—the one with the dark crack running down its center—is the Jinghong Hydroelectric Dam, in China's Yunnan Province. In Yunnan, there is a series of fourteen dams, of which six are operational at the time of writing. These are, in order from north to south, the Gushui, Wunonglong, Lidi, Tuoba, Huangdeng, Dahuaqiao, Miaowei, Gongguoqiao, Xiaowan, Manwan, Dachaoshan, Nuozhadu, Jinghong, and, planned, the Gantanba.

The area of Xishuangpanna, from where the Jinghong Dam stands and haunts Lert's dreams, is China's own "skeptical frontier"—space left over by colonizing powers and indigenous states alike. The name itself is perfectly legible in Thai as Sipsong Panna, the "twelve thousand rice fields" (*panna*, "a thousand rice fields," is an ancient political unit; *sipsong panna* might better be thought of as meaning "twelve princedoms"), and *jinghong* is a sinification of the Tai Lue *jiang hung* (Thai: *chiang rung*).

This region of China consists of inhospitable terrain, sharp mountain peaks, and "malarial valleys" (Osborne 2001) and, as such, forms a part of that ethnically diverse and politically divisive region of Southeast Asia that James Scott (2009) terms "Zomia."

My point in starting with this aspect of its history is to situate Xishuangpanna—as with Lanna, the Shan States, and Nan—as a skeptical frontier vis-à-vis the powers of the day. Non-Chinese to begin with, following Theravada Buddhism (as opposed to the East Asian Mahayana), it was already on the edge of the empire and, as such, became a central ground for various rebel groups—the Haw (the losers of the Taiping rebellion) and, later, the Kuomintang (the losers of Mao's revolution).[11] With this in mind, Xishuangpanna was relatively ignored by Beijing (as it was by other imperial capitals in London, Paris, and Bangkok) for years. It was where people went to be forgotten.

But this changed under the Deng administration, when Beijing began to actively court international partnerships. In the mid-1990s, the Asia Development Bank proposed, in partnership with the Chinese government, an "Economic Quadrangle" near Jinghong. The term played off the former "Golden Triangle" appellation and its association with the opium trade that dominated that region during the 1980s. But this new quadrangle aimed at increasing connections, industry, and tourism between China and its three southern neighbors.[12] It marked a turning point, a move away from seeing areas like the Golden Triangle as wild backwaters and toward seeing them as opportunities for investment. Indeed, this should not be so surprising—uncertainty is precisely what entrepreneurs seek. And that this investment would also lead to increased state presence was a benefit lost on neither planners nor observers (see Ferguson [1990] for a classic example).

As a promotional flyer read: "The Economic Quadrangle is now the focus of Asia. . . . This is a golden opportunity in doing business, in the area full of natural resources and labour with lower wages" (cited in Walker 2000, 122). But practically, the Quadrangle was something of a mixed bag. Actors on all sides grew frustrated with the poor delivery upon its utopian promises, as the kinds of corruption and patronage that regional businesses and border military had grown used to stood in the way of neoliberal fantasies (Walker 2000, 123).

Ten years later, the Quadrangle has radically changed, giving way to China's new Belt and Road model, one that seeks to create Chinese-controlled channels through which Chinese goods can move (Doig 2018; Ong 2017). With this new, much larger, plan in mind, the idea of a four-way cooperative region faded in importance against a narrative of an ascendant China. In the later 1990s, the Chinese state increasingly pursued bilateral negotiations with Mekong countries, where it could assert more pressure on weaker neighbors, as opposed to multilateral relations, where weaker countries could band together. As such, while the notion of a free-trade zone at the nexus of East and Southeast Asia withered, the dream of the Mekong as a commercial highway has become more and more realized.

The Luang Prabang airport's international terminal is one such marker of Chinese presence in the region. It is, for a city of 56,000 people, stunning. The entrance hall is cavernous and air-conditioned; the immigration counters are state-of-the-art. But the electrical outlets do not accept Laotian plugs. Rather, they are made by the airport's Chinese builders for Chinese appliances. Builders either did not care to check, or intentionally made the heart of Laos's cultural tourist industry a Chinese space in ways that easily parallel the (intentional or not) lack of care in hydropower projects planned for the region.

Within the Mekong region, a Chinese presence is more and more evident, thanks in part to the success of a Chinese comedy film, *Lost in Thailand* (Xu 2012), set in Thailand's north, as well as new highways connecting Thailand with China. Chinese tourists are ubiquitous. Based upon numbers from the Tourist Authority of Thailand, in 2016, Chinese tourists constituted 8.7 million arrivals, compared to 3.5 million from Malaysia and 1.5 million from South Korea (only 600,000 tourists came from the United States).

In this new context, the Xi administration has sought new friends in the region, and found them in Hun Sen's Cambodia and the Communist Party of Laos. In the latter case, border tensions and the ongoing antipathy between Vietnam and China have moderated Laotian partnership with China, but Hun

Sen has proven himself to be a willing partner. Elsewhere, the Thai military government of Prayuth Chan-o-cha, finding itself criticized by traditional allies in the United States and Japan, has warmed to the Chinese influence in the region as one that doesn't pressure the Thai military too much over human rights.

The river itself, too, has changed with the rise of China. Currently, the Chinese government is sponsoring the demolition of rapids (*kaeng*—a term that will become significant in a subsequent chapter) along the Mekong between Yunnan and Luang Prabang, allowing ships of up to 500 tons to pass (Cochrane 2017). With the rapids in place, one motivation for releasing water from Jinghong or keeping water levels artificially high has been not just power generation, but allowing cargo ships to move. "Blasting the rapids to make a canal," as the project is termed in Thai, would obviate this need.

The view from Beijing, then, sees the Mekong as untapped potential, both standing reserve to be mobilized for China's urban expansion and new opportunities for Chinese industry or tourists. And this notion of the Mekong as Chinese standing reserve is what makes the dams north of the border so controversial: Xi's policy on the Mekong is that water in China is China's to do with as the state sees fit. Thus, dams built in China are not beholden to any kind of international oversight. Chinese media reports downplay negative impacts downstream, and instead bring forth the commonly repeated narratives of flood control, carbon-neutral energy generation, and national development.

One Thai NGO activist in Bangkok expressed to me his frustration at Chinese data on hydropower: "China is not helpful [in mitigating the damage from dams]. They provide tainted data—for instance, they might say that their dams only affect [total] outflow [from the Mekong] by 18 percent, but they take these measurements [from the mouth of the Mekong] in Vietnam! If you measure in Chiang Khong [on the Thai-Lao border, very close to Jinghong], the level is more [like] 70 percent. And also, they only measure in the rainy season [when Mekong levels are swelled by local runoff]."

The Jinghong Dam sits just at the border between China, Burma, and Laos, where the Mekong prepares to exit China and flow between the latter two countries. It, according to International Rivers (2017), produces 1,750 megawatts of electricity, a significant proportion of which is sold to the Electricity Generating Authority of Thailand (EGAT). Construction on Jinghong began in 2003 and was completed in 2008, and it was in the intervening years that Lert and others began to notice its effects—a precipitous drop in water level followed by a sudden flood, and the disappearance of fish species, especially the large *pa beuk* (*Pangasianodon gigas*; see discussion in chapter 2).

That dams should lead to a collapse in the ecology of the region should come as no surprise. Richter et al. (2010) note the common experience of those living downstream of major dam projects, in terms of the loss of fisheries as well as a drop in the fertility of riverbank cultivation. In Richter et al.'s analysis of such a project in Laos, they note that the loss of fisheries was far more significant than simply the loss of income from fishing. Rather, the capture of small aquatic biota (Richter et al. [2010, 27] mentions snails, shrimp, and crabs along with fish; I might add frogs and algae) was vital to everyday consumption. As these animals (and algae) declined, villagers turned toward the consumption of livestock, animals that had been kept as "banks" against future famine, rendering populations increasingly vulnerable to future shocks, ecological or economic.

Yos Santasombat (2009, 26), in his study of fishing on the Mekong, notes the dependence of Lao and Thai-Lao riverbank communities on fish protein, as well as that of fishing techniques upon the monsoon cycle of ebb and flood (27). While different species of fish migrate in different ways, beuk and other large fish tend to hide in deep pools (nong) in the main channel during the dry season and migrate out to tributaries or flooded forests during the wet. Such a movement makes sense: as areas that were land are steadily claimed by rising water, the nutrients thus covered are available for fish to consume.

Yos describes how the effects from the closures of Jinghong's predecessor, Manwan, were catastrophic for Mekong fishermen near the city of Chiang Khong, a community, like Ban Beuk, that focused around the capture of gigas in deep channels at a narrow point in the river. In 1994, just after the closure of Manwan, water levels reached unprecedented lows. Afterward, and intensifying in 1999, as subsequent dam projects began construction in China, water levels became erratic, with record highs and lows. At the same time, capture of gigas stopped entirely in 1994, and has only sporadically happened since.

The Chinese dams are inseparable from the way the river operates. Owing to their size and their openings and closures, these dams have a profound impact upon the river. But they are also products of the border. Jinghong straddles the river just kilometers away from the border, and claims to absolute ownership of Chinese water are immediately complicated when this water becomes Lao. Sovereign claims are bound up in the water, water that by its very materiality elides these claims.

Sayaburi

Past Jinghong, the Mekong River weaves in and out of the Lao People's Democratic Republic, at times forming the Thai-Lao border, and at times disappearing into Laos proper. Here, any unitary claim to the river becomes complicated, as, for much of its length, the river forms the border between two countries. As such, projects south of the Chinese border inevitably concern the Mekong River Commission (MRC), an international organization based in Vientiane.

The MRC is an organization established in 1995 and built on the bones of previous colonial and postcolonial organizations intended to comanage the river. The MRC was to be a place where Southeast Asian countries could balance environmental and economic impacts upon the river in a multilateral way. Its member states include Thailand, Laos, Cambodia, and Vietnam, with China and Myanmar as "dialogue partners."

However, these goals of mitigating environmental and economic impact have largely gone unmet. Whereas the MRC publishes a wide body of knowledge on the Mekong and the impact of dams, even to the point of criticizing member states' failures in implementation of environmental controls, the organization faces an apathetic response to environmentalism from Thai, Lao, and Cambodian interests who seek their own dam projects, and outright antipathy from China. Indeed, as Middleton et al. (2009) point out, the emergence and emboldening of a China-centric political model in Southeast Asia has led to an embrace of actors with lower environmental standards and a transformation of the MRC into a rubber stamp for new projects.

Chief among those seeking hydropower for national development is Laos. Landlocked Laos is a country of mountain ranges cut through by river valleys. It belongs largely to those areas left out of state formation processes in the region, and shares with Myanmar traits of ethnic diversity split between animist upland and Buddhist lowland zones.

After independence from France and a brief period of American hegemony, Laos remained dominated by Vietnam. Although the Vietnamese-style communist rule of the Pathet Lao was more isolationist and controlling than its form in Vietnam (at least in the lowlands), the state remained generally weak compared to its neighbors. Laos is, on the geopolitical scale, still a hinterland.

But what Laos lacked in economy, it made up for in natural resources. Hydropower was to be chief among these. Laos would use the very geography that rendered it difficult terrain for lowland states to master as the engine of its ascendancy into the, as the slogan went, "battery of Asia." Indeed, the Lao PDR official seal features a hydropower dam.

Major Lao dams—thirteen in total at the time of writing—were built largely by and for foreign interests. Investing companies included Norwegian, US, French, and Korean firms as well as the expected Chinese, Thai, and Lao firms. Most of the power generated is aimed at the Thai market, in order to feed the growing demand for power south of the Mekong, although other analyses have suggested that the Thai market could generate power more cheaply in other ways (Trandem 2011).

This is certainly true for the Sayaburi Dam, Laos's first along the Mekong's mainstream. Proposed in 2010 and begun in 2012 by Thai construction company CH Karnchang, the dam was expected to be completed in 2019, although it already spans most of the river at the time of writing (2018).

The Sayaburi Dam is different from the Chinese dams, which are tall, with big reservoirs. Sayaburi is short. It will release water every day, unlike the Chinese dams that release water once a season. What will happen, river activists anticipate, is that the region from China to Sayaburi will be affected by periodic great floods, while land downstream from Sayaburi will be affected by daily differences. Both are catastrophic for river ecology.

Sayaburi ignited a firestorm of criticism from international groups, Vietnam, and from activists on the Thai side of the Mekong. These last were outgrowths of Thailand's active civil society, protest groups already fired up over years of protesting the expansion of business interests and dam construction in Thailand.

But in Laos, environmental groups languished owing to strict state control. Indeed, Lao environmental activist Sombath Somphone became a cause célèbre when he was abducted from downtown Vientiane in 2012 and presumably killed, despite taking pains to mute criticism of the Lao state.

Sombath's case—where criticism of illegal logging and predatory business activities becomes a sore point for state interests—highlights the messy intertwining of business interests, mafia, and state interests that plagues all of the Mekong countries mentioned here, especially Laos. Back in Ban Beuk, shipments of illegal lumber from Laos passed the docks frequently, enabled by cutting the local police in on the profits. Thus, guarantees of environmental protection at one level may be undercut at another, even by the same person, and figures powerful in one sphere may be equally influential in another. My survey of the processes and considerations that go into any major project is necessarily limited—in other words, I do not have informants among the Laotian mafia.

In a related note, Sombath's disappearance was crucial to the planning of this study as well. I had originally envisioned doing this research in Laos, but was repeatedly warned away after it happened.

Chief among the criticisms of Lao hydropower are not only the expected critique of upstream (flooding) effects of the dams, but also the paucity of data that went into the downstream effects of Sayaburi—unsurprising given the sheer lack of environmental studies done on the Mekong (Baran, Guerin, and Nasielski 2007). Planners from the Finnish engineering company Pöyry conducted an environmental impact assessment for the dam, but only included a 10 km stretch of the Mekong downstream (Hogan 2011). The company concluded that, while not all concerns were known or could be anticipated, any unknowns could easily be addressed after construction had begun (Herbertson 2012; see also Whitington 2018). For instance, the MRC evaluation of Sayaburi states that a "modest increase in flood water levels" would result, and advocates the vague "further consideration" (MRC 2011, 21). As an example of such an ad hoc measure, facing criticism about the dam blocking fish migrations, Pöyry proposed fish ladders modeled after those in temperate climates. These ladders (later built), as a number of fisheries scientists concluded, do not work for the kinds of migrations that Mekong fish undergo (Dugan et al. 2010).

In the end, Pöyry concluded that the dam was in accord with MRC protocols and could safely proceed. Immediately afterward, provoking accusations of conflicts of interest, Pöyry was awarded an engineering contract on the dam by the Thai construction firm in charge of it.

Sayaburi cannot be seen as a product of Laos's national ambitions alone. Jakkrit Sangkhamanee (2017b) points to the interlinking of desires and demands—like the Xepian-Xe Nam Noy Dam, Sayaburi is a Thai-built structure supplying electricity largely (95 percent) to Thailand in response to growing demand for power in Bangkok. Thus, projects such as Sayaburi are "spillover" effects—faced with an emboldened environmental movement in Thailand, the search for hydropower projects was outsourced to areas with a complicit government, curbs on civil society, and little regulation.

Thai civil society grew out of a variety of protest movements that became united in opposition to the business-centered and crony capitalist policies of Thaksin Shinawatra (prime minister 1999–2006). Thaksin, a relative outsider who brought his own blend of nouveau riche, ethnic Chinese-Thai business networks, and police connections into competition with established military and monarchy-allied groups, reshaped the Thai political system. In contrast to previous administrations, he advocated for development projects outside of Bangkok, projects that often disregarded environmental standards, but which won him favor with many in the provinces.

Thaksin advanced megaprojects, repression of NGOs, and curbs upon the media, actions that led environmental and health NGOs to join forces with royalist and military-aligned groups, groups that were already opposed to Thaksin. This opposition was galvanized into a number of protest groups arguing against electoral democracy and toward a political system based around a fusion of scientific expertise and traditional authority (see Funahashi 2016)—what Paul Handley (2009) terms *dhammocracy*. Environmentalism, then, acquires a conservative cast.

Here we must pause before we cast such environmentalist movements along a left-right axis imported from the West. For many health and environmental movements, Thai democracy itself was the problem. Instead, many advocated for a rule by "good people," those with access to barami and elite sources of knowledge, rather than by messy popular opinion. Royals and other elites would be guardians of national patrimony, rather than having the nation's natural resources in the hands of profit-minded capitalists. In other words, in a clash between crony capitalism and feudal noblesse oblige, civil society chose the latter.

Sparked by such a notion of national patrimony, the Thai military deposed Thaksin in 2006, but the next elections brought his sister, Yingluck, into power in 2011. Environmental groups rallied against her, and hydropower became a particular flashpoint, especially with regard to endangered tiger habitat near the Mae Wong Dam. In Thailand's northeast, these anti-hydropower groups gave fuel to the already existing concern over Sayaburi.

And these groups got what they wished for—in a sense. In 2014, Yingluck was deposed in another military coup d'état, but this one established a far more authoritarian and repressive regime (one that persists to the time of writing).[13] While many of my interlocutors (Pla and Kai, for instance) in environmental groups initially cheered Yingluck's ouster, it soon became apparent that junta leader Prayuth Chan-o-cha was as committed to the dams as his predecessor. In 2016, Prayuth visited Mae Wong and concluded that the dam was necessary, and his administration similarly showed no interest in changing Thailand's stance on Sayaburi. The military government passed laws prohibiting assembly, cracked down on protests, and, in a final move, passed the notorious Section 44, a law which stated that any new order could be passed without review, "for the sake of the reforms in any field, the promotion of love and harmony amongst the people in the nation, or the prevention, abatement or suppression of any act detrimental to national order or security, royal throne, national economy or public administration, whether the act occurs inside or outside the kingdom" (Constitution of Thailand 2015). Among other things, Section 44 was used to push through the interests of mining firms and other businesses against environmental concerns. Thailand's protest movements got what they wanted, but ended up in a worse situation.

Rivers and Borders

In the center of downtown Bangkok, Rama I Road runs between row after row of luxury shopping malls. These are glorious spaces, from the glittering scaled façade of Central Embassy to the giant outdoor screen at Siam Paragon to the floors and floors of luxury goods and high-end restaurants in Central World. Walking into the mall from the heat of the Bangkok street and hitting the wall of frigid air conditioning is a pleasure that I and many Bangkok residents have savored.

The malls at an intersection on Rama I Road called Ratchaprasong have replaced Sanam Luang, the ground in front of the Grand Palace, as the new town square of Bangkok, where public protests are held and displays of power marshaled. In 2014, shortly after the coup, students gathered at Siam Paragon to eat sandwiches (as a protest against national calls to "Thai-ness") and read George Orwell's *1984*. In 2010, in protests for democratic rule and the return of Thaksin Shinawatra, the Red Shirts seized the road just next to Central World.

In this light, Ratchaprasong is the new center of Bangkok, marking a move from the mandala not toward the absolute monarchy that the Grand Palace oversaw, but toward one fixed in flows of capital. One might be tempted to move the mantle of palladium from the Emerald Buddha to the Erawan Shrine, a shrine to Brahma in the center of all of downtown Bangkok's opulence and a center for worship for Chinese tourists in between shopping excursions.

But these malls are costly. A news report released in 2016 compared power consumption between downtown Bangkok's malls and entire provinces, finding that Siam Paragon (just one of these malls) used 123 gigawatt-hours (GWh) annually. This is more than the entire provinces of Amnat Charoen (110 GWh) and Mae Hong Son (65 GWh). And Paragon isn't alone; its neighbors, Central World (75 GWh) and MBK (81 GWh) also use tremendous amounts of power—not to mention the many other giant malls elsewhere in Bangkok (Marks 2014).[14] And the malls are expanding: this study did not factor in the new Central Embassy or Siam Discovery, also on the same road, or Icon Siam elsewhere.

The demand for power, then, is a demand from the center. But it is one that exploits the opacity of the border as it does so. A watershed does not recognize boundaries. The runoff from the Xepian-Xe Nam Noy Dam flows directly into Cambodia. But the existence of the border allows one to think about victims of the disaster in particular ways. Is the Lao government responsible for Cambodians washed out by the dam? Is SK Construction responsible for its rupture? Is the Korean government itself responsible, as many South Korean civil society groups claimed?

Just as the border takes the intimacy of living in a shared watershed and divides it into nation-states, the border also places the sovereignty of a distant capital over the hinterland. For the region surrounding the Jinghong Dam, Beijing asserts its authority over Xishuangpanna, a region over 3,000 km distant, a region with a different language, ethnicity, and history. But on the map, Jinghong is unquestionably Chinese. The imagination of the border allows dam builders to perceive the river before the dam in Jinghong also as wholly Chinese, and the river after the dam as wholly Lao. It is a fictive divide atop a continuity of material and history alike.

Similarly, the fiction of the border allows one to say that power generation is going to Thailand, and as such would presumably benefit all Thais, whereas in reality the expansion of consumption in the center has fallen out of pace with the periphery. The border, and its concomitant fiction of national development, allows projects intended for specific interests (builders, politicians, the capital) to be cast as benefiting the nation.

Here, then, we should see the exploitation enabled by the border (e.g., "this is Chinese water," "this is done for the good of Thailand") as also dependent upon the borderlands' historical marginality. If ethnic Tai Lue or Lao (in China and Thailand, respectively) have their lives disrupted, it makes less impactful headlines than if they were Han or Thai. Already marginal, already precarious, the border allows power to be further wielded over the skeptical frontier.

But how do these two notions of the border—the skeptical frontier and the skinworld—work in practice? In Ban Beuk, while people were quick to talk of abstractions like "Laos" or "Thailand," the border itself was a more complicated factor in people's day-to-day lives.

ON THE WATERFRONT

For now, let us turn to this periphery. I do so from two sites on the Thai-Lao border in Ban Beuk: my own home in Mon's compound by Bird Island, and a few hundred meters past the temple at the Ban Beuk docks. The two places are close enough to walk easily. Here, I present a series of vignettes seemingly unrelated at first, but each of which sheds a different perspective on what the border does.

Borders and Development

On paper, the border at Bird Island, the island onto which the door of my hut opened, is closed. No representatives of the Thai or Lao states monitor the banks of the Mekong there. But this does not mean that no one watches the river.

In the early morning, when the fog still hangs low over the river, Yai headed up to check on the crops. This involved hiking on foot up a winding dirt track to the top of the ridgeline behind Mon's compound. As we walked, we passed rubber orchards, papaya trees, and other plots apportioned to Mon's family or other families nearby. Yai described most such mornings as cold; I did not concur.

Mostly I was there to carry things. Yai would find a papaya that had fallen or was about to fall and pluck it off, tossing it into my arms while she carried nothing herself. On the first trip, this was charming. Later, it became labor. One morning, as I was sleeping off a hangover occasioned by one of Mon's late-night riverside drinking bouts, Yai burst into my one-room home. "I will show you a papaya," she exclaimed as she held up her arms in a circle as big as they would go, "as big as *this*."

We hiked up, me dreading having to lug a barrel-sized papaya fruit back down the mountain and nursing a splitting headache, but the "papaya" in question turned out to be the trunk of a papaya tree, not the fruit. And, at the top of the ridge, we came to a suddenly clear concrete platform. It was a high vantage point overlooking the river, and a central place for me to rest and wait for Yai to find more fruit. I looked down across the Mekong, into Laos, and could see smoke rising from fires in fields across the way. "The army made this for the villagers," Yai proclaimed as we looked out across the border, but I knew this already: copious signs along the path had indicated it as a "development project" undertaken by the Thai army "for the villagers." "They knew it was a good view, that here you could see the fog in the valley below [*tale mok*]" (figure 1.1). Yai here referred both to the phenomenon of morning river fog and to a local tourist attraction an hour to the south, where tourists (normally Thais from Bangkok) travel to a high temple to look down on the fog along the river. Yai envisioned, bolstered by my presence, a similar platform here for tourists, all thanks to the kindness of the Thai military. But the trail wasn't originally for cloud gazing nor for Yai's orchard trips.

The district in which Ban Beuk sat was one heavily scrutinized by the Thai military, and had been for years. The region was, during the 1970s, the heart of the CPT. This was especially so following American losses in Vietnam, the communist takeover of Laos, and the massacre of university students in 1976 (which in turn led to many of these students "entering the jungle" [*khao pa*] to join the insurgency). For a place like Ban Beuk, the communist cause was immediately sympathetic, and many joined the CPT (Pattana 2015). As a result, in the 1980s, the military assumed direct control over the district, and used development as a means for both convincing villagers of Bangkok's good intentions and expanding state surveillance. Indeed, as US military reports

Figure 1.1: Yai's overlook

indicate, development units were targets for attacks by insurgents in Nong Khai during the war, indicating that the CPT saw development clearly as a part of Bangkok's military strategy and not as assistance of any kind (Alpern 1975, 692; regarding "help," see Ssorin-Chaikov 2017).

It is easy to be cynical about the military's purposes in developing Ban Beuk: from Yai's platform, one could see—and shoot—straight into Laos and monitor the river traffic on the other side of Bird Island. But the discourse of development was a significant presence in twentieth-century Thailand. Royal propaganda placed the former king, in both military and civilian clothes, at the head of development projects, often using photos from his 1950s- and 1960s-era trips to the countryside. Royal projects were touted as rural, especially agricultural interventions. And, significantly, most major dams in Thailand bear royal names—development, the body of the monarch, and the military are linked here.

In 1980, the ending of Chinese funding to the CPT largely ended the communist insurgency, and when, seven years later, there was another conflict between Laos and Thailand, few took part. Villagers remembered a heightened sense of surveillance on the border from that time, describing how they feared to go out upon the water, and would instead make clandestine trips to shrines midstream to ask for protection. Around this time, too, new concrete border posts were constructed, and Bangkokian soldiers returned to the riverbank.

Here, the very danger posed by the border causes it to be a target for development. As Ferguson (1990) indicates, this is not unusual. The seemingly neutral category of development, of implementing projects for the villagers, as Yai suggests, is a means of control and surveillance over the frontier. But is that all that it is? Might not infrastructure intended by its builders serve alternative purposes? Platforms intended for artillery launches are also tourist locations, and roads built to move military convoys can also move trucks. And not all eyes on the river seek threats—some are there to look at clouds.

Borders and the Status of Strangers

At the base of the mountain, most afternoons Nu reclined in the hammock under Mon's house. With the morning's labor either done or waiting, and the day too hot to fish, Nu smoked hand-rolled Lao cigarettes and watched the water. Many days, I, too, sat, smoked, and watched with him.

Boats first announce themselves by their motors long before you see them. As you listen, you can immediately tell a number of things about what they are up to—a slow *putt-putt* indicates a fisherman going to check on the nets, or perhaps a heavily laden boat moving freight from one bank to the next. These latter boats never passed by Nu's perch, although they were frequent sights farther down the river. During the cold season, many fishermen would take Thai tourists out to the sandy islands in the center of the river (technically over the border), and these, too, moved at a meandering pace. A high-pitched whine means someone traveling at a fast clip—trouble, maybe, or a fisherman with a load of tourists that had goaded him into cranking the engine. Sometimes an old fisherman would paddle his craft, making his way slowly down the river at a fraction of other boats' speed. A few times a month, a large, luxury river cruise ship came down the river, presenting an incongruous sight: colonial-decor cabins, speakers playing soft traditional Lao music, and well-heeled tourists sitting on the deck, watching postcolonial Lao fishermen blasting loud contemporary Lao country music watching them back.

Once, after a Buddhist holiday when villagers would take donations to the temple, Nu saw the abbot of the temple next door, boat loaded with the donations intended for the maintenance of his monks, head over to the Laotian bank in order to sell these donations at a profit. At other times, a friend would pass by, stop, hail Nu, and invite him to one of the new grilled fish and beer places just built on the Lao bank.

Nu laconically rattled off the people coming and going: "This person is from Ban Beuk; he owns a fishing site on the other side of the island. This person is from Ban Ngoen, a Lao. This person I don't know [*boh hu*]—probably from the other bank [in Laos]. Just a person looking for fish [*peun ha pa*]."

Sometimes there would be a series of low pops, indicating someone fishing with explosives. In these cases, even when the boat was directly visible from the land, only Nu's eyes followed the activity, along with his vociferous complaints. I questioned him on this—Nu would complain loudly about the depredations of those fishing with explosives at other times, and proclaim that we needed to call the police, so why did he not react now?

> Maybe it is a person detonating fish. People like this, they don't really care about consequences. It's not good to be seen. Even if you don't call the police, if they see you running around they might think you are calling the police. Then they might come back at night. It is like at night when you hear a boat engine. That is a [fish] shocker, or someone taking things between banks [i.e., a smuggler]. You cannot shine a flashlight toward the sound! You will be shot! Anyway, maybe the person is from over there [i.e., Laos]. There's nothing we can do. If we call the Thai police, they will simply say that it might be a Lao person [over which they have no jurisdiction].

Here, Nu deliberately does not react physically to examples of what he termed a present threat to fishing on the Mekong. Instead, he uses the indeterminacy presented by the border to justify inaction. Because the fisherman might be Lao, the normal means of law enforcement fail. Here, again, is the power of "maybe."

Because the person might retaliate with violence, Nu must stay very still, to avoid seeming like he notices the explosives. Indeed, what Nu presents is a feeling of threat enabled by the opacity that the border provides. Someone who might be "just a person looking for fish" might also be a potential killer. This indeterminacy—the possibility that Nu might not know, or might not care to know, someone driving by, allows for his inaction in the face of what he verbally alleges to be terrible crimes. "Maybe" opens the potential for killers in boats otherwise entirely familiar.

Borders and Possibility

As Nu's observations indicate, the river is not a closed border as the line on a map might indicate. Here, the Mekong is a highway. And just downstream of Bird Island are the Ban Beuk docks (figure 1.2).

Figure 1.2: Ban Beuk docks

In the center of Ban Beuk is a low, flat, concrete foundation, largely exposed to the sky. Ringing it are restaurants and sundry stores that are sporadically open. This is the market square, open on Wednesdays and Saturdays and catering mostly to visitors from Laos. At the end of the square is a squat concrete structure, big enough for one or two rooms—the military post. Soldiers there rarely mix with the locals and virtually never seem to come out. Past this, the road drops down a sloping track and disappears into river mud. On this mud are the boats that ferry people and goods back and forth from Ban Beuk to Ban Ngoen.

On market days, Mon and his friend Lo would get up early to sit at one of the restaurants near the docks. They—and I—would sit and watch people disembark and stroll among the Thai vendors who had laid out tarps and goods in the market square. These goods—what Lao visitors called *khreuang*[15]—were usually cheap clothing or electronics (rice cookers, etc.) or sacks of food.

The two men would—predictably—make a point to carefully watch young women in the market. "You can tell the ones that are Lao," Mon explained to me one day, with a thrust of his head toward a pale young woman walking on the other side of the market. "The way they dress, the way they move. They are more elegant, more well-dressed [*taeng tua di-di*]. Like how Thais were fifty years ago." He then, to my extreme embarrassment, began to whistle at the woman. Although Mon had a fiancée, Fa, he speculated that, should they split up, he might marry a "pale, beautiful" Lao woman and bring her to this bank.

Lo watched, but remained silent. He made it a point not to speak to any-one until he'd had at least two beers, enough to take the edge off his hangover. He'd been on a bender since his incense manufacturing business fell through, a victim of increased border controls after the military coup of 2014. He had run his business employing workers coming over the border, but now he had been told that such cross-border work required permits he couldn't afford.

Lo told me, two beers later, "[The chief inspector] said if it were only a couple employees, that this would be acceptable, that he would permit it to pass. He said if I cut my business in half, then he would permit it. But I need to do more than that in order to stay in business. So now I wait." And while he waited, he drank.

Lo cast his gaze down to the military post, following a group of three young men in green with a sullen stare. "I hate soldiers," said Lo. By *tahan* (sol-dier), Lo did not mean just the young men in green who passed by his table. He meant the military coup of 2014 and administration of Prayuth Chan-o-cha. "Ever since they seized power, nothing has worked. I try to make money, try to keep money . . ." Lo, still hung over, made a dismissive wave with his hands.

Here, Lo is referring to stricter cross-border controls implemented by the Prayuth (2014–present) regime, aimed at cracking down on cross-border corrup-tion, something rather ironic, given that Prayuth's own wealth began through trading gems across the Cambodian border with the Khmer Rouge (Strangio 2015). Stronger controls on the border were ways of limiting the cross-border mobility of small-scale businesses like Lo's and encouraging more centralized operations. I argued with Lo that it was a bid for Prayuth to look tough on cor-ruption. Lo simply concluded that Prayuth's band in the military "hated Isan."

Here, the border is a source of possibility and (exploitative) adventure. It allows Mon to fantasize about sexual conquests of women who might, in his mind, be more eager to pursue an Isan man than Thai women, and it allows Lo the chance to run his own business using cheaper Laotian labor. Both of these pos-sibilities are enabled by the fact that the border poses a barrier—it is Lao women's familiar unfamiliarity that makes them attractive to Mon, and it is the limits to labor rights and the inability of Laos to move freely that enables Lo's business to be profitable. As Nail (2016) would have it, the border enables new flows.

BORDERS AND POLITICAL POWER

At the Ban Beuk docks, the border also provides a focal point to contest power at the village level. Here, I take up a conflict between two authority figures at the border, both of whom made claims toward their own patronage network, but who constructed their legitimacy along very different lines. This conflict reflected different orientations toward the border, across multiple ways of understanding authority and sovereignty.

Thailand's recent political strife has been color-coded, with Yellow Shirts arguing against the forces of neoliberal capitalism and electoral democracy (problematically embodied by the Shinawatras), and Red Shirts largely for. These in turn were regional conflicts as well, with Isan and the north deep red and central and southern Thailand yellow. Since 2012, these colors and the Red-Yellow divide have largely fallen out of use, after a massacre of nearly a hundred Red protesters outside of the shopping malls at Ratchaprasong (Sopranzetti 2014; see Saowanee [2019] for a contrary view), but a more everyday divide between an appeal to the moral and traditional authority of leaders and an appeal to popular mandate persists—even at the Ban Beuk docks.

Buddhist activist Sulak Sivaraksa (2009) paints a clear picture of what he means by a true democracy, and a clear picture of what many on the Yellow side of the political fence were fighting for. Using Britain as an example, Sulak writes, "Before citizens [in supposed democracies like the UK] go to cast their votes, all kinds of means are used during the election campaigns—lies, vote-buying, misinformation, etc. in various degrees . . . therefore [voters] may interpret the world according to the dictates of the ruling interests—e.g. capitalism, consumerism, neoliberalism, imperialism, etc. People everywhere are increasingly finding this version of democracy revolting. No doubt, this is not the kind of democracy that Thais should aim for; it is not good enough for us" (2009, 124–25). For Sulak, although he has been no advocate of coups d'état, Thaksin epitomized this false democracy, using trickery and corruption in order to achieve electoral victory (133). Ideally, Sulak imagines an enlightened despot, a morally just and wise leader who rules in accordance with Buddhist principles.

For those in the NGO community, Sulak was a leader. This was especially so among environmental movements, as moral outrage mounted against the corruption and damage caused by Thaksin's megaprojects. Along with the moral dimensions of this pressure, though, there was a sense of noblesse oblige, with traditional elites casting themselves as safeguarding Thailand's resources against rapacious businessmen (see also Pattana 2006). This color coding of activist movements became so extreme that once, when describing my research project to a Thai academic and outspoken advocate for democracy, I had the premise of this book rudely dismissed as it involved writing about environmental issues: "Environment! This is a *Yellow* issue. Environmentalists don't care about people. They don't care about democracy."

For this academic, and for many of my interlocutors, the appeal of the traditional elites had soured. As I have described elsewhere (see Johnson 2013), many of my interlocutors dismissed claims to barami as hypocritical attempts to justify inequality and corruptly cling to power, using elite trappings to gain currency among ignorant villages. They pointed to international observers and reports that detailed the corruption in royal and military projects and the injustice of lèse-majesté laws (see Handley 2009; Streckfuss 2010; Ünaldi 2013; Walker 2011).[16] These Thais rejected calls for a special Thai-style democracy as simple authoritarianism and Bangkok-centered elitism under a new name.

Here, then, is a binary that was in the process of playing out in Ban Beuk. Many of my interlocutors were former Red Shirts, and some were former Yellow Shirts. Most had supported Thaksin in the 2000s, but this support had flagged in recent years. With recent environmental crises and the movement of NGO groups into the area, new Yellow influences had begun to spread at least until the military takeover of 2014, when Prayuth's dramatically unpopular regime came to power.

But, as for left-right divisions elsewhere, we must not rush to categorize actions or people as essentially Red or Yellow. These are complicated political positions, based around patronage networks. Instead, here I take a cue from Michael Herzfeld's (2016) work on sources of authority in Thailand. For Herzfeld, negotiations of power and authority in Thailand rely upon both an appeal to a discourse of egalitarianism (e.g., "we are all Thais") and an appeal toward patronage networks (e.g., "we have powerful allies"). The former is an appeal to national belonging, and the latter to discourses like barami.

But there is more to this binary than simply a political one of moral authoritarianism and electoral democracy. On a personal level, such claims are also wrapped up in issues of self-presentation and identity. Therefore, here, I bring Yellow/Red and authority/egalitarianism in line with one more binary, one that reflects Thai masculinity.

Peter Vail (1998) describes two ideal types at the poles of Thai masculinity— the monk and the gangster (*nakleng*). The first is removed from the world, accrues merit instead of money, and cultivates a calm, "cool heart" (*jai yen*; see Cassaniti 2014) demeanor. Famous monks are said to accrue the semimagical charismatic power barami, associated with righteous action. The gangster, in contrast, is violent but loyal, cultivating *ittiphon* (influence) and *amnaaj* (power), and has a demeanor that is direct and true.

These two qualities in turn draw upon dual notions of the power of leaders: leaders balance the potency of figures removed from the world (*phra-khun*) as well as that of those engaged with this world (*phra-dej*). The ideal king, for instance, is both "world-conqueror" and "world-renouncer" (see Tambiah 1977). Following this tradition, Thai leaders have often walked the line between the two, relying upon the monarchy, which, in the age of Bhumibol Adulyadej (r. 1946–2016) was the ultimate source of barami in Thai society, and the military, the ultimate source of amnaaj.

Here, then, are three binaries of moral legitimacy. First there is the Red-Yellow divide—a political appeal to a democratic mandate versus a notion of loyalty to the monarchy. Related is Herzfeld's notion of claims based on egalitarian principles versus patron/client connections. And, finally, Vail presents us with contrasting models of masculinity that emphasize strength and action versus passive wisdom. With these in mind, I turn now to the two figures in question—two older men who vied for the role of my patron in the field.

The Gangster Cop

The chief inspector spent most of his time in a resort next to where the boats pull up at the docks. "Resort" here is a joke—the inspector had written "Lisort" in Thai over the bamboo shelter in which he normally sat.[17] It was shabby, but comfortable, a woven mat raised about three feet off the ground with a thatched roof for shade and a bucket of ice for cold drinks, of which there were plenty. This platform provided a focal point for the five or six ferrymen who normally stayed on the docks waiting for fares heading to Laos.

While the army post at the top of the hill was the marker of the hard border—dissuading any large-scale incursions by foreign forces—the chief inspector is the day-to-day barrier to entry. His official duties involve overseeing the entry of persons and goods from Laos into Ban Beuk. Informally, it was rumored that he ran a lumber-smuggling ring and likely was involved in other forms of trafficking (wildlife, people, and methamphetamine would be chief among them).

The chief inspector was originally from the southern part of Isan, from Buriram Province, and was appointed by the police to this station. He spoke Lao as his native tongue, but the kind of Lao spoken in Buriram is significantly different from the Vientiane Lao spoken in Ban Beuk. He was significantly better educated than most in Ban Beuk—with me, he spoke flawless Central Thai, and once introduced me to his son, who was planning to go on a student exchange in New Zealand and who spoke perfect English.[18] But he was intimidating. He always kept his pistol close at hand—occasionally *in* hand—and had a habit of leaning in and staring into my eyes whenever something less than toward was happening at the docks. "Andrew," he said to me, on a day when two Lao sex workers sat in the resort pouring drinks and haggling with the village head of a nearby town over prices, "you don't have to write *everything* down."

Like Nu, the chief inspector's job largely had to do with visual identification. Most days, he sat, feet dangling over the edge of the resort platform, and watched people arrive. While he did so, the ferrymen poured him (and themselves) liberal helpings of Johnny Walker Red (or, at times, SangSom or Mae-Khong) and soda. Occasionally, local men would join him there, as well as the sex workers who poured drinks and chatted with the men, flirting and arranging assignations. Children at the docks (most often the sons of ferrymen) were omnipresent, diving into the river and back out, and were occasionally cajoled into running up to the market to buy alcohol or food for the men.

When a boat arrived, the chief inspector gave its occupants a long look before going back to his drink. "I look for people that don't belong. Sometimes I ask people to empty their pockets, looking for [methamphetamine] pills. Sometimes I look for people—young women—with men who don't look like their fathers."

"So what do you do [if you see such a person]?" I asked him.

"I call them over and question them," he replied. Immediately, he called to a man disembarking and motioned him over to the resort. "Can I look into your pockets? We just have to check to see if you have pills in there." The man, smiling, obliged, and the chief inspector turned back to me. "You see?"

We kept drinking. This was the only time I saw the chief inspector search someone.

The chief inspector also was responsible for the bureaucratic face of the Thai state at the border. Most Lao arrivals were supposed to present a permit. When I asked the two women if they had brought their permits, they produced theirs and assured me that their documentation had been well examined by the chief inspector. "He inspects very well," one said with a smirk.

If we see the chief inspector as simply a guard, though, enforcing the laws of the state or, alternately, as a symbol of petty corruption, we miss the point. To be sure, he fulfills these roles. He checks identification and watches the border, although he lets those who seem to belong, or those in whose cross-border traffic he participates, slip by. He guards against human trafficking, although he participates in the sex industry. And, as with Lo, he enforces the laws of the state (albeit in his own idiosyncratic way—demanding Lo pay lip service to the law and recognize his own authority, but not that he submit entirely). But there are other aspects of power that the chief inspector carries out as well that should be taken into consideration.

First of all, he is the head of the ferrymen at the docks. That is to say, he personally controls nearly all transportation that comes and goes in Ban Beuk.

This is a role unrelated to his status as chief inspector, and the group has no official status or name, nor does he collect dues from its members (insofar as I know) outside of their permit (*win*; see Sopranzetti 2017a, 2017b). But they are a coherent group, with matching T-shirts that read "'Love Ban Beuk' Group." And they do things other than ferry—at night, after the ferries stopped running, the ferrymen would get together and have semimandatory high-stakes games of *hi-lo* (cards), run by the chief inspector, who took a cut. On the weekends the chief inspector ran *muay thai* matches with betting on all sides.

Second, the chief inspector had appointed himself the enforcer of a cross-border ban on fish electrocution. As I detail in chapter 2, many in the community had taken to fishing with an industrial battery and a pair of jumper cables, an activity that was frowned upon owing to its catastrophic effects upon fish stocks in the river. The chief inspector had taken it upon himself to stop this. He would head out in the middle of the night, armed with his service pistol, and fire at boats that he thought were engaged in poaching in the river. "They escape most of the time, back to Laos. But we scare them off."

My point here is that the chief inspector, owing to his control over the border at the docks and, thus, the flow of Laotians to the market, had become one such source of legitimacy. He framed himself as a loyal enforcer of the Thai state far beyond his official capacity, enforcing the spirit of the rules with little patience for claims to traditional authority. But he is no bureaucrat—his flagrant violation of the laws he was to enforce was a clear message to those nearby that he was the arbiter of their power, that he was the source of authority and legitimacy, a position made strikingly clear in his role as the head of weekly gambling and muay thai rings. In this way, he fits rather well into Vail's nakleng (gangster), and as a figure striking a clear—if strange—balance between authoritarianism and egalitarianism (i.e., he advocates for democratic rule in a military-dominated society, but at the same time cultivates an image as a nakleng).

In addition, the chief inspector was a former Thaksin sympathizer and an outspoken democrat—he considered military rule an abomination, and the Thai royalty as puppets of the generals, both aspects that held Thailand back from entering the world stage. These were sentiments that people occasionally shared in Ban Beuk. Some men had been a part of the Red Shirt movement in 2010, and had seen friends die at the hands of the Thai military, and were privately derisive of the monarchy; nearly all of the men in town hated the military. But the chief inspector was verbose on the topic; he would go into detail about the failings of the military and the monarchy and their inability to usher in a truly democratic society. For all that he made me nervous, I shared his view: we understood each other in terms of politics.

The Holy Bureaucrat

The subdistrict head, Pong, presented a sharp contrast. Pong was hardly the intimidating figure that the chief inspector cut. He was short and quiet, and leaned back when speaking. Much as the chief inspector cultivated an image as a nakleng, Pong was scrupulously clean—he rarely drank and had a seemingly perfect marriage. Additionally, Pong was from Ban Beuk, unlike the chief inspector. He had made his initial capital working in a factory in Taiwan as a migrant worker, back in the 1980s when such labor was a guarantee of success. While not everyone liked Pong (many wished he would be less judgmental of others' drinking and gambling), nearly all with whom I spoke respected him.

Pong presented a sort of Jeffersonian figure in that he had a large, well-appointed farm and experimented with different ways to keep it. Unlike the chief inspector, whose house was a few miles inland, Pong had a large house right at the border, in the village of Ban Thong. He was clearly the most wealthy person in the district, owning rubber orchards, a galangal plot, and banana and papaya trees, and even raising huskies and boar. In addition, he owned a large number of designated fishing sites (*luang mong*) in the river.

As an outgrowth of both his gentleman farmer habitus and his status as subdistrict head, Pong's house and the Community Development Office—an open-air building across the road from his home—became a focal point for community, NGO, and academic activities. At times, Pong would host ecotourist groups from Bangkok, government ministers touring the Mekong region, farmers' meetings to promote new cash crops, college student groups studying rural development, and other such initiatives. He was, too, the first person that I contacted in Ban Beuk, having had a meeting arranged by Pla, the Mekong environmental activist.

In short, Pong framed himself as the custodian of Ban Beuk. Rather than engaging the population in the social sphere and indulging in common vices, Pong sought to frame himself as a moral (via refraining from vices like womanizing and drinking) and charismatic leader, a framing that had some success in cultivating a sense of barami.

And the two hated each other. Pong, normally reserved, would let criticisms fly when I mentioned that I was going to see the chief inspector. "Do you mean that bastard chief inspector [*ai sarawat yai*] that is a drunk [*khi mao*] and gambles down at the docks? Andrew, you have to talk to everyone. You should talk to everyone. Just come back before dark, before they start gambling. They will take all your money." Similarly, the chief inspector said of Pong, with a laugh, "I see you with that subdistrict head that thinks he is such a good person [*phu di*]. He's not! If you only knew what I do about him."

The attacks that each figure levied at the other reflected these characterizations. Pong criticized the chief inspector for moral vices: corruption, gambling, impiety. He accused the chief inspector of taking advantage of ignorant or corruptible villagers in much the same way as Thaksin had been accused. In turn, the chief inspector accused Pong of hypocrisy, of acting pious when in fact he'd known Pong to be just as corrupt.

At the chief inspector's resort, he leaned in close when I mentioned that I was going to see Pong the next day. "Are you? Then I have some questions that I want you to ask him! Ask him if his boat [which he uses to take tourists out] is insured or not. Ask him if he has a registration for it."

At this, one of the ferrymen came to my defense, making the case that the chief inspector was setting me up for personal embarrassment, asking such confrontational questions of such a respected man. "OK," he said, backing down, "but you must ask him about shocking fish. Notice that behind me [behind the resort] hang nets. Any other post at the edge of the river will hang jumper cables." The chief inspector smiled and looked me in the eyes. "Tomorrow, look at what the subdistrict head has hanging in his house."[19]

He continued. "If you go up there, past [Ban Thong], past that damn subdistrict head's [*man kamnan*] house, you'll see. Andrew, you have to *look*. Look where they have their tools. Every one of them has a set of jumper cables. And it's worse. When I go out on the river to stop the fish shockers [by shooting at them], that damn subdistrict head tells me that I can't, that if I shot a Laotian fish shocker, it would start an international incident. And do you know why?"

I looked at him blankly. The chief inspector knew that I was close with Pong but was sharing this with me anyway. "He takes their electrocuted fish and sells them in the market. He is all intermarried with them. His family is so wrapped up with that other side [i.e., Laos, *faeng noon*] that he wants to help them and get rich at the same time!"

I asked Pong obliquely about these issues. He admitted that "some fishermen would make sure that [shocked] fish [from across the border] would not go to waste," and that some fishmongers would sell shocked fish, although he fervently denied engaging in or tolerating shocking fish himself.

Here, the chief inspector makes the same accusation as those Red Shirts who claim that all barami—that charismatic, righteous authority—is a veneer over corruption (Johnson 2013). It is a claim to egalitarianism, and an authority based upon the rule of law. Even though this rule of law is routinely violated by none other than the chief inspector himself, it is a claim to honesty. In hearing the chief inspector's complaints against the subdistrict head, I was reminded of Nu's complaint against the neighboring abbot who resold his religious donations—that a person with a veneer of righteousness was in fact just as corrupt as the next man.

The chief inspector's other accusation—that Pong was too close with Lao families across the river—deserves some unpacking.

Ban Thong, Pong's home, was founded at some point during the last century, when a group of Laotian nobles came across the bank to settle. The exact terms of what they were escaping and their exact rank were unclear to Pong and anyone else that I asked in Ban Thong. But since that founding, the village had always maintained relationships with Ban Ngoen, across the river. Pong had uncles, in-laws, and cousins across the border and had maintained these relationships even through the 1980s, when Thailand and Laos engaged in a brief border war. When I expressed surprise at this, Pong directly said back to me, "Why is this surprising? We're family [hao phi nong kan]."

Indeed, the border seemed to mean little to Pong. During my stay, one of these family members died suddenly, and Pong invited me to the funeral. I balked, citing the danger of crossing the Laotian border and going to a public event when I had no Laotian visa nor was crossing at an official border point, and Pong nodded vaguely, not seeming to acknowledge what the big deal was.

Pong also worked closely with his fellow subdistrict head (the corresponding Lao district is simply called *meuang*) across the river. Fishing plots (*luang mong*) were specific sites within the river that were given to a particular person or family as an exclusive fishing zone. These sites had particular values and could be bought, sold, or rented just as landed property could. But these sites hung in the middle of the border, with sites owned by Lao fishermen occasionally hugging the Thai bank, and vice versa. Establishing who owned what and for how much was a task that involved local authorities from both sides.

In marked contrast to the chief inspector's politics (and that of many in the district), Pong was more sympathetic to royalists, and especially the environmentally focused Yellow Shirts. His fierce advocacy for environmentalism in the face of corporate interests extended to risking his own security. For instance, near his house was an ancient copper mine, now a cave where a holy hermit (*reusi*) lived. But the presence of copper meant the possibility of gold, and when a Japanese mining company made a bid for the land, Pong successfully argued that it was archaeological heritage, and thus off-limits. Later, when another company made a similarly legal claim upon mining rights in Ban Beuk, Pong and Mon spoke out against it. That night, soldiers dragged Mon out of his home and kept him in the barracks until morning—a warning against making too many such moral claims.

In sum, here the border reflects different sources of and challenges to legitimacy for these two men. For the chief inspector, the border was a line to be maintained as well as a resource to be managed. He worked to make the border a hard one, patrolled, if not by gunboats, then by himself in a boat with a handgun—to enforce the integrity of the border's skinworld while at the same time setting himself up as the privileged channel through which goods and people could move. For the chief inspector, Laotians, rather than being family members separated by an arbitrary line, were potentially dangerous others that needed policing. The other, in this sense, was those people across the border. This attention to the border as a legal entity allowed him to exercise leniency in the cases over which he could have power—what goods came and went across the border (e.g., Lo's incense business), what people came and went (e.g., the sex workers who poured drinks at his resort, fishermen who sought to shock fish in the night), and the infrastructure moving these goods and persons (e.g., the ferrymen). As such, he fought back, labeling as corrupt all the aspects of the border that ran in violation of the concept of it as an absolute boundary.

In turn, the subdistrict head, Pong, saw the border as a different condition under which the same people lived—what was foreign here was the border itself. He paid little heed to the legal aspects of crossing back and forth between two countries with a history of animosity and war, and pointed out the obvious continuities between the Thai and Lao sides instead of their differences. Laotians were fundamentally the same people under different conditions, and as such were another constituency over which his authority extended. In short, the chief inspector here gives voice to the nation-state, whereas Pong enacts the frontiers of the mandala.

While some in Ban Beuk identified strongly with one party or the other, most recognized the legitimacy of both the subdistrict head and the chief inspector. Mon, for instance, respected Pong's moral stance and was cautious of the chief inspector's drinking and gambling, but found himself politically aligned with the chief inspector's democratic ideals. Lo, on the other hand, found Pong too sanctimonious and respected the chief inspector's tolerance for fun, despite Pong's greater openness toward the cross-border trade that Lo relied upon. Pla detested the chief inspector and characterized him as taking advantage of the villagers and continually admonished me to steer clear.

POSSIBILITIES OF A RIVER BORDER

Thomas Nail (2016), in his *Theory of the Border*, asks us to rethink borders. Rather than seeing borders as static lines dividing nation-states, Nail proposes that borders are dynamic—they are maintained, contested, moved, subject to erosion. If we think of the border in a broad sense, that is, not simply the line itself but the processes and political positions that the line enables, then the border is itself highly productive.

So what have these vignettes from Ban Beuk told us, then, about the border?

The Mekong as border places a barrier to knowledge in the way of those who live alongside it. It permits hydropower plans to ignore downstream effects past a certain line in the map, or to consider only the effects upon one bank. It allows Nu, when he sees a strange face, to cast this face as Lao, and when the chief inspector fails to capture a fish poacher, he also assumes that the poacher has "escaped to Laos."

The border, in this light, enables indeterminacy. An unknown person is not a stranger, because he or she might be "just a fisherman" from the other bank. At the same time as Laos is the home of "fishermen" like "us," it is also the refuge of criminals. The border provides the possibility for both of these—strangers "like us," and dangerous strangers. Methamphetamines, for the chief inspector, come over the border in the pockets of such people who look "like us" but who pose a threat.

But the border is not just about fear of "them." The indeterminacy within the border allows for an escape for "us" as well. The Holy Man rebels can imagine a utopian new world summed up in the name Vientiane. Sex workers in Ban Beuk often come from Laos (and the two attending to the chief inspector were no exception). While Mon sees the act of selling off the donations received by villagers as monstrous, in Laos the abbot is able to do so (or, at least, is imagined to be able to do so). Mon and Nu can drink on holy days when the Thai government bans alcohol sales via escaping to Laos (and Laotians, for that matter, can do so in Thailand).

As such, it is little surprise that the border is a libidinal zone. Mon fantasizes about the possibility of marrying a "pale, beautiful girl" who will be more "elegant . . . like Thais were fifty years ago." This particular intra-Asian Orientalist fantasy is one replicated many times elsewhere—it is what Western sex tourists say of Thai women (see Johnson 2007), what Singaporeans say of Thai amulets (see Johnson 2016a), what Chinese tourists say of Hmong (Schein 1997), and so on. Following the link between such sexual fantasies and entrepreneurial fantasies (Johnson 2016a), the border presents a potential capitalist frontier.

Additionally, the border is a resource. The chief inspector is able to dole out permissions to border-crossers largely as he sees fit (disallowing Lo's business, for instance). But for the army, too, its presence allows intervention and building infrastructure when it has no such mandate elsewhere. The lookout point on the mountain and the army post at the border were hardly the only places where army capital was spent on the border—the roads in Ban Beuk were sealed asphalt, roads that quickly became concrete or red dirt once one turned away from the border and toward the Isan heartland. On the geopolitical scale, too, the border allows floods to become Lao or Cambodian problems (not Chinese problems). The fiction of the border allows the framing of hydropower as a national good, rather than as one that benefits some regions to the detriment of others.

Thus, the border enables certain flows of goods, people, capital, and fantasies, both across it and internally. Jakkrit, drawing upon Nail, describes the border by virtue of its "in-betweenness" (*nai-rawang*), by which he means the way the border overlies ethnic or political indeterminacy (Jakkrit 2017a). This is certainly the case for the Thai-Lao border, where a recent history of antagonism belies a deeper, deeply intertwined history—as Thai historian Sujit Wongthes (2016) puts it (in a way intended to abrade nationalistic sentiments), "Thai are those Lao that happened to settle in the Chao Phraya river valley and marry Chinese men." From the opposite political angle, but also affirming a sense of unity, is fascist-era propagandist Wichit Wathakan, who writes, "our brothers and sisters on the bank of the Mekong are genuine Thais with no less Thai blood than we Siamese" (cited in Ivarsson 2008, 76).

In short, claims to borders are claims to a certainty that belies their messiness. It is an act of naming (Siegel 2005), the designation of a person or place as belonging somewhere. But as Siegel points out, in the act of naming we open ourselves up to possibilities otherwise. Here, the establishment of a Thai Isan is drawn into question by those on Isan's "skeptical frontier" that dream of a "new Vientiane." The sovereignty of national borders means little to the downstream effects of hydropower, even if the act of naming allows one to judge water on one side of the border Chinese and on the other Lao. It is a fixity that belies opacity.

In chapter 5, I address the issue of the productive power of opacity, an opacity enabled by the establishment of boundaries and barriers—to sensorial exploration, to vision, to understanding. But in chapter 2, I stay with this issue of opacity to look at the change in materiality that the river undergoes below the dam. The river is changed, Pong tells me, and they don't know what to do with it.

2

RIVER BEINGS

In April 2015, during an ebb following one of the recent irregular gluts of water from Jinghong, Pong and I took his boat to look for a lost net. As he guided us through the maze of islands and rocks exposed by the Mekong's retreat, we moved through clumps of bushes with branches bare except for a thin green line of foliage marking the highest extent of the recent water. These shrubs would ordinarily be submerged for the extent of the rainy season, leaf and bear fruit during the dry season, and then be resubmerged in time for their fruits to be eaten and seeds distributed by catfish during the next flood. But the rapid rise and fall of the river gave little time for this. The buds were smothered before they had a chance to grow, and fruit never appeared. The network is in flux, and relations are uncertain.

Looking at the bare branches while sitting in Pong's boat, Pong said to me, "They are confused [ngong] like the fish are confused, like the Lord of the Fish [jao pa beuk] is confused, like we are confused. They [the fish] are here [in the water] but we don't know how to get to them. The water is changed."

"So [the fish are] still there?" I asked him.

Pong replied, "They are hiding until things get better. They are pissed off at us [man beua hao], but they will come back."

As he steered the boat through the river's narrow channels, Pong related to me the multiple different techniques that he had used in fishing only ten years ago that had since stopped working: the use of road-killed dog flesh, pickled in urine, to catch the giant catfish's slightly smaller, carnivorous cousin

(*Pangasianodon hypophthalmus* or possibly a *P. gigas/hypophthalmus* hybrid—see discussion elsewhere in this chapter). The use of a drop of opium on a hook for certain kinds of large fish. Spells (*khatha*) that could coax a catfish to the net. A petition to the naga to guide fish toward him. A specific request to the Lord of the Fish (jao pa beuk)—a spirit who ruled over and managed the local giant catfish—to catch one of his subjects (see Giles 1932; and discussion in chapter 3). Finding "red" water in which nets could be invisible to passing fish.

Pong points to a failure of technique across multiple levels. His own technologies for catching fish no longer work. These techniques include both those that rely upon material qualities (e.g., bait), his own personal prowess (e.g., spells), his relationships with religious figures (e.g., the Lord of the Fish or the naga), or his skillful reading of the environment (e.g., "red" water). Each of these, for Pong, is interlinked, and each has failed. But this is a failure of old knowledge, an attempt to dwell in a place that is no longer extant. A new river requires new knowledge, new means to access the potency that had changed.

Analyzing Pong's sense of loss on the river requires addressing a few distinct points. The attempt to live with the changed Mekong and its other beings involves negotiating four factors: time, material, technique, and potency. For instance, Pong's fishing involves knowing what time a particular fish would be active, what material bait would draw the fish to him, and what traps to set for the fish, but also accessing some further means to ensure that the fish actually comes.

Each of these qualities—material, time, technique, and potency—are in flux. Accordingly, here, I address the material qualities of the Mekong land/water-scape, including its temporality, water itself, fish, and the changing techniques used to access them. This in turn involves Mekong concepts of time, as time and space become vital to how potential fish become actual fish, and what it means to dwell in this new landscape.

I spent most of my fieldwork on a boat, going to and from nets in the Mekong, and talking to fishermen about the river, its alterations, and its contents. In early 2015, I supplemented this ethnographic work with a series of surveys of fishermen aimed at understanding their fishing techniques, as well as informal conversations about other—less often spoken about—techniques (e.g., magic, electrocution, explosives). Here, we talked about the mutual entanglement between all the beings on the river—material, immaterial, human, nonhuman, and inhuman.

Much as seasonal variation marks life in the Arctic (Mauss 2004), monsoon-related variation in the flow of the Mekong River marks life along it. Time, for fishermen, is based upon the great river's rise and fall, a movement that indicates when actions (fishing, farming, etc.) will be efficacious and when they will not. Reading and responding to the river is a vital part of living with it.

However, the relationship between the river and river folk is not unidirectional. In his study of the Amazon River, Hugh Raffles (2002) sets the relationship between rivers and people—by extension, nature and culture—in context. Via the action of those living on its banks, felling trees, cutting channels, and so on, the Amazon has been altered time and again in ways that fundamentally change its nature. The river is constantly becoming something other than what it was. It is only later, in the nineteenth century, that the Amazon comes to be touted as untouched nature: something separate from the work of humans. Similarly, on the Mekong, the river is a thing with which one interacts, physically as well as socially (e.g., with the Lao on the other bank, with the chief inspector, or with the Lord of the Fish). But this is social as well as physical labor. Just as one learns to deal with their materiality, rapids, eddies, and fish alike become beings with which one has a personal kind of relationship. One may come to know a fearsome rapid, but that rapid might also come to know us.

But now is different. Whereas the kinds of alterations about which Raffles writes on the Amazon are incremental, the new, dammed Mekong, with an irregular flow, collapsing banks, and disappearing fish, is something else. It is a "blasted landscape," to draw a term from Anna Tsing (2015)—a term literally true for those stretches marred by dynamite fishermen or, farther upstream, the Chinese blasting of boulders to make the river more navigable. For Tsing, blasted landscapes are environmentally ravaged but also productive places, where the dispossessed and vulnerable are able to reforge a relationship with the land, a land damaged by capitalism. This is a form of dwelling that is not ideal, nor is it in some kind of imagined perfect harmony. Rather, Tsing emphasizes how we make do with ruins. Tsing (2015, viii) describes the matsutake (mushroom) as taking hold in ruined postindustrial landscapes worked by migrants, giving rise to a new "natureculture," one that is neither a multispecies *Mitsein* nor a modernist "management" of natural resources but rather simply "what manages to live despite capitalism."

Raffles and Tsing both focus on the intertwining worlds of human and nonhuman, complicating nature and culture. But they do not venture into the ghostly or the imagined. What of the poetics of material? Gaston Bachelard (1999), in his *Water and Dreams*, focuses on the way that water carries with it a poetics. He, in a very different way, also complicates the distinction between nature and culture: nature, via its very materiality, suggests certain meanings to us in ways that are both psychoanalytically relevant and prelinguistic. Of course, Bachelard's link falls victim to a kind of reification based upon his own speculation—what a river suggests to Bachelard (i.e., what he claims the river "suggests" in general) is not quite what a river would suggest to another. But communication exists between people and their environment within the intangible, the occulted, the poetic—in short, that which transcends the material conditions of life. I, too, am compelled by the relationship between rivers and the imaginative worlds that they bring into being.

MATERIAL

I know rivers. I grew up on the Nansemond, on the brackish stretch just where it combines with the James and the York to make Hampton Roads, a section of the Chesapeake Bay near Norfolk, Virginia. My parents owned a house on the water, and I spent a lot of time in kayaks, sailboats, or swimming in the current. Or just sitting on the back porch, looking over the river and salt marsh, watching the animals, the colors of the marsh grass, and the play of light in the distance. Sometimes dolphin would come up the river, or cownose rays. Other times, striped bass (rockfish, in the local terminology) would run the river, and anglers followed them. My father, a retired engineer, seeded local oysters after the devastating influx of *Perkinsus marinus*, a marine parasite. My parents were not what Virginians call "watermen," being transplants from the northeast, but we knew the Nansemond well.[1]

The Mekong, where it flows past Ban Beuk, is nothing like the Nansemond. Its surface is in constant motion in three directions; its flow is hypnotic. It normally flows from west to east, until the monsoons engorge it, when, at least farther downstream in Cambodia, it reverses and flows from east to west. It flows up and down, too: whirlpools the size of a fist form on the surface with great sucking sounds, travel a few meters downstream, then dissipate. Plateaus of water bubble up from underneath. These are expected when the river flows over a great rock (*kaeng* or, to refer more directly to the rock and less to the rapid, *hin*), but many are unpredictable: they form seemingly from nowhere and disappear into the swirl. There is an endless churn in the red-brown flow.

For fishermen, the water is a constant topic of conversation. It is little (*noy*) or much (*lai*). It runs either red with sediment (*daeng*) or clear (*sai*), meaning with a few inches of visibility. At nights of the full moon, those living on its banks report fireballs (*bang fai*) erupting from the water that they attribute to nagas living in its depths.

The topography of the river is mediated by its rapids—those kaeng over, under, and around which the water flows. One navigates by reference to this or that kaeng, which, in Ban Beuk, have names and stories. Some, like the great *kaeng phan*, have personalities, and this particular rock, despite its reputation (its name means Cruel Rapid), guards the best fishing in the area. Local fishermen such as Lert navigate the rapid with relative ease—even if they fall silent and hold tight to the rudder of their boat when going through. A decade ago, the rapid tore the bottom out of a Chinese cargo vessel attempting to traverse it. Cargo and oil floated down the river for days.

At another, Corpse Rapid (*kaeng phi*), Pong (and other fishermen) occasionally find bodies that have floated down from upstream, caught within a particular eddy that somehow chooses to float human flesh and ignore other flotsam. While I was conducting my research in 2015, Lert found the bodies of a young man and woman in the same week. "They had tied wrists," he said, shaking his head sadly. By this, *mat meu*, he means that they had rows and rows of strings around their wrists: not signs of bondage, but blessings from the elders in a Lao ritual. Everyone traveling a long distance—myself included—would ask for such a blessing before leaving home, and Lao travelers often had entire sleeves of string bracelets running from wrist to mid-forearm. It showed that one was loved, and was the result of a ritual intended to stay safe and keep one's *khwan* (spirit, soul, essence) firmly bound to the body. Lert's grief at discovering the bodies was one of recognition: they were Lao people, like him, with parents and grandparents who loved them and wished them well. And they ended up in the swirl of Corpse Rapid.

Two years later, in 2017, Mon found a similar body, too badly decomposed for identification, at the kaeng. Normally sober-minded, he was frightened of the corpse and revolted by its putrescence, but he made a broad effort to get in touch with anyone who knew of anyone missing upstream. He even reached out to me, teaching then in New Jersey. "I think it is a woman," he said to me in a Facebook chat. "It is waiting on the kaeng. I don't know what to do. I cannot bring it ashore and I cannot send it off. What should I do with it?"

The body was a part of his disquiet, but the kaeng, too, marked a place in the river where unknown others seemed to collect. Unlike in my previous studies of accidental death in Thailand (Johnson 2012, 2014), Pong and Mon did not speak of ghosts;[2] rather, what was concerning about kaeng phi was its ability to cause others' deaths to become Ban Beuk's problem.

Thus, kaeng like the vicious kaeng phan and the corpse-collecting kaeng phi mark the river and are the means toward navigation. One refers to places in the river with respect to kaeng or other hydrological features—one can even talk about the shoreline like this: Lert lived just across from kaeng phan. Pong could see kaeng phi from his house. Near *khok hae* was a Laotian pub that one could boat up to. Most towns on the river have names derived from such features: *ban khok mai, ban nong, ban khok huay.*

Fish also appreciate kaeng. Crocodile fish, *Bagarius suchus* (Lao: *pa khae*), stick close to the boulders of a kaeng, in that eddy just next to the rush of water. This suits them: they are ambush predators and sport a nasty-looking mouthful of teeth, hence the name. Especially when the current drops in the dry season, these fish are the largest that are regularly caught, although they are nothing compared to the Mekong giant catfish (*Pangasianodon gigas*). Theoretically, one could net a large pa khae by leaning out over a rapid with a dip net strung between two bamboo poles. Assuming that the weight of the fish—at times over 50 kilograms—did not tip the fisherman into the rapid, the profits would be sizeable despite the poor quality of crocodile fish meat—especially since this kind of fishing was normally done by less-well-off fishermen without their own designated fishing ground.

Sometimes a kaeng is more than just a rock. A pocket of sand might grow into a beach (*hat*) when the water drops. Sometimes larger plants might colonize it and create an island (Lao: *don*; Thai: *koh*), like my own Bird Island. Some islands are inhabited (and, following the tradition of marking the border at the Thai bank, their residents are nationally Lao); most are not. The dividing line between kaeng and don seems, to Mon and others, to be the presence of trees— such as the fruit-bearing shrubs that Pong pointed out to me—rather than the year-round emergence of the island from the flow.

Don are useful for a number of things. Mon, for instance, as a relatively young public official, was interested in promoting domestic ecotourism, and had a long mental list of hat and don where Thai tourists could go to take selfies on the sand. Chomchai, Pong's neighbor, cultivated a seasonal watermelon patch on a sandy don (appropriately, "watermelon island" [*don mo*]) that emerged only during the dry season.

Don are named many things, but mostly have names that indicate what sorts of resources might be available there: *don kluay* (Banana Island) had bananas; *don nok* (Bird Island) had birds, and so on. *Don phi* had, not corpses like *kaeng phi*, but another kind of *phi*, a guardian spirit.[3]

These islands break up the flow of the river, turning a flat linear course into a maze, slowing the water and enabling silt to fall out of the stream. As such, they present an obstacle to navigation: Mon was especially concerned with Chinese plans to fund the Laotian demolition of the kaeng and don of the Mekong, something that had been planned for zones upstream. This would affect not only the ecology of those zones marked for detonation, but the speed of the water: hydrologically, rapids and islands slow the flow of the river. Ban Beuk sits at a transition point, where the Mekong pours out of the Laotian mountains, and a last series of rock escarpments jut out and disrupt its flow

Figure 2.1: Mekong water

before it widens into the flat, muddy expanse that flows past Vientiane, Nong Khai, and points farther downstream.

As these rapids and islands slow the river, the water does many things in response (figure 2.1). Released into a broader, flatter stretch after being pinched by kaeng into a few fast streams, the water might make a slow, churning, oval eddy (*wern*). This long, lazy swirl makes for good hunting with a throw net or a place to fence off a part of the river in which to store live fish. More common is a faster, rounder eddy (*khok*), marking a brief moment of respite between kaeng. Most owned fishing grounds of my interlocutors were in a specific khok, where fishermen caught sheatfish (*Hemisilurus mekongensis* or *pa nang daeng*), tilapia, or a place to swim.

Finally, there are deep pools (*nong*). Here is where the water persists in the dry season, when the rest of the river drops to a trickle, or where the water remains relatively still in the wet season, when the kaeng are raging. Here, too, is where the *beuk* fish (*Pangasianodon gigas*, the Mekong giant catfish) live, and from where their divine king, the Lord of the Fish, ruled (see Giles 1932). At one such pool, the mayor of Ban Beuk boasted that the pool was so deep that the bottom was never found—"they" (researchers? tourists?) had sent a man in scuba gear to see the bottom, and he swam to the limits of his ability without finding it. The mayor speculated that there was a secret tunnel that led from the bottom of the nong to an underground series of caves linked far below and behind Ban Beuk, something proved by the fact that tall bamboo stalks would suddenly erupt into the surface of the nong, despite the fact that these plants only grew on the back side of the nearby hills, away from the river.

Indeed, Mon, during a fieldwork stretch in 2019, showed me a schematic of how he imagined nong to work. The deep pool, at its lowest extent, turned into a cave underlying the bank, partially filled with air. As the cave stretched farther back, chimneys letting in fresh air broke through the Mekong-side hills. These submerged caves would, for Mon, provide a refuge for catfish and naga alike, and a reason why the catfish might be still present, even if they were not found for years at a time. As he asked me, "How is it that a 200-kilogram fish is suddenly caught in Ban Beuk? We have nets strung up everywhere. People are shocking fish everywhere. The smallest fish has a hard time getting past here—just like that tiny fish you threw away four years ago.[4] And then suddenly someone finds a huge beuk? They must still be here, hiding."

Solid Authority on a Moving Medium

Riding along with Pong multiple times in different seasons, I sketched out a map of the river as it flows past Ban Beuk, marking down the the names of each kaeng, khok, and wern, photographing each and detailing the kinds of fish caught and at what time of the year they were caught.

On a typical such outing, Pong would pilot his boat alongside a rapid or, gearing up enough momentum, straight up some of the less precipitous ones. We would pull into the eddy alongside one of the great boulders that marked a kaeng. Sometimes there would be a rope dangling in the water for mooring, at other times the slope would be shallow enough that Pong could pull the boat atop the rock. We would get out and clamber up the rock, at that time of the year looming ten or twenty feet above the water. But as the tops of many of these rocks indicated, this was only a temporary height—nets, logs, bits of boat, and other wrack were markers that what was now a cliff was once underwater. Indeed, at times after a surprise flood, there were pools of standing water on the top. From that vantage point, Pong would peer out from under the brim of his cowboy hat and list the names of various sites in the water before returning to his boat.

Pong's map did not just stop at the names of sites. Instead, he detailed who owned each spot in the river, showing me the legal grid that overlaid the river. Certain places were designated as public or private, determining who had the right to fish where. These locations, termed *luang mong* (traps), were also affixed to a particular khok, wern, kaeng, or other hydrological feature. The richest fishermen—Pong included—owned the rights to fish at several sites, and luang mong could be bought, sold, inherited, or leased on a monthly or yearly basis, just like land-based property. A good luang mong can go for several tens of thousands of *baht* ($300–$1,000). For those without, throw-net fishing in public wern was an option, or some public boulders offered a precarious perch with a dip net (*tak-ton*).

But here is a legal issue. Lao fishermen claimed the Mekong up to the point where the water meets the Thai shore and suggested that they were simply being generous neighbors in allowing Thai nationals such as Pong upon its waters. Indeed, Bird Island shows just such an arrangement: although only separated by a small strand of the river, and not its main channel, Mon didn't think to farm it and left it for someone from the other bank. But, contradicting this principle, Lao military-erected concrete pyramids on kaeng midstream mark another boundary, one following the deepest channel. This boundary was the one that Pong pointed out to me. But this, too, was ignored by all involved. Pong and Mon crossed this line regularly on their boats (often taking me with them) and went for social engagements in Ban Ngoen, in Laos, without any kind of paperwork. When I pressed Pong on the competing national definitions of what constitutes Lao or Thai places in the water, Pong replied simply, "Boh kiaw khong"—"[the nations are] not applicable [here]."

Thus, claims to plots of water within this border are recognized by no authority higher than the village headmen of Ban Beuk and Ban Ngoen. These two authorities agree upon who owns what luang mong at what time and are responsible for adjudicating disputes over them. Here, too, the police do not and cannot get involved—indeed, a Thai policeman would have questionable authority over property rights claimed by another country, not to mention midstream.

The village head of Ban Thong showed me his records, which constituted a college-ruled notebook of some age, with carefully written lines indicating the owner's name and address, location of the luang mong, and occasionally purchase or rental price. These owners were nearly always residents from a nearby town—either Ban Thong itself or Ban Ngeun, on the Lao bank, or one of the other Thai or Lao villages within a few minutes' travel up or down the river.

Thus, luang mong as well as public throw- and dip-net sites constitute another way of seeing ownership and authority in the river. In this respect, because of the Mekong's unclear status vis-à-vis international law, customary law administered by local authorities takes precedence. In short, effective legal authority in Mekong fishing is proximate; it is administered not from Bangkok or Vientiane, not from the provincial seat in Nong Khai, and not even from the district head.

But luang mong fisheries have been the hardest hit by recent hydropower projects. When unexpected floods rip through Ban Beuk, the most common casualty is the nets strung within these fishing grounds. These nets, already prone to tangling, become a pale blue mess as they are torn from the eddies in which they float. Most often, they end up the morning after the flood stranded atop one of those boulders that Pong and I climbed, often with fish rotting in the sun too ensnared to be removed. Most nets thus swept away and stranded were too damaged to be repaired and constituted the majority of losses from minor floods.

Thus, of the sites that Pong pointed out to me, many if not most were devoid of nets. Here, either nets had been swept away or, equally often, Pong described the owners as "waiting" (Lao: *lo du*). Some had lost nets and were waiting to have the time or money to replace them, but some were simply waiting for the instability in the river to be over. As in rubber farming, as I detail elsewhere, such a moment of flux is one that calls for inaction. Fishing, and by extension the realm managed by local authority, is changing. The new landscape of potency is uncertain, and only after this new world emerges can decisions be made.

Navigating the Flow

A typical fishing trip (figure 2.2) began with a stop at Mon's luang mong. These were nets stretched in a wide, slow eddy (wern) or slow pool (khok), or at the mouth of a stream (*pak huay*). Empty water bottles kept the nets afloat, and most of the time fishermen kept a few dangling in the river. These nets held the greatest chance to catch something large, and to increase these chances, Mon would strategically set his nets according to a particular calendar.

Mon would pull up the fine polyester fiber of the net, rhythmically shaking out the water as he did so with a firm slap to the side of the boat. He would carefully draw it up, hand over hand, feeling its weight. Usually there was something in it, from a small, hand-sized *Probarbus* to a typical good catch—a tilapia of a few kilograms. These were hard to disentangle from the gill nets, which was a job Mon delegated to me. Often, I fumbled with the fish, turning it this way and that trying to angle its head out of the net and only getting myself stuck with its spines.

Sometimes the fish was dead and rotten. This was especially the case if Mon had not visited this particular net for a few days. In these cases, the fish

Figure 2.2: Mon, fishing

would not necessarily go to waste but could be tossed into a vat underneath Mon's house. Here it was repurposed as stock for fermented fish sauce (*pa daek*). This ingredient sharply marks Lao food as different from Thai food. The dark, savory pa daek (Thai: *pla ra*) transforms the bright, sour tastes of central Thai food (in papaya salad, for instance) into a more earthy, fragrant (Bangkokians might say "stinky") experience. If national cuisines are defined by one staple ingredient, pa daek defines Lao and Isan palates.

Luang mong failing, we might, in the wet season, when the water had flooded the riverbanks, go to a shallow wern that had formed atop a grassy field, where fish might be trapped at one end. One of us, preferably me, would stand in the deeper water and splash, while the other, preferably Mon, would be ready with a weighted throw net. As I flailed in the water, a pleasant, cool experience, Mon flung the net with a spin, so that it opened in midair and made a great circle in the water. Inside, hopefully, would be smaller fish.

I learned the lesson of what to keep and what to throw back quickly on my fishing trips with Mon. The first fish that I caught was a hand-sized *pa eun* (*Probarbus* sp.) in a throw-net cast. After struggling to free it from the net without either damaging the net or sticking my palm with its spines, I held up the violently wriggling thing doubtfully. This would not have qualified as legal on the Nansemond, and it was just the size of the tiny croaker (*Micropogonias undulatus*) that I used to catch off my parents' dock. I knew from experience that there was not enough meat on it to filet the thing, and it needed some years to grow. Without much thought, I tossed it back into the water.

Mon was stunned. "We could have done so much with it!" he began, after which he launched into a lecture lasting the entire trip back to the dock on all the things one could do with a small fish.

"We could have deep-fried it!" Mon announced, "And eaten it with sticky rice and [store-bought] dipping sauce."

A minute went by while I watched the shoreline go past and Mon looked ahead, over my shoulder.

"We could have put it on a bamboo skewer and grilled it [over a coal fire]."

I watched the water.

"We could have minced it raw to make *koi.*"

Feeling defensive, I retorted, "Even that small?"

"Of course that small! Even if none of these things, we could still have thrown it into the clay container to make fermented pa daek."[5]

Maybe, Mon wondered, I wasn't ready for the throw net and should just stick to standing in the shallows and splashing the fish into his net. That, at least, I could do.

When the water was high, as it was that day, the fishing was more difficult in the wern. Bigger fish were deeper and had spawned already. This was the time of smaller fish like that lucky *Probarbus* that I had let go.

But the rains brought other kinds of food, too. At night, as we came back with only some rotten fish for pa daek, Mon tied up the boat and immediately guided me farther down the riverbank, on the sandy bank where the city had been building its embankment. "Let's see what's there [to catch]." He stood, listening for frogs, knee-deep in the fine sand. We scoured the industrially cut granite boulders and sandy artificial embankment, but the construction site was too arid and artificial for frogs. But later, as we ate our bamboo-shoot curry (Mon's sister, Yai, had harvested some bamboo shoots and mushrooms from a neighbor's plot), giant cockchafers (*Holotrichia* sp. or Lao: *mengjinoon*) began to throw themselves against our electric lights. Thip sprang up to capture them in order to pan fry them.

This particular day was in June, when the fishing season normally would be beginning to slack off and, in some places (Yos 2012, 9), fishermen would observe a moratorium on fishing. But Ban Beuk had ceased observing this moratorium in the years since 2003. I give one example here of a typical day out with Mon to show the sheer variety of experiences that one engages with during such an outing. Mon checks luang mong for large fish, tosses a throw net for smaller fish, improvises a use for an otherwise useless unskilled fisherman (me), hunts frogs, and eventually catches beetles. In each, he deploys particular techniques, none of which work excepting the unintentional use of his porch light to attract beetles. He is a *bricoleur* of the river.

BIOTA

As with the water, life in the Mekong is constantly in flux. With the water's rise, riverbank areas and the plants growing on them are submerged, becoming a part of the river's food chain. In turn, as these banks are exposed, a thick layer of silt is deposited. This is a reddish-orange sand with surprisingly bright flakes of mica and other metals—seeing flakes glitter in the water, one remembers that a gold seam cuts straight under the town, and some residents still pan for gold in the silt in their free time.

The silt makes the water almost opaque. For most of the year, and especially during times of red water (*nam daeng*), the water is opaque enough that visibility only extends for a few inches. When pulling up nets, Mon anticipates what is inside of them by weight and feel, not by sight.[6]

The water is a trade-off for plants: it is rich in nutrients, but to be submerged is to be entirely choked off from light. A number of plants live part of their lives submerged and part exposed, including those shrubs with the bright red fruit that Pong pointed out to me, along with wild floating rice and a kind of algae that villagers elsewhere collect and eat. But primarily, my interlocutors spoke about fish.

The fish in the Mekong are, again, nothing like those of the Nansemond. The murky water means that everything tends to look like a catfish: muscular, sinuous bodies designed for quick bursts of speed; mouth barbels to sense prey in the gloom; migration patterns that depend upon the ebb and flow of the river between rainy and dry seasons.

While I describe fish that were significant to my interlocutors in context, this is no guide to fishes of the middle Mekong. Indeed, in-depth study of Mekong fish lags behind that of better-researched rivers. That said, Yos Santasombat's (2012) *River of Life* contains a fantastic list (in Thai, Latin, and English) of fish caught in upland fisheries, wetlands, and main-channel fisheries at a number of sites along the river, the closest of which is just upstream of the Sayaburi Dam at a site similar (in other respects) to Ban Beuk. Similarly, Walter Rainboth (1996) has written an exemplary field guide to fishes of the Cambodian Mekong with names in Khmer, English, and Latin as well as images. If the reader wishes to learn in detail the kinds of fishes that one might catch along the Mekong, please turn to those volumes.

My interlocutors divided fish into two main varieties: those with scales (*mi kret*) and those without. Of these, while scaly fish were numerous, it was the catfish that really captured people's attention.

Most scaly fish in the Mekong are cyprinids, the family that includes carp: indeed, all of the members of these are thick-bodied, slow-moving fish with gulping mouthparts and barbels. These fish live in slow-moving parts of the river and, during the seasonal flood, take advantage of the newly inundated regions to feed. This is precisely the environment in which Mon and I were using his throw net—a wern where water had backed up and overflowed land on the Laotian bank.

Species of scaly fish here include silver barbs (*pa mang, Barbonymus goniono-tus*), black sharkminnow (*pa i-tu, Labeo chrysophekadion*), the Siamese mud carp (*pa soi khao* or *pa bok, Henichorynchus siamensis*), and *pa eun* (*Probarbus* sp.), like the one that I had caught. These latter are particularly vulnerable to barriers to migration, and *Probarbus jullieni*, exterminated in the Chao Phraya (Bangkok region) river basin, cannot be expected to survive the current hydropower developments on the Mekong (Rainboth 1996, 83).

Additionally, there are invasive scaly species, including Nile tilapia (*Oreo-chromis niloticus* or *pa nin*) and common carp (*Carpio carpio* or *pa nai*). The former is a relatively recent introduction, having escaped from flooded fish farms in turn promoted by royal development projects.

But the kinds of fish that make the Mekong distinctive are its catfish and sheatfishes (a catfish from the Siluridae family). These latter, called *pa neua on* (literally "soft-fleshed fish" or *Phalacronotus apogon*), make up a great deal of the wet-season gill-net catch and are popular in riverside restaurants as well as for fish balls, although on a later visit in 2019, fishermen reported an ominous, precipitous drop in *Phalacronotus* catches. Other popular catfish include red-tail catfish (*pa kot, Hemibagrus* sp.), the "crocodile fish" (*pa khae, Bagarius suchus*; figure 2.3), and others.

Mon was pleased when he had the opportunity to bring home a tilapia or pa neua on. But such a catch wouldn't be a subject of conversation on the bamboo platform where we sat and drank rice whisky at night. Instead, there, we would talk about the bigger catfish: shark catfish, faster-moving fish with torpedo-shaped bodies and firm, pink flesh. These include *pa pho* (*Pangasius bocourti*), *pa sai* (*Helicophagus* sp.), or especially the large iridescent shark (*pa sawai, Pangasianodon hypophthalmus*). These latter made good donations to the temple, especially the more prestigious temple at Ban Thong, and Mon would save his pa sawai alive in nets awaiting holy days when the temple might be crowded, and his presentation would reach an audience.

Figure 2.3: Crocodile fish

Of course, this list of fish neglects the Mekong giant catfish (pa beuk, *Pangasianodon gigas*) and the river's new species, a hybrid of *P. hypophthalmus* and *P. gigas*. But I will return to these shortly.

Nearly all of these species are endangered (excepting, of course, those that are introduced), some of them (*P. gigas*) critically so. This status seemed to matter little to fishermen, who did not distinguish between an endangered sheatfish or a common tilapia in their nets. Both yielded meat, and both yielded profit. Additionally, many fishing techniques do not discriminate: nets as well as explosives or electricity kill or stun all fish in a radius. Indeed, fishermen could not discriminate if they wanted to: in the murky river's flow, one cannot see what one catches. One makes a guess, chooses a kind of bait or net (or both), and gives the rest up to chance, fate, or something else beyond one's control.

Posing another risk to fish, many of these fishes have distinct migratory patterns. Catfish often spawn up smaller tributaries during the rainy season (June–September), and many cyprinids migrate up the main stream to spawn as well. These movements are triggered by water flow, and as such are particularly sensitive to its fluctuation, notwithstanding the direct barrier that hydropower projects place in the path of migrating fish.

But of the biota in the river, two deserve particular mention, one the largest fish in the river,[7] and the other microscopic: the pa beuk (*Pangasianodon gigas*, hereafter beuk) and a bile duct fluke (*Opisthorchis viverrini*). Each of these is a being with which fishermen have particular intimate relationships. The beuk is that fish that is both animal and subject of a religious focus: the Lord of the Fish (jao pa beuk) of which Pong speaks. The fluke is more insidious.

The Case of the Uncertain Fish (Part 1)

Mekong giant catfish—pa beuk—are enormous beasts that feed largely on algae. On the large end, they can push 300 kilograms in weight, although most are much smaller. Catching a beuk is a cause for celebration—they can net tens of thousands of baht. Indeed, this is all they bring; owing to their expense, and owing to the—privately acknowledged—poor quality of the meat, villagers who talked about catching a beuk never mentioned eating it, but always sold it off elsewhere.

This is illegal. The beuk is critically endangered and nearly extinct in the wild. At the same time, fish farms growing beuk exist in Thailand, with a market for beuk meat across the region. Indeed, when I mentioned my fieldwork, many in Bangkok encouraged me to try to find beuk meat, not seeming to know about the ban.

The beuk is, in Jakkrit's terms (2017a), a "quasi-object" that crystallizes certain networks: for instance, Pong related to me a story that illustrates the role of the beuk vis-à-vis the region, religious power, and the law. He had a government delegation from Bangkok visiting Ban Beuk and he, as subdistrict head, was supposed to entertain them. They had been asking to eat beuk, and Pong felt obligated to serve it to them, but no one had caught one in years. He went to the shrine to the Lord of Nagas (jao inthranagaraja) behind the temple in Ban Beuk, where a newly arrived medium had set up business in a cave. He asked the naga what to do about the visit, and the naga (via the medium) called on him to check his nets in the morning. Sure enough, that morning there were two (small) beuk in his nets! He served the fish to the visiting officials, who were pleased to eat it. No one seemed to question the status of the beuk: illegal or legal, critically endangered *gigas* or introduced hybrid, and so on.

Legality aside, catching a beuk is still the desired goal of any Mekong fisherman. Even if one was not to sell the beuk on the open market, state-run beuk farms are ready to buy any fish in order to harvest the eggs. Mon told me darkly that the fish thus caught, while they could be rereleased, are then slaughtered by the fish farm owner for meat, thus returning far more profit than what he paid to the fisherman who originally caught the animal but at a cost to the ecology of the river.

While a smaller beuk can be brought straight into a boat, one cannot lift a several-hundred-kilogram fish straight out of the water. Thus, catching a beuk involves at least several men in at least two boats. The men might tow the net into the shallows and lift the thrashing fish up from there, where it can be brought onto land and harvested. It is a community effort.

As Durkheim would have it, such a communally significant creature is also religiously significant. In 1932, F. H. Giles reported in the *Journal of the Siam Society* the rites and practices involved in catching the giant *pla beuk*. Specifically, he identifies by name two of Ban Beuk's neighboring towns and points out not only the topography of the pool (nong) in which the giant fish lives, but also the fact that the fish requires propitiation. In this pool, the "Golden Basin," the "chief of Viang Chandr [Vientiane]" presides over offerings to the "spirit chief," offerings that are in turn passed through a spirit medium (*nang tiam*). The spirit "replies that if the fishermen act in a right and proper way, the catch will be numerous, but if their behavior falls below the proper standard, the catch will be small, that you may not return home empty handed with your feelings bruised and hurt" (Giles 1932, 99).

Some in Ban Beuk (Pong, but significantly not Mon) still make an offering to a divine catfish—what I here refer to as the Lord of the Fish (jao pa beuk). Above the deep, bottomless pool (nong) famous for beuk was a concrete statue of the fish, as well as an altar where one could make offerings to the fish (or the naga) in order to ask for its help in trapping one of its subjects.

Farther down the river, by the district head, was a temple devoted to the beuk. There, monks with whom I spoke recounted a festival (see Giles 1932) from their grandfathers' time that the temple had put on in collaboration with the Lao bank (under the French, at that time) centered around the propitiation of the Lord of the Fish as well as its capture. For several days, villagers from either bank of the river (from the Siamese or the French-Lao side) would come out on their boats, floating offerings in the current and stretching nets across the river. This continued until politics intervened: as Laos fought for its independence from France and, later, for a Communist Laos, this idea of large-scale cross-border celebrations ceased (although smaller-scale events continue).

So the beuk have been ritually and socially important in Mekong fisheries for years. But in addition to their precipitous decline in the present, the beuk has changed in another, important way: there are now new, different beuk in the river. Seeing the demand for beuk flesh as well as the rapid decline in beuk catches, fish scientists under Kriangsak Mengamphan of Mae Jo University in

Chiang Mai developed a hybrid between the beuk and a related species of iridescent shark catfish, also native to the river (*Pangasianodon hypophthalmus* or *pa sawai*). The resultant, nationalistically named "Siam [Thai] *beuk*" was raised in fish farms, but hybrid fish escaped or were intentionally released into the Mekong. Now, nearly all of the beuk that fishermen catch are hybrid. Interestingly, Mon and Pong referred to these fish neither by their nationalistic name (*beuk siam*) nor by the alternative name of "white-flesh catfish" (*pla nang neua khao*), but simply as "beuk" at first, or, occasionally, "mixed beuk" (*beuk phrasom*) if I pressed them.

This hesitation is more than just a reluctance to admit to catching a smaller fish. Instead, the hesitation speaks to uncertainty: it was hard to tell the difference between a small real beuk and a full-grown mixed beuk. Different fishermen had different ideas (anal fins, for instance, on the real beuk were claimed to be farther back than on the mixed, but how far back was unclear). I have stated, following the claims of my interlocutors, that all beuk caught during my fieldwork were hybrid, but in truth a 50-kilogram fish pulled up out of the water might be either. To put it another way, the mixed beuk as possibility confused the ontological presence of pure *gigas*. Whereas before, the Mekong River's water was a mysterious place where creatures might be seen (e.g., the naga), here is the presence of new possibilities, new mysterious creatures engendered by that word: "maybe."

Tsing et al. (2017) refer to the "monsters of the Anthropocene" as just such hybrid and introduced species. For Tsing, these are beings that, like the mythological chimera, are monstrous amalgams of existing species and disrupt the environments into which they come. On the Mekong, this mixed beuk presents a mystery, as little is known about the impact of the new beuk on the river. While iridescent shark are carnivorous and beuk are algae feeders, fishermen reported that the new mixed beuk could be both: maybe it eats like an iridescent shark, maybe it eats like a beuk. Indeed, mixed beuk sometimes looked like a beuk and sometimes like an iridescent shark. While they worried about the impact of the new fish upon the river and bemoaned the loss of a fish as beloved as the old beuk, Mon still celebrated when he caught two (presumed to be mixed) beuk (small ones, about 20 kilograms each). Like Tsing et al.'s monsters, the new fish are a new, unknown entry into the river. They might operate for good or ill: devouring all the other fish, or reviving the crashing beuk populations, or both.

Or they might legitimate the consumption of the rest of the beuk. While no fishermen with whom I spoke mentioned the possibility of throwing back a pure beuk once they had caught it, all suggested that they would sell such a fish to a Thai state-run fisheries research lab. But this never happened during my fieldwork, as, even if colloquially fishermen would refer to their catches as simply "beuk," they were identified to any authoritative voice asking for more detail as "mixed." While original beuk would be illegal to keep for sale on the market, mixed beuk, as introduced species, were perfectly acceptable. Thus, pulling a fish that looks like a beuk out of a net is now always acceptable so long as one thinks of it as a mixed beuk. Legality is in intention, and "maybe" provides a way out.

In this indeterminacy, too, is resistance. Pong grumbled to me that the fish research lab, after harvesting the eggs, would simply butcher a beuk and sell its meat for profit—something that they did even if the fish were delivered to them alive. Here, Pong presents the fisheries lab as a profit-minded arm of Bangkok, claiming to exist to assist Mekong villagers but exploiting them instead.

Here, it is the indeterminacy of the fish that leads to its profit. Were the fish definitely a beuk (*P. gigas*), it would be illegal to sell except to a Thai state-run fish research institution. Were the fish an iridescent shark (*P. hypophthalmus*), it could not command the prices and prestige of a beuk. But the category of Siamese beuk, and the indeterminacy which it causes, allows for the fish to be sold or eaten without penalty. Because of the doubt that the idea of Siamese beuk introduces, the promise of landing a giant, profitable fish exists, and catches can remain between sacred (unable to be caught) beuk and profane (common) sawai.

In other words, just as certainty in what fishermen know or do not about the river erodes, this very doubt enables potency. But this is a theme to which I will return.

The Case of the Uncertain Fish (Part 2)

If the case of the ontologically unclear beuk demonstrated how the new river system called for a failure of situated knowledge, there is another being on the river that also demonstrates the uncertainty newly inherent in Mekong lives. Here, I return to that tiny, fist-sized fish flapping in my hand. "We could mince it for koi," Mon suggested to me after I'd already thrown the fish back. Koi is a Lao dish involving raw minced meat mixed with mint, garlic, lime, and chili, and served fresh. It can be made of pork, beef, or, here, fish. But it presents a problem.

Underneath the scales of particular freshwater fish in the Mekong region lives a fluke, *Opisthorchis viverrini* (Banchob et al. 2007). This parasitic flatworm is endemic to Isan and Laos, and has in the past also been a problem elsewhere in Asia. The fluke lives part of its life in the human bile duct. Its eggs, passed out in feces, are able to in turn infect freshwater snails and hatch as a kind of larva (something for which the technical term is *cercariae*). These free-swimming worms embed themselves on the skin of fish, especially at the attachment point of scales. Thus, they pose a risk with particular kinds of fish (e.g., tilapia, carp) and not with others (e.g., catfish). The extremely common mud carp (*pa soi*, *Henicorhynchus* sp.) was singled out by my interlocutors as being particularly risky.

The problem with *O. viverrini* is in its link with bile duct cancer. Many in high-risk *O. viverrini* regions become infected, purge with antiparasite medication, then become infected again. This cycle in turn becomes closely linked with cholangiocarcinoma (cancer of the bile duct), a particularly painful and fast-acting disease.

Infection with *O. viverrini* is widespread in the Mekong area, especially around some of Isan's inland lakes, and can reach nearly 70 percent of the population (Banchob et al. 2007). In Ban Beuk, this rate is lower, at 8.8 percent, largely owing to fish coming from the Mekong's fast-flowing waters—while the doctors in the hospital at the district head cast cholangiocarcinoma as a major issue, there was only one case on the books.

Opisthorchis viverrini infections come from the consumption of raw fish, especially in dishes such as koi, and public health campaigns against *O. viverrini* infection focused on educating ethnic Lao villagers against eating koi. But these attempts failed again and again, leading researchers to reach out to anthropologists—like myself—in order to explain the failure of such efforts. In 2016, I, along with Daena Funahashi, was invited to London to discuss Mekong fishing with a cholangiocarcinoma research group seeking to, as they put it, find out why villagers persisted in eating koi when they knew the risks.

"Bullshit" (*ku bo seua wa*), Mon said in response to my explanation of *O. viverrini* risk. It wasn't that Mon denied the existence of *O. viverrini* in scaly fish, but he dismissed the entire campaign to stop the consumption of koi. In response to his negation, I offered the (incorrect) oft-repeated rejoinder that getting drunk on rice whisky while eating koi killed the parasite. Mon disagreed with that, too: "They didn't use enough lime! When you make koi, if you make it right, you have to put enough lime in it to make it properly 'cook' [*tham hai man suk*]. It's only people who don't know anything about koi who get sick from it."

Back in London, I had suggested just the same thing. The physician on the team denied that acid killed all of the parasites and suggested that abstention from koi was the only way to eradicate the disease. But, as Echaubard et al. (2016) show, Mon is onto something in suggesting that "it's only people who don't know anything about koi who get sick from it." Echaubard argues that it is the cycle of purge and reinfection—especially infection at high levels—that poses a risk for cancer. At the same time, low levels of infection have some health benefits, including a reduction in inflammatory diseases (Echaubard et al. 2016). The risk, for Echaubard and Mon alike, lies in lack of correct knowledge about flukes and how to live with them. It is in the disruption, in the simultaneous introduction of antifluke medication and the loss of proper cooking techniques, that danger emerges.

The conflict is exacerbated by anti-koi campaigns. The Thai medical system, already dangerously Bangkok-centered, has a hard time dealing with rural regions. Funahashi (2016), in a study of the intersections of politics and health, points out the misrepresentation of rural livelihoods by those creating public health campaigns. These ranged from the innocently naive (e.g., assuming that farmers did not have electricity) to the aggressive (e.g., suggesting that rural villagers needed to be educated by force).

Similarly, health professionals working on eradicating bile duct cancer focused on the irrationality of eating koi as another dumb move by obstinate villagers. And, in response, Mon's answer of "bullshit" makes clear that obstinacy is born not out of irrationality or ignorance, but active rejection. But here, I want to underline the human/nonhuman relationship thrown into flux in the present, and introduce the cancer-causing fluke (as opposed to the fluke in moderation) as another "monster" (Tsing et al. 2017) of the Mekong's present—the medical solution offered by repeated antifluke medication ironically opens the door for greater and more harmful infections.

This (mis)understanding of regional technologies is indicative of knowledge and power relations in Thailand. Knowledge and solutions come from the center, from Bangkok, and even local knowledge (as I show below) only serves as such if it, too, has been vetted and approved. As with the Mekong itself, knowledge relations, power relations, and medical relations are spatial.

Biota

Here, then, is an ecology in flux. What at times was a fishery dominated by a yearly pulse, with giant catfish promising occasional windfalls and, in some areas, endemic bile duct infection, has become one with intermittent pulses of water and crashing fish stocks largely owing to disrupted migrations, hybrid catfish replacing pure stock, and cancer-causing cycles of infection and purge. Here, following Tsing et al. (2017) and taking a phrase attributed to Gramsci, is a time of monsters—monsters defined by uncertainty.

I address the link between these new forms of monstrosity in the river—the water's own deformation as well as that of the beings within it—further in subsequent chapters, when I bring to bear the effects of disruption of the new river upon the cosmological beings within it. But I do not wish to lose sight of my interlocutors here. Fishermen do not vanish in this new river; rather, when the material world—the river, its temporality, and the biota within it—alters, those who seek to dwell in a place must alter their own techniques. Here, then, I turn to technology.

TECHNOLOGY

In Ban Beuk, it is easy to recognize a fisherman's house—it is strung with nets, basket-like traps, and occasionally jumper cables. It most often sits on the river's edge, but not always. And there is often a boat tethered to the water's edge nearby.

Many—not all—fishermen have their own boats, and boats on the river are mostly fishing vessels. The term *sampan* is Cantonese in origin and is certainly not used on this stretch of the Mekong (instead, the word used was the Lao *heua* or its Thai variant *reua*) but might conjure up the right image in an unfamiliar reader's mind: a long, narrow boat with a raised, rectangular front. Alternately, imagine a banana peel of wood about twenty feet long with an outboard motor. This motor is both rudder and engine, connected as it is to a long driveshaft with a propeller at the end. Boats like these cost between several thousand baht (about $80) to about ten thousand (about $300), with most of that expense in the engine. In the right hands, the boats are fast and nimble, and expert steersmen like Mon or Pong dart in and out of violent rapids with relative ease.

On very rare occasions, at the height of the wet season or when the dam controller at Jinghong released water, larger ships would come down the river, most often from Laos but potentially from farther upstream. These multistory affairs were always a topic of discussion. Fishermen would watch the boat navigate the river as it went, especially after kaeng phan gutted the Chinese cargo ship.

Traps, too, define a fisherman. Fishing traps are laid out, generally, underneath a house. It is often an impressive and sometimes confusing display. Light blue polyester gill nets are rolled in cloudlike bundles or hung to dry. Barrel-shaped shrimp traps stand in a corner like kegs of beer at a bar. Other, handmade traps woven from palm leaves suggest Greek amphorae.

I use *traps* (*luang mong*, literally "fool the eye") here instead of *gear* (*upakon*) in order to follow the Lao word. *Mong*, a word synonymous with "to gaze," is different from *net*, as the latter emphasizes the interlacing of strands, and the former emphasizes trickery. Nets entangle fish as they would any other object, but referring to luang mong imagines a conscious actor that is fooled into being caught. One can knowingly be caught in a net, but a trap is sprung without foreknowledge.

In March 2015, I conducted a survey of fishermen and their equipment, supplemented with follow-up conversations throughout my fieldwork. In this, I was assisted in the field by Pla and Kai, two activists from a larger Mekong-oriented environmentalist group, who had helped to arrange my fieldwork in Ban Beuk to some extent. While not originally from Ban Beuk (instead, she was from closer to Nong Khai proper), Pla had gotten to know Pong and others in the town owing to their shared concerns over Chinese dams, and, further, Pla and I shared a mutual friend in the late anthropologist Pattana Kitiarsa. Pla's presence and familiarity with Pattana's work helped me to explain in Ban Beuk what exactly an anthropologist was and what one did. Later, other anthropologists (most notably Chayan Vaddhanaphuti) visited the town and taught some of the fishermen basic anthropological research techniques, another factor that greatly helped in explaining what it was that I intended to do.

In early 2015, Pla and Kai helped to organize a group of high school students from Ban Beuk who, accompanied by either Pla, Kai, or me, interviewed their neighbors and collected survey data on fishing techniques, income, and household information. In subsequent months and years, I then conducted follow-up interviews with some of these residents and accompanied still others on fishing trips.

These data, like any interview or survey data, were naturally selective. We asked about kinds and numbers of fish traps, estimated yields per month, changes after the dams, pressing concerns, migrant work, and the ultimate fate of fish caught (sold on the market, eaten at home, used for pa daek, donated to the Buddhist temple). We also asked about other sources of income: rice fields (*na*) or rubber or other cash crop orchard (*rai, suan*).

This work revealed a wide variety of fishing techniques and gave an indication of who most of the active fishermen on the river were. This portrait yielded unsurprising results—fishing is an old man's game, something one does after returning from migrant work. Of the thirty-one surveyed, the median age was fifty-eight, including a few in their nineties. All were men. All also relied to a varying extent upon income from kin engaged in migrant work.

Naturally, a key topic of conversation in the interviews and survey was fish. Discussions of fishing gear, locations, bait, seasons, spells, and patron spirits all detailed what kind of fish would be caught by such techniques, and asking fishermen to reflect on the changes in fishing practice revealed the scale of the decline—nearly all fishermen reported a loss in fish yields since the dams were built (although some attributed the loss to overfishing or electrical shock fishing), and an increasing reliance upon cash crop orchards.

But fishing techniques were the cornerstone of the conversations. Here, then, is a catalog of fish traps along the Mekong.

Gill nets, or the aforementioned luang mong, were the most popular fishing tool for Ban Beuk's wealthier fishermen. Luang mong can be suspended in a particular owned or leased location and checked every few days, or can be deployed in a public place or group-owned place. These are responsible for most of the fish that my interlocutors reported caught, and checking luang mong was a cornerstone of any trip out with Mon or Pong.

Other fishermen preferred to target a particular, especially carnivorous, fish with a hook (bed khan, bed sam) strung in the water or left to drift (bed phiak). Occasionally these would be strung out in fishing sites where luang mong would normally go, especially if fish had been reluctant to be caught in the nets—baiting hooks was a secondary alternative.

For these, one needed to have a boat and, normally, a dedicated fishing site assigned to one's family. This was the sort of fishing of which Pong spoke—reading the water, learning the kinds of bait, using the right spells and prayers. But the need for equipment placed many fishermen, like Lert, at a disadvantage, as they lacked the capital or social standing to purchase such a site. Instead, these fishermen had to rely upon fishing from the water's edge. These techniques precluded certain kinds of catches—no one is going to catch a 30-kilogram crocodile catfish with a throw net, but one might just get a good enough tilapia.

Lert relied upon a throw net (hae), of the sort that I used to catch the Probarbus in my vignette above, as well as dip nets (sa-wing) with a handle. Mon, too, threw a hae when his gill nets did not pan out. But the water's edge was not the only place one could use such a net—there were several large boulders near Ban Beuk where fishermen could wait in line to try swinging a dip net in a large arc through the rapids. Additionally, most fishermen had shrimp traps (lop kung) and fish traps (lop pla), barrel-shaped nets tossed into shallow water and used especially for smaller fish.

Finally, another category of traps includes fish traps woven from bamboo, including tower-like woven structures with an entrance at the bottom and an opening at the top (tum lan); "reclining tiger" traps (seua non kin), woven traps that might look like baskets; and what I might term a sluice trap (jang), a wooden structure that looks like a rectangular corridor with a gate at one end, where fish in narrow creeks are flushed through and trapped when the gate shuts. Each of these is deployed near the mouths of creeks (huai) in times of flood, as surprisingly large fish—especially Asian redtail catfish (Hemibagrus sp. or pa kot)—travel up smaller tributaries to spawn and are easily captured.

While gear was relatively homogenous, bait was not. Previously, I mentioned Pong's cocktails involving opium or dog flesh, but others had their own personal recipes. For instance, Uncle Oi, a fisherman with no personal luang mong, could nevertheless bring in a sizeable catch in a public site by using a special cocktail for bait: a mash of vegetables (*pak kum luak*) and rice bran oil for the large vegetarian fish, such as Basa fish (*Pangasius bocourti* or *pa pho*) that were sought after in May and June.

Finally, there were other techniques. Pong described—but did not give details of—a secret khatha, a mantra that would ensure that fish would come to his nets. In addition, one of his luang mong was strung within an eddy that had its own guardian, a Buddhist angelic being (*thaevadda*) with which he had cultivated a close relationship. Other fishermen intimated that they, too, had such secret techniques, although they were loath to reveal them.

They were especially loath to reveal them to me. While I protested that I was no fisherman and couldn't possibly gain from knowing a spell to ensure a plentiful catch, one fisherman asked me, "Well then, why do you want to know it?" It was a valid question, and my response, "I am writing a book," drew knowing laughter. "That's even worse [than if you were a rival fisherman]! Then everyone who reads [your book] will know [the spell]!"

What is important here is that these conversations about spells and spirits emerged not during a discussion of religious practices along the river, but instead while discussing bait. In short, they are not belief (*khwam chuea*) but technique (*withi*), a (lack of a) distinction that problematizes local knowledge as it is seen in much of the literature. Framing magic along with religion (e.g., as in B. J. Terwiel's [2012] otherwise encyclopedic *Monks and Magic*) misses the link that magic has with technology.

Local Knowledge

Here, it helps to distinguish local knowledge from situated knowledge. "Situated knowledge" is a term that I take here from Donna Haraway (1988). It refers to having a perspective from somewhere—all knowledge, for Haraway, is situated knowledge. She intends it as a critique of supposedly objective science, but here I take it to mean the subjectivity of perception: Thip develops her own understanding of spirits and place in ways that are not necessarily shared by Mon or me. It speaks to the knowledge created by individuals that does not always overlap with others.

Phumipanya thong-thin is the Thai translation of "local knowledge." But not all local knowledge is "local knowledge." For many social scientists in Thailand, studying local practices is important only inasmuch as it highlights practices that have been ignored by a center-oriented development model but which nonetheless are beneficial. In this way, phumipanya thong-thin has become reified into meaning something like "that part of local practice that anticipates present-day desired practices." For instance, elsewhere (Johnson 2014) I detail how northern Thai housing prohibitions (*kheut*) are recast by those who would classify them as "local knowledge" as sensible admonitions against the dangers of suburban sprawl and concrete architecture, thus erasing kheut's ritual and symbolic aspect in favor of a northern Thai cosmology that is already coterminous with bourgeois ways of living. In other words, "local knowledge" never problematizes expert knowledge or presents us with real difference; rather, it serves the political purpose of critiquing capitalist interests via invoking locality. At times, especially among Marxist Thai intellectuals of a certain generation (cf. Chatthip 1999) or, on the other political side, royalist Thais touting the "Sufficiency Economy" (see Walker 2008), this representation has veered into the realm of wholesale invention.

The cataloging and valorization of local knowledge for the benefit of a larger society is precisely how many of my interlocutors, especially Pla and Kai, interpreted my own research project. What they sought from me was an accounting of local practices that were rendered obsolete by the Chinese dams. While I share their commitment to a sustainable Mekong, I cannot be a full participant in this project. To create an archive of "local knowledge" is to edit: to take up some practices and not others, or to alter the meanings of certain practices so that it corresponds with present-day social mores (downplaying supernatural elements, for instance, in favor of those that would be ecologically productive).

In his extensive work on fishermen's lives along the Mekong, Yos Santasombat (2012, 134) details the use and decline of local knowledge (which he uses as synonymous with situated knowledge). He defines local knowledge as "a repertoire of situated experience developed in particular physical and cultural contexts, from intimate interactions between humans and the environment" (11). While Yos emphasizes the similarities between local knowledge and scientific knowledge, local knowledge is more desirable in that it "represents a shift away from [a] preoccupation with centralized, technically-oriented solutions" (11).

The location most similar to Ban Beuk in Yos's extensive work is Ban Pak Ing, near Chiang Khong in northern Thailand (and not Isan). Ban Beuk and Ban Pak Ing are both Middle Mekong settlements, in that section of the river where rapids still define its course and before it broadens to its maximum extent. While residents of Ban Pak Ing speak a dialect close to that of Luang Prabang, and residents of Ban Beuk speak something more like Vientiane, both are Lao speakers. The most notable difference between the two villages is their relationship to the Sayaburi Dam: Ban Pak Ing is upstream; Ban Beuk is downstream. Like Ban Beuk, Ban Pak Ing is a riparian, fishing-oriented town that historically was associated with the capture of the beuk, but, as in Ban Beuk, after the construction of Chinese dams the beuk largely disappeared (Yos 2012, 114). According to Yos's data, beuk catches fell from forty-eight caught in 1993 to eighteen the year after, following the closure of the first dam in Yunnan (the Manwan). In 1999, as more dams appeared on the river, the catches fell further. During the 2000s, most years went by with no beuk caught.

Yos shows how, as I too found, fishermen orient their activities based around a ritual calendar. The *liang luang*, a ceremony of feeding those spirits who are responsible for guarding the beuk, marks an end to periods of abstention from fishing (Yos 2012, 113). These ceremonies, held in mid-April, are at the height of the dry season and about a month before the summer monsoon begins. Yos only mentions briefly the identities of the spirits and the means of sacrifice to them: the spirits of boats as well as, as one can interpret from the name, spirits of fishermen's fishing sites (luang, as in luang mong)—these aspects are not significant for Yos.

Yet here is a question of anthropological interpretation and the status of knowledge. What is knowledge, here? For Yos, local knowledge is a certain imperfect capture of scientific knowledge. Villagers may imagine that they are abstaining owing to a debt to spirits or out of fear of such spirits, but in fact they are observing good ecological management in limiting fishing time to just the month or two before the rains begin, in April and May. The benefit of local knowledge is that it removes a capitalist, technically oriented bias and sees local populations as effective data collectors in their own right. Yos's is at once a scientific and a political endeavor. He is arguing that community practices and ways of dwelling, while their true import might be obscure to those carrying them out, constitute sound environmental practice. But constructions of local knowledge as always already sensible fishing practices foreclose alternate systems of knowledge. And there are those systems of knowledge that do not make ecological sense.

Heretical techniques

If Yos and others downplay the supernatural aspects of riparian life, he ignores entirely other aspects of fishing—namely, those systems of knowledge that involve ecologically harmful practices: fish shocking, for instance. Some people catch fish with explosives—one can hear the muffled pops late at night. Some people catch fish with Lannate, an insecticide that often poisons the meat. But let us here take as our example car batteries.

If there was one politically controversial issue in Ban Beuk, it was not monarchical succession (people were generally apathetic) nor the military coup d'état of 2014 (people were generally opposed), but rather the practice of fish shocking (*sok pa*).

As the chief inspector indicated to me, fish shocking was rampant in Ban Beuk, although very few of my interlocutors confessed their practice of shocking to me (and, here, I do not reveal in more detail even the pseudonyms of those who did). The accusation of fish shocking at times felt like Azande accusations of witchcraft. To me, people accused their neighbors of having secret equipment, even as at times they admitted to having engaged in the practice themselves—as the chief inspector told me, regarding Pong: "His village is full of shockers; they are all shockers. They come to him with shocked fish and he sells them for a profit. He himself is one!" Elsewhere in town, many villagers admitted to buying and reselling fish they suspected of being shocked—"You can tell that the muscle becomes detached from the bone. It is less delicious this way, but it is hard to find a fish that is not shocked."

A fish shocker begins with an industrial battery.[8] "Chinese," suggested the chief inspector, "or Vietnamese. You can tell by the language on the sides. Not the kind of thing you would use in a car—this is for larger equipment. They get them from Laos, from who knows where." The shocker then takes a set of jumper cables and removes the clamps, shearing off a bit of the rubber until a few inches of wire are exposed at each tip. These wires are then wrapped around either end of a large boom, in order to spread the voltage out over as wide an area as possible.

Then, the shocker and a companion load the battery into the bed of a boat and cover it with a cloth and some nets. A careful observer might note that the boat rides a bit lower in the water than usual, but it will pass a quick glance. As a shocker told me, "Everyone else has [a boat rigged] just like this!"

The fish most pursued via explosives or shocking were *Pangasianodon hypophthalmus* (or *pa sawai*) and the hybrid beuk—these were big, meaty, rare, expensive fish that one could quickly sweep up and load into a boat, landing a day's profit in the course of an hour. Yet these large fish were the most likely to survive at the edges of the shock, sterilized or crippled, but able to escape.

On the docks, the inspector painted a brutal image of fish shocking syndicates. "If you hear a boat at night, it is a shocker [*khon sok pa*] for sure! They are very dangerous. If they think that you have seen them, they won't hesitate to shoot at you. If you are on the water at night, you should be armed." He then went into a story of getting into an open firefight across the water with fish shockers, ending with scaring them off, back to—he guessed—either Laos or Thai villages farther upstream. There were other risks as well: sometimes, the electricity would turn deadly. Shortly before I arrived, two Laotian fish shockers were killed as the current arced into their boat, killing them instantly.

But shockers themselves were more phlegmatic. You didn't necessarily have to go out at night; you just needed a quiet place, preferably one that did not border a village where someone important might see you. You might spread some bait around to attract fish, or you simply might go where you know fish are, and then you drop the cables in and connect the electricity. Fish rise to the surface, awkwardly flopping on their sides. Those near the cables die outright, and those farther away might be permanently damaged. "I saw a catfish that looked like a naga—it swam like a snake!" Nu told me, "[It had] been shocked, the meat stripped from the bones so it couldn't swim."

In addition to the term "shocking fish," villagers condemning the practice (and NGO workers such as Pla) referred to fish shocking and fishing with explosives as "sucking the fish [dood pa]." Pla explained, "It kills the fish in a wide ring. And when they draw the fish to them [with bait, or with sound], it kills and sterilizes all of the fish in that eddy [khok]. It is wiping the Mekong clean of fish!"

But here is a conundrum. With fish increasingly difficult to find in the wake of overfishing and in the wake of the dams, shocking becomes one of the only ways that fishermen can reliably find fish. It is a technique taught in secret, a kind of survival strategy that nonetheless makes survival more difficult. It is in this way very like certain kinds of hostile magic (mont dam). In other words, as Anna Tsing (2015) describes how one lives in the ruins of postindustrial landscapes, she imagines new, productive networks that arise— matsutake worlds, so to speak. Here, though, is a new "blasted" world that is more Cormac McCarthy and less Anna Tsing[9]—as the Mekong's ecology crumbles, the ways that people live with its new reality can be more destructive than ever before.

But this destructive practice overlies other destructive practices. In invoking witchcraft accusations in accusations of shocking, I was not giving in to a flight of anthropological fancy. In Ban Beuk, the practice of shocking takes on a characteristic similar to the practice of learning aggressive magic. Just as some fishermen studied particular spells to draw fish to them (katha) or others cultivated dangerous relationships with malevolent spirits (liang phi) via secret chants and rituals, shocking becomes a kind of hidden knowledge—a secret that all cultivate but which all agree is antisocial (see Terwiel 2012).

Thus, shocking becomes a kind of local knowledge that runs counter to the positive, sustainability-focused models promoted by NGOs such as Pla's and accounts such as Yos's, or even in Tsing's "what lives despite . . ." It is, rather, "what lives because . . ."—a destructive sort of knowledge, but one that requires study and an understanding of dangerous forces and special techniques nonetheless. And it is one way in which individuals seek to sustain life in the midst of blasted landscapes, even if the technique blasts the landscape even further.

TIME

Here, the changed materiality of the water requires changed techniques in order to bring forth its potential. But technique also involves a consideration of time, time that also depends upon the materiality of the river. Pong needs to wait for the water to turn red before he can set his nets.

The picture that I have painted of Ban Beuk and the Mekong that runs past it has been misleading. I have called the river a "river," which it not always is. I have referred to particular points in the river as kaeng or hin or khok, but they are not always such. Instead, they change into other things over the course of the year: open water turns to scrub forest when the water retreats, hin and kaeng submerge, the lazy swirl of a khok becomes a torrent. The river follows a rhythm, one dictated by the seasons and the yearly monsoon.

Urban philosopher Henri Lefebvre (2013), in his *Rhythmanalysis*, asks us to see places as subject to particular flows: cyclical flows as well as linear ones. Indeed, the Mekong presents to us a dramatic example of both: the river rises and falls cyclically in its great monsoon pulse, even as the same water rushes past on its journey to the sea. Whether or not the Mekong is a river or a forest, then, depends on when you are there.

Seen during a flood, either one that arises from the twice-yearly monsoon or from a release of water from the Chinese dams, the river makes a flat line stretching from bank to bank, broken perhaps by a few large islands (like Bird Island). Seen during an ebb, the river looks like a thin reddish-silver line through a broad valley of scrubland. From the surface of the water, this dry-season river bed looks like a forest of large bushes—some with thick red fruit, sandy soil, and creeks over which one must jump or wade. Standing on the edge of one of these is a stark reminder of the instability of this environment. As one watches, the water rises a few inches, then might drop as much in the span of a few minutes.

The defining feature of the Mekong is its yearly pulse. During the rainy season, a time beginning in June and running until September, and for a few months following, water melting from the Himalayas joins water pouring in from all of its tributaries to rush down the course of the river. According to historical data from the Mekong River Commission, at its peak in September, the river at Chiang Khan (near Ban Beuk) averaged a pulse of about 9 meters (with a historical high of near 12 and low of just over 5). This pulse begins in

June, peaks in September, and trails away in November and December. To put this pulse in context, in the dry season the river averages only 1 meter—the yearly pulse raises the water level nearly tenfold.

This pulse does a number of things (see Baran, Guerin, and Nasielski 2015). First, it expands the world of the fish. As the pulse covers over riverbanks and fruit-bearing trees, and deepens tributaries, fish gain access to new feeding and spawning grounds. It is at this time that some catfish breed by moving up smaller streams (*huay*). These movements are vital for fishermen to note, as the time of year (my interlocutors referred to Buddhist festivals as markers) determines the kind of trap one might use. Second, the pulse first inundates, erodes, and then slowly deposits a layer of fine silt down the banks of the river, fortifying its banks and spreading nutrients.

This is important not only for those plants growing in the water (Arias et al. 2013), but also for those living alongside the river, as farmers plant various crops following the water's retreat (what is termed flood-retreat agriculture). This involves some risk, especially as the rains become more frequent, but the richness of the soil more than makes up for it. The slope of the bank becomes a kind of measure of the time it takes something to grow: large, permanent trees such as papaya are at the top, and smaller and faster-growing plants predominate farther down. It is a planting schedule that can be incredibly productive, but which also has risks when the flood cycle is unpredictable.

And now is a moment far riskier than ever. The new Mekong has a different time from the old one, and with it, what was once efficacious no longer is. If we were to reframe this statement in Deleuzean terms, the Mekong becoming-dammed opens onto a new, uncertain field of potentiality.

Whereas before 2003 the Mekong rose and fell seasonally, in the years since it has been different: rising and falling, in Mon's words, "against nature." By this, Mon refers to surges in the water level in violation of normal seasonal cycles—such as a flood in the absence of rain in March 2015 and an ebb that dropped the river to record low levels in March 2016.

I should note here that the river still does ebb and flood dramatically (nearly 10 meters) along with the monsoon. Here, the ebbs and floods that I discuss are on the order of a meter or two—sizeable floods, and enough to severely disrupt the life of the Mekong.

These new rhythms originate when the Chinese controller of the Jinghong Dam decides to release or retain water, decisions that are on principle not communicated downstream. Without the ability to communicate with the Chinese, Mon and others in Ban Beuk can only closely watch the water level for indication that the dam controller has acted.

When the floodgates opened, water surges came suddenly in the night, wiping out fishing boats, nets, and even livestock tethered too close to the water's edge. No lives were lost in Ban Beuk, but fishermen at times found a number of corpses floating in the water, coming down from somewhere upstream and often collecting in kaeng phi. Fish disappeared—Mon and other fishermen in Ban Beuk estimated that their 2015 fish yield was only 30 percent of what was normal in years before the dam, and linked the disappearance of the beuk to these changes.

The changes in the river also produced changes to popular Buddhist practice. During the height of the dry season, Ban Beuk, along with Lao villages from across the river, constructed a temporary village on the sandy islands exposed by the water's retreat for the celebration of the Buddhist New Year festival of Songkran. But in April 2014, one of the sudden and unannounced releases of water from Jinghong descended upon the revelers, sweeping away the festival grounds and destroying millions of baht worth of property. During a lull in 2015, the debris from this surge remained: dead timber and hopelessly tangled nets piled high atop rocks midstream.

As the festival village indicates, patterns of rise and fall on the Mekong are one strand in the way that one marks time on the river: a yearly, cyclical calendar punctuated by Buddhist holidays, fishing and farming practices, and the monsoon. The dry season, when the festival village is at its height and sandy islands emerge from the Mekong's flow, coincides with an abundance of fish, as large fish are easy to catch. In turn, these fish catches fuel temple donations, sacrifices to river beings, and social events, and ritual activity centered upon mobilizing villagers' own potency. Around this time, the villagers hold a rocket festival (bun bang fai) where large, phallic rockets are fired into the sky, triggering the monsoon.

By being mapped onto the monsoon cycle, rituals also gain the power to yield rain. Later, when the water is near its height, other beings in turn act, discharging their own potential—when the rains end at the festival of ok pansa, nagas come to the river's surface and spit fire into the air. These fireballs that herald the beginning of the cold and dry season and the decline of the Mekong are, notably, given the same name (bang fai) as those rockets that began the wet. In this way, land beings act to bring the rise of the water; river beings act to bring about its ebb. Thus, the water-based calendar of the Mekong mobilizes the potency of particular technologies.

The dam, then, alters time along the Mekong. Here, I see time in the sense that Laura Bear (2014, 6) puts it—the "dynamic simultaneity" of different rhythms that shed light on the complexities of the present day. Here, monsoon time and Buddhist time become disrupted via new modes of time (when the

Figure 2.4: Erosion caused by a weeklong release from Jinghong

dam controller opens the gates, for instance). In the wake of the dam, the river and those within it become disentangled from these rhythms. The Mekong water level is no longer linked to the rain, which in turn delinks it from ritual activity meant to provoke the rains. Fish follow suit, and, as the naga shows, so do river beings. So now, in the wake of the new Mekong, this situated knowledge fails and new practices arise. Moratoriums on fishing in particular seasons have elapsed in Ban Beuk, and in response to the falling yield, fishermen, to compensate for this lack of knowledge of how to handle the new river, turn to other forms of fishing—like electricity. Indeed, the metaphor of "sucking fish" points toward linear flows (fish moving from the river to boats) as opposed to cyclical ones (fish returning). As fishermen can no longer trap fish with old methods, and as naga fireballs (while they still appear) do not bring a lowering of the water, and as high water comes with or without phallic rockets, river time is disentangled from Buddhist time, monsoon time, and calendrical time. Events that were previously simultaneous (rockets, clear water, big fish) are now not. The changes in river time alter the way that fishermen and riverbank farmers deal with the river—red water comes without fish, and the rising river sweeps away crops planted in anticipation of its decline (figure 2.4).

In short, now is a different time in which to dwell.

What does it mean to know a place? When I say, "I know the Nansemond," I mean a number of things. I know that on a low-draft boat, one can go into the salt marshes at flood tide or at high tide, but that the little channels in the reeds dry very quickly and can leave any boat stranded. I know that deer like to jump through the tall grass around dawn, and that they have little place to hide there from someone up on the bank. I know what season striped bass (rockfish) head up the narrow channels, and that they are good when cooked in an outdoor smoker. I know about how much storm surge a hurricane will bring, and where one shouldn't swim because of oyster shells, snapping turtles, or cottonmouths.

I know, too, that a parasite in bilge water has made most local oysters inedible, and that poultry runoff creates algae blooms that in turn give rise to giant rolling dead zones across the floor of the Chesapeake Bay. I know that swimming in such a zone can give you a rash (at best) and make you very sick (at worst). In short, as my hometown changes, the kind of knowledge that one has about it does as well. But sometimes change happens too rapidly to keep up.

What is this knowledge? Here, I turn to Lert: "Our problem today is a problem of decreasing *niwet* [home, oversight, ecology]. [The river is] nothing like before. . . . [What has changed] is everything! The fish—all kinds of food—are decreasing. Now the water . . . every seven days it rises, every seven days it falls. When it does, fish disappear. Equipment [upakon] disappears."

Lert's *niwet* is a complicated word, as it simultaneously suggests a sense of belonging, husbandry, but also ecological coexistence. It points to a sense of dwelling that dovetails with Heidegger's. One might be tempted to see local knowledge as that adaptation to dealing with the material qualities of a place—as dwelling, in other words. But dwelling, for Heidegger, goes further than this. In "Building Dwelling Thinking," Heidegger (1993) explores a notion of being in a place that seeks not to alter its characteristics, but to recognize the role of the human within the bounds of a place. This, for Heidegger, points toward a unity of being with the "fourfold"—the material (earth), the transcendent (sky), the finiteness of our own existence (mortals), and presences concealed (divinities). To dwell, one does not seek to alter the environment overmuch; rather, one seamlessly integrates oneself into it.

This is fine in the ideal, but as the Anthropocene shows, such a model of equilibrium has not come to pass. We exist in an altered world, and via our presence we alter it further (see also Baird and Green 2016). Lert, sitting mending nets under his house, bemoaned the loss of niwet in the new Ban Beuk—a loss of a capacity to be at home, to dwell. It is a loss of biodiversity just as it is a loss of knowledge about fishing equipment (upakon) and the river. As I show here, this is no simple matter. Hydropower on the Mekong throws notions of land, nonhumans, labor, and time, among many other things, into flux, and what ontologically exists in the world is no longer certain.

But that does not stop our drive to dwell. We continue to create knowledge about and adapt ourselves to places even as they alter around us. Additionally, in his invocation of "presences concealed," Heidegger's dwelling recognizes a boundary beyond which our knowledge and experience of the world are incomplete. There exist limits to human perception—mortality being one—but Heidegger also urges us toward recognizing limits beyond the human.

In chapter 3, then, I explore other ways to dwell: namely, how migrant laborers from Ban Beuk develop their own ways of dealing with a changing ecology and economy, and how those left at home cultivate waiting as a way to deal with the uncertainty involved in being reliant upon a distant, but still powerful, entity—an entity here which is one's son, husband, daughter, or wife.

3

DWELLING UNDER
DISTANT SUNS

Dwelling on the Mekong involves a certain degree of knowing, preserving, and cultivating a being-in-common with its material, biota, and inhuman elements, even as those elements change. But fishermen do not simply fish. Ban Beuk is embedded within larger political and economic systems, and the most important of these for families on the Mekong is labor migration. As fishermen prepare to leave and work in construction overseas, they must acquire new techniques of knowledge, ones that enable them to live in another ever-changing and dangerous environment. Knowledge about fish traps is supplemented by knowledge about human traffickers and labor recruiters. Requests to the Lord of the Fish turn into requests from dangerous nature spirits that offer boons to migrants at a cost to their safety and health. But it is the very uncertainty and precarity of the capitalist system built upon international migrant work that renders it another space of potential. Just like the hybrid beuk that enables fishing profits owing to its very uncertainty, the potentiality inherent in migrant work renders it seductive.

Labor migration, just like the Mekong, has its ebbs and floods. In the wake of the 1997 Asian economic crisis, formal labor migration from Isan to Bangkok factories was replaced by international migrants from Myanmar and Cambodia (see Campbell 2019). As a result, many Isan workers were driven into either the informal (Sopranzetti 2017b) or the international economy—or both (i.e., "illegal" migrant work). Claudio Sopranzetti (2017a; 2017b), Stephen Campbell (2019), Pattana Kitiarsa (2014), and Mary Beth Mills (1999) have all written fantastic volumes on the political economy of labor migration in and out of Thailand. This book, however, focuses on those techniques of dealing with uncertainty, and learning to dwell with the *maybe* inherent in risky work such as migrant labor.

Tui was preparing to leave. He is a slim, serious man, the same age as me (in 2015, in his late thirties), with stylish rectangular-frame glasses. At that time, in 2016, he was a fisherman, a rubber farmer, a petty government official (assistant village head, *phu chuai phu yai ban*[1]), a photography enthusiast, and he often volunteered to help local students with projects about the river.

But what Tui is famous for is divination. He plays the lottery nearly every week and has elaborate schemes for figuring out what winning numbers might be. He posts on Facebook the numbers and letters from vehicle license plates involved in traffic accidents, or that he sees in the coils of ash from incense at the shrine to the Lord of the Fish, which his house overlooks. These in turn are intended to be tools for further calculation—for instance, 33 revealed in ash might indeed indicate that 33 was a likely lottery number, but it might also suggest 23 (as there were two 3s). Or 32. Or 6. Or a broken 8.

In early 2016, though, his fortunes were running dry. His fishing nets, never very profitable, were now so useless that he did not bother laying them in the river—besides, with the water so unpredictable, he risked losing them each time he did. Unlike many in Ban Beuk, he worked his rubber orchard, but an out-of-control fire in the hot season of 2014 struck his crop hard. Then, he stayed up for nearly forty-eight hours straight fighting the fires, but lost a great deal of an already unprofitable harvest.

Finally, despite his effort at divination, his luck at the lottery was nonexistent. When I won (and gave my winnings to Thip and Yai), I did so with a clear show of disregard for the kinds of careful calculations that Tui made. Gift giving in Thailand should be done without much fuss, to show both the giver's ease with generosity and the receiver's lack of greed for the gift. But Tui did not take my careless purchase and gift giving well. He grew frustrated and sullen for weeks after the results came out, not at me, but at a universe where his technique did not work and some cavalier foreigner's random pick did.

So, in 2016, he shaved his head as part of his ritual to ordain briefly as a Buddhist monk. This was no long-term commitment to the Buddhist *sangha*; rather, Tui would ordain for a limited time. Yet even such a brief ordination would yield merit (*bun*), merit that Tui intended to mobilize as better fortune for his journey. He changed his Facebook photo to an idyllic, glossy shot of a house like the one he planned to build with his remittances, complete with a rainbow overhead. And then he signed up with a labor recruiter. For the next few years, he would be an undocumented factory worker in South Korea.[2]

In the years that followed (2016 until the time of writing), he stayed in touch with his wife, child, and friends in Ban Beuk via digital media: phone calls, chats using the online service Line, and Facebook. His posts were a litany of nostalgia and regret:

> How should I feel? Every time I tell someone that [my wife and I] work in two separate places and are not together right now . . . [I] get so exhausted [*phlia jai lai deu*] (July 29, 2018).
>
> [Standing at a] corner in Korea . . . I miss home (July 29, 2018).
>
> I miss my little fattie [*i uan*]! . . . Now she is so thin (July 25, 2018).
>
> [This] life seems like a happy one, but it is not a happy one [*chiwit muean mi khwam suk. Tae mai mi khwam suk*] (July 14, 2018).
>
> I had a horrible thought: that it was my karma [that said that] wherever I'd go, I wouldn't have happiness (April 26, 2018).

And, disturbingly, during a cold snap that killed over sixty-six Thai workers (Asaree 2017), Tui wrote, "[Tonight it is] −10 degrees [centigrade]. Sweet dreams" (December 11, 2017).

In addition to the heartbreak of being separated, Tui lamented poor food, a lack of promised pay, poor shelter, and difficult working conditions. But he remained.

Working conditions for Thais abroad (in South Korea, Singapore, Dubai, and elsewhere) have received a great deal of popular media attention. Thai news reports describe the dangers of inadequate housing for overseas Thais (Asaree 2017), the legal troubles of Thais working without permits (Jintamas 2018), poor wages ($0.75/hour, for example, in Singapore), and lack of rights of Thais abroad (TWC2 2017).

Going abroad is dangerous. It is also, as Tui indicates, heartbreaking. Often literally—Pattana Kitiarsa (2009; 2011; 2014), perhaps the most prolific and sensitive writer on men's migrant work in Southeast Asia, describes in a series of volumes the personal and professional struggles of labor migrants from Isan. For instance, Pattana (2011, 75) describes one man who fell victim to *lai tai*, or what in medical terms is called sudden unexplained nocturnal death syndrome (SUNDS). For medical experts, SUNDS is essentially a stress-related heart attack suffered by an otherwise healthy man while sleeping. Others in Isan explain it differently—the result of an attack of a "widow ghost" (Mills 1995). The man's friend brought the body back to his wife in Isan, but she did not come to receive her husband's corpse. Instead, she sent her new lover to pick up the remains.

This theme—selfless labor on behalf of a home that may forget you—is reflected time and again in the *mor lam* popular music enjoyed by workers (Pattana 2009). In a place like the Golden Mile, the shopping mall frequented by Thai construction workers in Singapore and where Pattana did the majority of his fieldwork (and where I myself spent a great deal of time between 2012 and 2016; see Pattana [2011] in Thai; Pattana [2014] in English), the sounds of mor lam echo from a dozen or so karaoke bars and Isan restaurants, especially on Sundays, when workers have the day off. Groups of men sit on the ground in circles, drinking and talking in the same way that men did in Ban Beuk at the roadside platform. They ate dishes unavailable anywhere else outside of Isan: papaya salad soaked in pungent fermented fish sauce (*tam mak hung*), ant larva salad (*khai mot daeng*), Isan mushroom curry (*kaeng hed*). It is worlds away from Isan, surrounded by the glass and steel of the high-modern east coast of Singapore, but it sounds and smells of home. Or, rather, a specter of home.

Tui risks the unknown dangers of migrant work in order to harness the prosperity that it offers. Would he fall victim to a labor recruiter? Would he die in his sleep from the Korean cold? Would his wife leave him? Would he win the lottery? Would he return rich and be able to buy the house that he dreamed of? Maybe.

LIVES IN FOREIGNNESS

Tui, the migrant worker, holds a very different perspective on borders than Nu, who watched the Mekong border from his hammock and speculated upon the identities of fishermen going by. As I argue in chapter 1, in Ban Beuk, the opacity of the border allows a space for fantasy regarding the other side. One can imagine Laos, despite its familiarity, to be full of criminals, potential romantic interests, or riches. But such borders can also be temporal: the river's change demands new, less certain ways of dwelling. Each of these revolves around distance, physical or metaphysical, as it becomes a quality that renders a thing powerful even as it becomes less visible.

But what happens when this distance emerges between people? Here, migrant workers are those that willingly engage with other realms, realms that hide behind certain layers of opacity. This engagement in turn fuels certain booms back home, ones that themselves contain risk. And, finally, with migrant work, migrants risk becoming distant themselves—more economically powerful, but no longer a full part of their home communities.

Migrant work—national and international—is the cornerstone of Ban Beuk's economy and, indeed, has been vital to Isan for years. This work may involve factory labor, sex work, construction work, or work at sea, and may be on the books or off. It always involves an immersion in otherness and fantasy surrounding this otherness. Villagers who were relatively well off (owning a home, for instance) had often done a few years of migrant work, and even the local elite Pong had worked for some years in a factory in Taiwan. Migrant work acts as a means of accumulating an initial sum of wealth or, as in Tui's case, supplementing income when times at home are hard. As the stories I describe here attest, many migrant workers seek to transform their wealth into similar sources of ready cash—namely, setting up a cash crop plantation.

Tui was *thiaw* or *nok*, terms for a state of being that is simply out or abroad. It is a word that also means "to go out" for fun in the same sense as it is used colloquially in English. Whereas academic literature on labor migration is replete with terms like *khai raengngaan* (selling labor), *khai phed* (selling sex), or the issue of *kammakon* (laborers), Tui and others in Ban Beuk simply referred to migrant work—even for years—as "going out" (*pai nok*; Pattana 2014, 29), or *pai thiaw*, for instance, *thiaw kao-li* (going to Korea), or even *thiaw thai* (going to Thailand). This last term was used to refer to working in Bangkok, the implication being that Bangkok is Thailand (and Isan is not).

As Mary Beth Mills (1995; 1999) notes, these currents of labor are gendered. In Ban Beuk, women generally ran shops or market stalls, whereas men fished in the Mekong, or planted and maintained cash crops. This gendered labor has made Isan one of the few places in the world where women's work (e.g., teaching, bureaucratic positions, market vending) yields more income than men's work (e.g., construction, fishing, rubber). Before the 1990s, the individuals going abroad or to Bangkok for labor were primarily men (see Mills 1995, 268), but as factories began to actively seek out women's labor, as it was thought to be more temporary and exploitable (see Ong 1987), women left Isan in greater numbers.

Mary Beth Mills (1995), in her work on women in labor migration, describes thiaw as an engagement with a dangerous and exciting field. It carries with it a sense of being away from home, engaging with adversity, and sexual adventure. Indeed, as traditional Lao society is uxorilocal, meaning that a man marries into his wife's household, a young man going thiaw for labor in the past was also a means of finding a spouse and settling down. Traditionally, women maintained the family household, and men wandered off. For women, marriage migration offers a similar idea of sexual adventure in going thiaw.

As Pattana points out, in places such as Singapore, this sense of thiaw as a space for adventure, especially sexual adventure, was still strong. Singaporean law seeks to discourage families from forming among migrant workers by only bringing in mass labor of one gender from a particular country. For instance, construction workers given temporary permits in Singapore are Thai or Bangladeshi men, while domestic workers are Filipina, Sri Lankan, or Indonesian women. In other words, the kinds of sexual adventure men imagined in Singapore involved foreigners. Thai men in Singapore's Golden Mile exchanged speculation and stories about the sexual appetites or proclivities of women from the Philippines versus Indonesia with—often too much—gusto. Many also sought to enter into a relationship with a Singaporean woman and acquire all of the status that entailed vis-à-vis other migrants.[3]

Pong, the subdistrict head who cultivated such a moral exterior, was no different when it came to such talk. In the 1990s, Pong worked in a factory in Taiwan for several years, and when he returned in 2001, he had enough capital to buy and build his riverside farm and house. It was only in reminiscing about migrant work that Pong displayed any sort of propensity for impiety—he asked me in all seriousness once why it was that Taiwanese women did not like to have their breasts squeezed. I had to reply that I had no idea, that this was out of the purview of my body of anthropological knowledge.

Mills also points out that going thiaw is also an opportunity for sexual adventure for women. Mor lam featuring female singers praises the desirability of foreign (especially Korean) men. This is especially true when women in communities such as Ban Beuk rely not only on factory work, but also marriage migration as a source of income. However, for those marriage migrants that I met in Ban Beuk, marriage migration, too, was simply another form of migrant labor, of engaging with the foreign in order to bring back prosperity. Fern, whom I introduce in more detail later in this chapter, described her job to me as "working as a foreigner's wife" (ku thamngan pen mia farang) after having married a European man whom she had met at a hostess bar in Bangkok. Dang, an elderly woman who tended a bamboo plot near the docks, told me with a sense of pride about her daughter's sexual adventures: "My daughter has brought home [to Ban Beuk, as boyfriends] men from all around! Arab men. Black men [nikro]. Now she is married to a Korean man, who is very nice."

Crossing borders, engaging in this world of cash and danger, involves a certain familiarity with risk. It is, like fishing, an active intervention into an unknown realm, a foray beyond the point where one can see with the hopes of mobilizing one's skill and fortune in order to draw something back. In this chapter, I analyze stories that my interlocutors told about migrant work, sex work, and cash crops as an engagement with this opaque realm, as a search for potency. But further, as these figures sending remittances back stay longer and longer away from home, they become in a sense spectral figures like the Lord of the Fish or the naga. They bring prosperity, but their motivations become less and less understandable.

Migrant Stories

I spent much of my fieldwork sitting on a raised bamboo platform on the side of the Mekong highway with a group of four or five men, sharing bottles of rice wine (*lao khao* or, as most of the men called it, "forty degrees") or Leo beer and sharing stories of work abroad.

Lo—the man who waited at the market for border restrictions to allow his joss stick assembly line to function again—had a typical story. He worked at a farm in on the Israeli-Gaza border for years.

"It was full of violence," he said, going on to refer to the threats he felt when he was in public in Israel. "But none of this has to do with us. I'm just a Thai, a Buddhist. I don't care about Jerusalem. Let anyone have it." These feelings of fear were not imagined—in 2018, a rocket attack killed a Thai worker on just such a farm (Breiner 2018).

But there was other violence. In addition to the threat he felt constantly from the conflict, Lo complained of poor wages, dilapidated quarters, and constant exposure to harsh pesticides. But he returned, having saved approximately 50,000 baht (about $1,500). This, along with his family's land, was enough to purchase a grove of banana trees, Ban Beuk's first cash crop. But the banana market in Ban Beuk quickly grew oversaturated, and Lo's savings ran out.

He went abroad again at the age of twenty-six, working for three more years in a plastics factory in Taiwan making fake leather products. This time, he saved enough to start his cross-border incense work, work that ended after the Prayuth regime's crackdown on cross-border labor.

Now, after this recent failure, he drank, and waited.

Ink was similarly a self-styled entrepreneur. He was a slender young man in his early twenties and Mon's cousin. He worked land that belonged within their family, and his strip—a plantation that ran from the riverbank up the steep slope of the nearby hill—was primarily Pará rubber. Younger than Mon, and having heard stories from older men like Lo, Ink expressed little interest in working in migrant labor. He even dismissed prospects in Bangkok, facing as he did comparatively increased competition in the informal sector from cheaper Myanmar (see Campbell 2018) or Khmer migrants as well as other Isan workers who had been in Bangkok longer and therefore had better connections. For instance, Stephen Campbell (2018, 28) finds that Myanmar workers are paid from one-fourth to one-half the wages of a comparably skilled Thai national. Ink saw himself as avoiding the stressful, hectic (*wun wai*) life of a migrant via skillfully riding the market for new agricultural cash crops. He had traded the physical insecurity of dealing with a foreign land for the biological uncertainty of experimenting with new, foreign plants.

But this did not mean that Ink was independent of the remittance economy. Ink's crops were funded by the migrant work of Nong, his fiancée. Nong was slightly older than Ink and initially went to Bangkok to be a domestic worker for a wealthy couple—"Chinese people," in Nong's description, by which she meant wealthy Bangkok-born Thais (many of whom have Chinese ancestry). Her employers were, compared to the stories of her friends who were also domestic workers, not the worst, but she made little money (approximately 1,000 baht/month—about $30) and described her employers as continually scolding her. The last straw came when she was asked to clean her employer's underwear and noticed that it was stained with menses. "[Giving me that underwear] was deliberate," Nong told me as we sat drinking with Ink, Fern, and Aek. "She knew that it was disgusting and still made me wash them."[4] After that, Nong quit domestic work and moved to a hostess bar in a place frequented by Western men, and made in an hour twice what she had previously made in a month. Coming as it did after living so long on very little, Nong's new wealth went everywhere—to her family, to her friends, to alcohol, but, significantly, to Ink, with the promise that he could build for them something lasting.

In these stories, engaging with this uncertain realm is necessary for prosperity, but it remains a realm fraught with risk and danger. While men often spoke in glowing terms about the adventures of thiaw and the sexual opportunities in foreign countries, or exchanged tips on good places for work or phrases in foreign tongues, there was a great deal of concern, as well. Accidents were common enough in the workplace, and, especially for those who, like Tui, were working illegally, there were few opportunities for recompense. But even for those working on the books, many countries that import labor (such as Singapore) have little to no legal protections for workers injured on the job (TWC2 2017), leaving the burden on the worker to find justice, compensation, or simply a way home without mounting debt.

But most uncertainty was financial and interpersonal. A popular saying, *pai sia na, ma sia mia* (you go and you lose your rice field; when you return you lose your wife) indicated the fear that many men had, both of the debt incurred in going abroad and in the damage to interpersonal relations that long distance brought (Pattana 2014, 35). And such debt might not even offer the opportunity to be repaid—as Mills (1995) and Pattana (2014, 35) both report, scams where labor recruiters simply absconded with deposits (or, in the case that Pattana reports, flew workers not to Saudi Arabia but simply back to Isan) were common enough.

Figure 3.1: Lert

While most in Ban Beuk either avoided such scams or did not speak of them to me, Lert, who had the foreboding dream of the Jinghong Dam, told me of being fleeced by labor recruiters before going to work for the shipping firm Maersk (figure 3.1).[5]

> L: I was a laborer on a ship. They flew me eighteen hours to Amsterdam! I'm sorry I can't speak English with you [i.e., even though I've lived abroad].[6]
>
> AAJ: So you used the cash to build all of this [house and small farm]?
>
> L: No. They paid me in US dollars and so I had to pay taxes [or other fees] as if I was a rich man. But I wasn't. It wasn't really a whole lot [of income], but I had to pay a lot [of fees]. Do you get what I mean? I didn't make a profit all those years! *Mai klia tang* [literally: I didn't clear the money]. I lost over 40,000 baht [about $1,250] in fees for things like checking for diseases [*truat rok*], investigating everything.
>
> AAJ: Maersk did this?
>
> L: No, once I got to Maersk everything was fine. This was before I got there [i.e., the labor recruiters].

AAJ: How did you like being abroad?

L: The difference is that here, we are free. Here, we are our own masters, with nature, with freedom [*seriphab*], independence [*itseriphab*]. The military can come in, they can take away everything, but here with the river we are still free. [Lert then turned back to the river.] But if the river changes, then we can't do anything. And China will make it change. You know the story of the high-speed rail? Everything—ASEAN has to be underneath the great power [*maha amnat*] of China. They will say to us: "OK, so if you don't let us do the rail lines, then we won't buy your rubber." Like that.[7]

Rubber Men

Lert's movement from migrant work to fishing to rubber is telling. Each of these involves a cash-dependent, high-risk activity. Rubber, for instance, had become the go-to crop for many in the region. But it involved a great deal of risk. After one plants saplings, the trees take approximately seven years to grow, meaning that one has to have alternative sources of income during that time. But while one is waiting, the market may change.

This was the case in Ban Beuk. In February 2011, rubber hit an all-time high price of $4.72/kg. Then, and soon after, many in Ban Beuk invested in seedlings, only to see the price repeatedly fall. Five years later, in 2016, it was down to a low of $1.31/kg. At this point, for many, the labor involved to cut and harvest the sap would not be worth the time and effort to do it. Some, like Tui, went abroad; some, like Lert, relied more on fishing; and some, like Lo, simply fell back on their savings and waited.[8] It was a time to reconfigure, to see what new forces were active in the world.

This moment of reconfiguration entailed experimentation with other, newer ways of dwelling in the global cash crop economy. One farmer in Ban Thong decided to try his hand at *kopi luwak*[9]—coffee beans fed to civet cats, whose digestion assists in the roasting process. Pong raised husky puppies in order to sell them as pets. Mon had the district build a platform overlooking the valley as an attempt to capture tourists. Each was casting nets (pardon the metaphor) in order to see what new forces were potent in the world: new cash crops, new pet trends (perhaps capitalizing on the Tibetan mastiff trend in China), tourism.

But most of these failed. For instance, OXFAM promoted *Plukenetia volubilis*, the Inca star bean, as a superfood, a movement taken up by a number of

Thai companies. Pong, ever enthusiastic to assist rural development in his role as subdistrict head, heard about the new trend and was eager to seize upon it. But, as Lert described to me, the system in which farmers found themselves was the problem. Lert bought the beans from the company that supplied them and then found himself needing to also buy fertilizer from that company. Then the company renegotiated the contract and, in the end, Lert paid more than he gained—just as with Maersk.

Others also fell victim to a softwood scam. Some years ago, "in the late Thaksin years," a truck came around to Ban Beuk selling seedlings. These were relatively expensive, at $1 per plant, but the expense was, the man said, owing to its status as a miracle plant, one developed by the United Nations as a part of a reforestation project. The trees would grow, said the man in the truck, extremely fast, and within five years would yield timber ready to harvest. At that time, he would return and pay impressive dividends. But after five years went by, no truck came back. The trees grew—slowly—and yielded wood so soft it was virtually useless, even were there people to buy.

Finally, even some of the largest companies in Thailand had business practices that many farmers in Ban Beuk considered to be scams of a similar kind. Charoen Pokpand (CP), one of Thailand's largest conglomerates, offered farmers pigs to raise and a comfortable set buy-back price. But farmers quickly found themselves needing to buy injections, pigpen upgrades, and specific feed directly from the company so that CP could, as they said, "ensure quality." The profit thus gleaned was a fraction of what farmers had expected.[10]

Capitalism, whether in migrant work or in cash crops, relies upon a certain sense of uncertainty, but with it freedom (as Lert describes, "here we are our own masters"). Claudio Sopranzetti writes about this lure of a freedom that reflects both vulnerability and "the changing structural configurations of capital and labor in post-crisis [he means the 1997 economic crisis] Thailand" (2017a, 69–70). For Sopranzetti's motorcycle taxi drivers, even if profits are lower and risks are higher, independent work holds an appeal over factory work and wage labor owing to its sense of freedom. This discourse is precisely how Lert and others characterize the life of a farmer—free, but subject to a constant menace from vague, outside forces.

Migrant labor, then, is not simply an economic matter of remittances. It involves a cycle, with risk at each point—indeed, as any entrepreneur knows, what is profit making is always risky. One goes abroad, an adventure laden with risk and reward that intertwines health, love, luck, and finances. And when one returns, one invests in a particular project (e.g., bananas, rubber, tourists) that is also cash- (and risk-) related. Going abroad (or planting an unknown seed) raises the specter of ruin, but without doing so one risks stagnation. In either case, one is alone upon this trip.

But migration also involves transformation. It often reveals a fundamental instability in both the migrant and those left behind.

THE PROBLEM OF TRANSFORMATION

"Which one of these two women is more beautiful?" Mon asked me with a conspiratorial smile, flipping between two images on his phone. One picture, with the grainy quality of a screenshot captured from a video call, showed a tanned, Eurasian-appearing woman with a high nose and big eyes looking alluringly into the camera. The other, clearly taken locally on the banks of the Mekong, showed a woman with pale skin, epicanthic folds, and a huge smile in a sweatshirt and knit cap.[11] Mon handed me the phone as I handed him the bottle of rice whisky that he and I, along with a small group of men, were passing around.

The question that Mon posed was one that recalls hegemonic norms of female beauty in Thailand about which scholars have already written (Hesse-Swain 2006; Mills 1995). It is a question that recalls issues of class, region, and colonialism and how they impact aesthetics of female beauty. While television and movie actresses were often of mixed Thai/Caucasian ancestry (*luk khreung*), since the rise to prominence of the Chinese-Thai middle classes (*luk chin*) in the 1990s and the popularity of East Asian television dramas and pop music, an East Asian appearance has increasingly become seen as desirable in Thailand. This was how I interpreted Mon's question—was I (and by extension all foreigners) old fashioned (and thus Western-oriented) in what I looked for in a romantic partner or trendy (and thus East Asia–oriented)? Or might I, despite my linguistic fluency, fall into the stereotype that many held about foreigners, that they preferred darker women whose appearance was considered undesirable in Thai notions of beauty? In some ways, it was a question that reflected shifting geopolitics, as Thailand moved out of the shadow of the United States in the 1990s and into a region dominated by East Asian influence. But Mon's was a trick question.

Before I could answer, Mon shouted, his voice overly loud in the still night, "They're the same person! My fiancée [*faen*]. This [indicating the second photo] was her before [plastic surgery], and this [indicating the screenshot] is her after."[12] Mon and I flipped the photos back and forth in silence. It was hard to see the resemblance, but once one knew what to look for, it was there. He abruptly put his phone away, smile gone. "I liked her better before," he said. "She did it because it helps her business. Her customers, Arabs [*khon arab*], like it."[13]

Fa had been living in the Persian Gulf region for five years. Both Fa and Mon had long had family fishing sites and farms in Ban Beuk and nearby, but in their young adulthood, they moved to Bangkok together to work for a construction company. Then, five years ago, Fa took a job as a masseuse in the Gulf, and Mon returned home to build a rubber plantation using Fa's remittances. It was privately acknowledged, but not publicly said, that Fa's job in the Gulf involved sexual services. Before they went separate ways, Fa agreed to return to Ban Beuk later, once her looks had faded (Mon: "When she is too old and no one but me wants her"), when they would get married. But later, Mon expressed his doubts. "Fa has tasted life in the city now and she doesn't want to come back to these boondocks [chonabot]. I like it here. But there's nothing to do; people aren't fashionable."

Here, Fa is not the same as when she left. Distance has changed her, even as it has given her the means to support Mon. Her tastes and desires are different—even her face has been altered to the point where it is not easily recognizable. The return point of her circular migration in terms of her previous goals (to live on Mon's rubber plantation and run his riverside hotel) is no longer an aspiration. What's more, Ban Beuk itself has changed, in both Mon's and Fa's eyes. What was appealing is now chonabot.

Distance here interposes itself in multiple ways. While the realization of the "we" has been deferred, those involved have changed so much that the "we" as first imagined is no longer possible. The intimacy that Mon lives over distance is an intimacy with an image of Fa, not the Fa that is, but one that has already passed. Thus, Mon's intimacy is one shared with something that, like the dam, exists in images and acts—sending money, words, love—at a distance.

Some transformations are more lasting than others. Fern became engaged to her boyfriend, Aek, before she went abroad to marry a European man, a customer at the snooker club where she was a hostess, while Aek stayed back in Ban Beuk.[14] In marrying another man, Fern paradoxically described herself as laying the foundations for a future together with Aek. She described her marriage as "work"—"I work as a white person's wife [ku thamngaan pen mia farang]," she told me—and she sent home remittances that fueled Aek's Pará rubber orchard.[15] Fern planned to marry Aek after the dissolution of her European marriage, and Aek planted rubber seedlings he hoped would yield profits once they matured. In the meantime, Aek and Fern would wait.

But in Fern's encounter with foreignness, plans and aspirations changed. Fern and Aek's lives diverged. Fern had a child with her European husband. As with Lert, when the price of rubber crashed, Aek's orchard was worthless. Fern and Aek continued to promise themselves to each other during Fern's yearly trips home at the Buddhist new year, but when Fern went back to Europe, Aek wondered about the future. "Why would she come back here [permanently]?" he asked me. "Would you?"

NEW WAYS OF DWELLING

During my fieldwork, the male-dominated productive spheres with which Ink, Mon, and Aek engaged were in crisis: upstream dams had destroyed fisheries, and, as with Ink, cash crop prices were so low few men bothered to maintain their rubber trees. A military coup d'état caused a sharp drop in the international segment of independent tourists Mon sought.[16] Along with this decline in local sources of income came an increase in the relative importance of migrant labor. Contra the massive outflows of migrant labor abroad or to Bangkok factories during Mon's father's time, and contra the wave of female factory labor in the 1990s (Mills 1999), much of this labor was in the informal sphere, a reaction to the economic crisis of 1997 and subsequent economic restructuring directed by the International Monetary Fund (see Sopranzetti 2017b). Women's jobs in Bangkok factories have now largely gone to migrant workers from neighboring Myanmar, Cambodia, and Laos in Special Economic Zones designed for this purpose (Campbell 2018; Kusakabe and Pearson 2012). Indeed, a new zone was planned for the Lao border an hour's drive downstream from Ban Beuk.

As a result of this restructuring, Isan's labor force turned international (Pattana 2014) and informal. In Ban Beuk, this split was clear: older residents, mostly male, had participated in international migrant work, while younger residents—some of the twenty-something men and nearly all of the town's twenty-something women—worked in the informal economy.

Informal here refers to a number of industries that exist outside of official recognition. Motorcycle taxi drivers, for instance, exploded in number as informal labor flooded the Bangkok market (see Sopranzetti 2017b). International migrant work, always important to Isan, became increasingly so (see Pattana 2014). Both of these forms of labor are precarious in the sense of lying outside of assurances given by the state or formal contracts with employers, although Thailand does not entirely fit the model of a crumbling welfare state that other scholars of precarity (Allison 2013; Funahashi 2012; Muehlebach 2013) highlight—while factory labor with contracts and unions was on the decline for Isan, the world of unregulated work has always been present, even if it spiked after 1997.

For women in Ban Beuk, work in this unpredictable, foreign sphere occasionally meant the sex industry, which both in Bangkok and abroad is an industry that relies primarily upon northeasterners (see Lyttleton 2000). This was certainly the case for Fa and Nong, just as it had been for Fern prior to her marriage. But seeing Fa's and Nong's work through the eyes of their partners back home complicates the predominating image of sex work in the academic literature, literature that remains focused primarily upon the sites where commercial sex transactions take place (cf. Bishop and Robinson 1998; O'Connell Davidson 1998; Wilson 2004), with a few exceptions (Cohen 1982; 1986; and 1993; Thompson, Pattana, and Suriya 2016). In this, perspectives such as Mon's or Aek's are largely lost, as is a perspective upon women's lives outside of these spaces.[17] In addition, left unexamined here is the ultimate fate of sex workers' remittances; my data here suggest that money sent even by long-term clients (relationships approaching marriage or an otherwise romantic ideal) goes not only to the woman's daily needs, but is also mobilized toward her own aspirations back home, aspirations that may (or, in my cases, may not) include a romantic life with the foreign client.

Marjorie Muecke (1992) touches upon this issue in dealing with the role of sex work in northern Thailand, where expectations of filial piety—where daughters are expected to support aging parents—override the social stigma attached to sex work, especially in light of increasing environmental and economic pressure placed upon rural livelihoods and subsequent increasing dependence upon cash remittances. It is a theme reinforced in other studies of female migrants that argue that women's remittances are focused more upon supporting a family back home (Le Mare, Buapun, and Rigg 2015) owing to cultural pressure upon women (as opposed to men). In a similar manner, I place sex work in its regional, familial, and economic context, but I also look at the family beyond parents or children. The remittances that Fern, Nong, or Fa send back go toward a possible future; not only an economic one, but a romantic one as well. Additionally, while Muecke's (1992) attempt to discuss sex work in women's home villages met with barriers of social stigma (leaving her thus to draw upon data from women's NGOs), here, my methodological approach using male partners, as well as my focus upon the migrant labor dimension of sex work (rather than the explicitly sexual dimension) allowed me to address these otherwise difficult topics.[18]

Internationally focused sex work in Thailand (as in the case of Fa, Nong, and Fern) is often characterized by its open-ended nature—relationships with foreign clients may transform into longer-term arrangements, even marriage (see Thompson, Pattana, and Suriya 2016; or Groes-Green 2013 for an African example). Indeed, in Ban Beuk, the only *farang* resident (other than me) was just such a client-turned-husband. He was a European man and former sex tourist married to a local woman who lived a few months out of the year in Thailand.[19] While he claimed to have settled down with his wife, he missed the sex tourist scene and intended to build a foreign-oriented brothel on the banks of the Mekong, although at present he had only cleared the land and poured the foundations for a few bungalows. His home was pointed out to me by Aek as one of the Caucasian houses (*ban farang*) that dot the Isan landscape, places where a foreign spouse's funds have built relatively luxurious accommodations. While Aek and Fern found him personally strange—especially his habit of working shirtless in the heat of the day and at the same time seeming never to make progress on his construction—they pointed to the house as the sort of place they expected to construct when Fern returned. Elsewhere in Ban Beuk, the fact that many marriage migrants were previously sex workers (see also Thompson, Pattana, and Suriya 2016) was only hinted at: in casual conversations, parents might say, for instance, "[Our daughter] worked at a bar in Bangkok," or "[My sister] met [her husband] playing snooker"—all situations that were assumed to be (but left unsaid) commercial sex work.

The continuum on which sex work and marriage exist (see Esara 2009 and Thompson, Pattana, and Suriya 2016 for a counterexample) can best be thought of as the "intimate relations" (Constable 2009) that form a key, if underexamined, part of transnational economic networks. Pilapa Esara (2009, 406) argues that, for rural, poorer Thai women, the two arrive at a similar end: a secure income and improved quality of life, as well as the ability for a woman to act as a provider for her parents back home. This latter feature of women's remittances underlines the role of traditional matrilocality in Thailand's northeast, where daughters continue to provide for parents (see Muecke 1992).

In Ban Beuk, in addition to Fern, there were many women who had married and emigrated abroad, to places including Australia, South Korea, Europe, Malaysia, France, and Canada, a stunning number of out-marriages within a relatively small town. Their remittances were important to the town's economy, and they embodied a certain kind of cosmopolitan possibility. Elsewhere, as Jennifer Cole (2014) observes for Malagasy migrants in France, the fantasy of being a foreigner's wife implies transforming into a wealthy, successful, and urbane woman—a lifestyle that clashes with the realities of lower- or lower-middle-class French lives. Similarly, in Ban Beuk, I heard stories about marriage migrants discovering, instead of a luxurious life abroad, alcoholism or domestic abuse. Especially in Isan, marriage migrants of a certain class that are identified as *mia farang* (wife of a Caucasian) are caught in a contradiction: she at once finds herself an upwardly mobile provider for her Thai family, but also subject to the lower end of both a Thai hierarchy of value (between Bangkok and the northeast, for instance) and an international one (between ethnic Europeans and Thai marriage migrants) (Esara 2009; see also Patcharin 2013).

This mismatch between local, national, and global hierarchies of value may highlight why Fern did not present herself as a potential immigrant assimilating into new European society, but rather as a kind of migrant laborer intending to return to Ban Beuk. She was not climbing an international ladder, or even a domestic one, but had her sights firmly on the locality. She remained—however physically distant—a presence in Ban Beuk. Indeed, recall how Fern described her role as mia farang as a kind of labor (*tham ngaan*) and her ultimate goal as relocating to Ban Beuk and building a "Caucasian house"—not necessarily with her Caucasian spouse.[20] Marriage migration was, in the way that she spoke to Aek and me about it, a kind of intimate labor aimed at refashioning herself and building a new identity in Ban Beuk itself.

The point here is that Fern seeks to return—at least one possible return—from international migration transformed. And here, too, is where the link between distant potency and labor migration comes to the fore. Fern could, like some women in Ban Beuk, have continued through high school, attended some degree of higher education, and pursued a career as a teacher or local administrator. This would lead to a stable career and respect within the village (e.g., Mon's sister-in-law had just such a trajectory). But she rejects this in favor of the potential for real wealth, experience, and personal transformation involved in marriage migration. When she returns, she does so changed, but also possessing access to particular powers—the ability, for instance, to create a Caucasian house and bring something home from Europe. Engagement with the dangerous world of the foreign has successfully transformed her into a source of potency herself.

Here, I should pause to address the love triangle between Fern, Aek, and Fern's European husband. In Ban Beuk, Fern clearly disregards any attachment that her husband may feel toward her, their child, or the marriage. The foreign husband is a source of money. This may seem callous of her and may fit into the worst stereotypes of such marriages in Thailand and abroad. But it is important here to suspend these judgments. Additionally, I am not a party to the details of her European marriage, and in conversations with other marriage migrants from the northeast, many expressed frustration with alcoholism, abuse, or other undesirable aspects of their lives in Europe. Finally, I should note that Fern should not be taken as emblematic of all Isan marriage migrants. Instead, my intention in telling Fern's story is to focus on how Fern's transformation enables access to particular sources of distant potency.

Her narrative expressed while sitting with Aek is not a permanent movement from Thailand to Europe, nor from rural to urban. Rather, it is circular. Many scholars (Le Mare 2015; Skeldon 2012; Soimart 2015; Thompson 2015) point toward Isan migrant labor as an example of circular migration: a system wherein the labor migrant does not (or, in the case of states such as Singapore or the Gulf, cannot; see Pattana 2014) remain, but seeks to return to his or her point of origin made into a new person. This certainly seems to be the case in Ban Beuk, where men often used money gained by working abroad in Singapore, Taiwan, Israel, or other places to build cash crop plantations, bars or restaurants, hotels, or other capital investments. Such circularity is one possibility for Fern, Fa, and Nong. But the very idea of circular migration is problematic. There is no real return. The Ban Beuk that one returns to is not the same. Additionally, both those who stay and those who leave are transformed. The "I" that promises "you" that there will one day be a "we" is not the same person when that time arrives.[21]

For Fern, one such person lives with Aek in a luxurious Mekong-side house paid for by Fern's (future) deceased European husband, but another is happily married and living in northern Europe, raising her half-Caucasian son. Both futures exist owing to the ambiguity of the present (see also Han 2011). And in the process, this end goal increasingly enters the realm of fantasy—that realm of *maybe*. It is only achievable by an engagement with the other, but through this engagement, new worlds are opened and old worlds changed. Opening oneself to *maybe* alters the self in unexpected ways.

In this light, I argue that Aek, Mon, Ink, and those others in Ban Beuk work at waiting (Kwon 2015)—accepting remittances, building homes, and preparing for a future life together—while at the same time considering the fragility of such relations and the mutability of their own and their partners' aspirations and desires. Time spent waiting expands, stretching across years and opening Isan lives to multiple new worlds while at the same time deferring them all. And as one waits, the other on whom one waits grows distant, grows strange.

THE RETURN

When Fern came back for Songkran, the Thai Buddhist new year, she threw a hell of a party. Because Aek still lived in his parents' compound, Fern rented one of Mon's riverside tourist bungalows for two weeks. She came accompanied by her year-old son (via her European husband), whom she left in the care of Mon's sisters and other residents. In the meantime, she and Aek, along with Ink and Nong, set up on the veranda of the hut and drank for a week straight. They began at around nine in the morning with bottles of whisky and soda and went until the midafternoon, when they would take a break and sleep for a few hours and then resume in the evening until late at night. Occasionally they would cajole one of the neighborhood children into driving a motorcycle to the market to pick up some food, and sometimes the largely happy reunion degenerated into arguing. These fights often became violent; Ink showed me a deep gash in his side, a scar from a knife wound suffered during a drunken fight during another such bender the previous year (figure 3.2).

The excess that Fern brought upon her return was not random. Rather, it was a display of wealthy homecoming familiar to many migrant workers—at Songkran, one returns from abroad or Bangkok dressed as well as one can and showers relatives and friends with gifts and parties as a way to mark a new, changed status and to solidify one's new, wealthier rank in the community. That said, the alcohol-fueled and explicitly extramarital nature of Fern's return raised some eyebrows among older community members. On one of the final nights, a drunken, machete-wielding man charged into the group of revelers believing that his wife and her new lover were drinking with the party, leading many in Ban Beuk to quietly caution me to steer clear of Fern's bender.[22]

During the week that Fern was present, Fern and Aek discussed their plans for the future. Seeing Fern's son fussed over by a group of older women, Aek suggested that her child would be happier in Ban Beuk than in Europe, as "here, he's surrounded by good food, beautiful nature, kind people," whereas in Europe one lacked such a sense of cohesion and wholeness. At another time, Aek told me that he had heard that Europeans (farang—i.e., white people, Christians[23]) severed all ties and communication with their parents upon turning eighteen (an idea I heard repeated in a Buddhist sermon a few days later). He stressed that Fern's son would not live that way—while the boy would be welcome to sever ties with his farang father, in Ban Beuk he was enmeshed in a system of kinship. But some days later, Aek expressed doubts about these self-assured statements. He asked me about life "in white countries" (mueang farang), expressing (as Mon did) his doubt that Fern would really want to return to a place like Ban Beuk. At other times, he would shrug helplessly when asked about his plantation and conclude, "For now, the only thing to do is drink."

Drinking here is significant. It is not work in the sense of taking Fern's remittances and fueling them into the deferred, anticipatable future, but rather what one does while one waits—waits for the afternoon to cool so one can fish, waits for one's rubber trees to mature, waits for rubber prices to rise again, and waits for Fern's older European husband to die. It is what one does when one is powerless to affect the *maybe*.

Here, then, is a model of potency adapted to migrant labor. One becomes distant, both geographically and in terms of being able to be understood, in order to access the potency of the distant. In the meantime, others wait, deferring the end point. But this end point is haunted by the idea that people, with

Figure 3.2: Ink's knife scar

distance, are mutable—they might become foreign entities themselves. They might love another; they might become parents; and, as Fa's appearance indicates, their very bodies might change. The assertion that a reunion will come to pass is undercut by the uncertainty inherent in that search for *maybe*, and an engagement directly with sources of distant potency means that one might become just such a source oneself.

SHE WHO SEES

If migrant work is fraught with this uncertainty, there must be techniques of knowing, just as there are for fishing. How does one know the risks in which one is embedded, and how does one better know the self, even as one is transformed?

Daena Funahashi (2012, 2021) examines Finnish rehabilitation programs that seek to instill a sense of economic rationality in their clients. Instead of a system of mutual obligations in the workplace, health professionals recast individual workers as possessing quantifiable amounts of resources that they must manage. But, as Funahashi shows, being told this triggers a crisis for some individuals—revealing themselves as caught in the grip of and moved by forces beyond their comprehension and control.

Migrant workers have no such illusions—they are fully aware that their personal resources are unknown quantities. These are resources like luck (Lao: *sok*; Thai: *chok*), fate (Lao: *satta*; Thai: *chatta*), merit (*bun*), and karmic store (*kam*), all of which we have in some quantifiable amount, but we do not have access to their totals.

These are different things. One's merit (bun) is accumulated in this life based upon good deeds one does—especially related to the practice of Theravada Buddhism. Donating to the temple was, for nearly all of my interlocutors, the way in which one accumulated merit (*tham bun*), and, in extreme cases like Tui's, ordaining temporarily as a monk would ensure a good deal of merit.[24] For my interlocutors, merit in turn influenced one's luck (sok), although such a link is not found in any official Buddhist canon. Someone who often made merit was likely to run into bouts of good luck, although occasionally people who rarely went to the temple (like me) would suddenly be inexplicably lucky. This, then, is the working of fate (satta) or the meritorious legacy of past lives (kam). Contra how the word is often used in everyday English, karma does not act in this lifetime—there is no "instant karma"—rather, it is payback for good or bad deeds done in past lives.

But, much as in a visit to a psychoanalyst, one does not know one's own qualities. Indeed, the self here is composed of qualities far beyond the indi-

Figure 3.3: Migrant workers search for numbers in a takhian tree, Bangkok

vidual. Karma is accrued over generations of past lives—our selves are made up of the actions of people who were and yet were not us. And, just as the past is out of our perception, Tui does not know if he is fated (satta) to die in a Korean cold snap, or if he will get the luck (sok) needed to win the lottery. These are pressing issues for those going abroad (or to Bangkok) and engaging in risky activity. One needs the technique and technology in order to be able to discover one's internal qualities. Luckily, there are ways to find out.

The shrine to Ya Nak Phra Khanong, a woman who died in childbirth, is perhaps Bangkok's most famous ghost shrine (Johnson 2016b). The spirit has been featured in multiple films (Nonzee 1999), stories, and even an opera. But a person attending the shrine on a night before the release of the lottery might be confused as to whose it was. On such nights, crowds gather not in front of the image to Ya Nak and her child (kuman), but at a greasy-looking tree trunk tucked in the back (figure 3.3).

These crowds were—nearly unanimously in the nights that I spent there—migrant workers from Isan. They included informal-economy construction workers, maids, sex workers, taxi drivers, and others—and it was my connection with these impromptu religious visits that initially sent me to work in Ban Beuk.

The trunk is from a takhian (Hopea odorata) tree, the same sort that loomed over my hut from Bird Island. Its bark had long since sloughed off, and its wood glistened from years of oily fingers rubbing it. This rubbing action had made deep wells and grooves in the wood, many of them the size and shape of a fingertip.

Various stories surround its origin. Some in the alleyway near the shrine tell a story of the ghost of Ya Nak being so restless that nothing could stop her except planting the tree directly on her forehead. Others said the tree had been dredged up from the nearby Phra Khanong canal and declared to be the abode of a beneficent spirit after it had given correct lottery numbers. The devotees to the shrine, however, cared little for its provenance. Instead, they were there for what it could do.

All agreed that the tree harbored a spirit—Lady Mother Takhian or *jao mae* Takhian. As in other such shrines, devotees, after giving minor offerings of incense or candles, rubbed the wood in order to reveal numbers. They also, like Tui, studied the swirls that incense ash made in the offering pots, seeing if one of them created a loop that might form part of a six or nine, or broke at an angle to make an Arabic seven.

Staring into the shining wood by candlelight, at times someone would see a face standing out in sharp relief. This would be a direct communication from the Lady Mother, but what exactly it meant would be more obscure. Interpretations here were entirely individual—Lek, the manager of the shrine who took care of devotees to Ya Nak, was indifferent to Takhian, and looked down upon her northeastern devotees. This despite the fact that the tree was at times more popular than Nak's shrine, and she profited by selling offerings such as Takhian dresses, rubbing oil, incense, and so on. She said, "People believe that they see a face. The tree is very popular." Looking at me, she added, "It's just a belief," in terms far removed from the glowing words that she had for Ya Nak (see Johnson 2016b).[25]

But the Lady Mother would not reveal these numbers to just anyone. She only favored people with correct numbers if they appealed to her in some way. This might be a pleasing physical appearance, especially a young man wearing a green shirt (green, of course, being a tree's favorite color). It might be the presence of something interesting and unusual (such as a foreign academic with a camera, who also happened to be a young-looking man wearing a green shirt). It might be a person who had made a particularly large donation to a temple and had a cloud of merit (bun) that no one else could see.

Jiap, a migrant domestic worker from Isan, described the process thus: "The Lady Mother, she knows. She can see if you have fate [to be wealthy, satta] or if you have merit [bun]. Things we do not know."

Here, Jiap presents a particular view of the world as fundamentally unknown. Jiap has no idea what lottery numbers will come out in the next drawing, but Lady Takhian does. And she might be persuaded to reveal them.

But, further, Lady Takhian sees Jiap better than she can see herself. While not knowing one's fate is understandable, Jiap does not even know her own store of good deeds (kam, bun)—were she a Catholic, she would not be able to deliver a confession. Instead, she must appeal to another power to see her true worth—if she is meritorious, she will receive a number.

In this way, too, Jiap reveals the fungibility of these unknown qualities of the self. Capital, via a temple donation, leads to merit. Merit can be used to entice Takhian into giving a windfall of luck (sok lab), which in turn yields cash. And if some of this cash is then donated back to the temple, the cycle begins again.

In short, those coming to Takhian are unknown to themselves, much as Takhian is also unknowable. Takhian, strangely like a psychoanalyst, is able to see beyond the everyday veneer of existence into more vital spheres ordinarily closed to view. Our hidden depths, then, do not just include our unconscious; rather, they also include a range of religious qualities as well. We may be traumatized by our upbringing, of course, but we are also potentially traumatized by our previous existences. We know this by staring into the bark of a tree, looking for signs.

This is a technique used to engage with an uncertain realm, one that requires skill in interpretation and in dealing with the unknown, as much as the informal conversations about evading unscrupulous labor recruiters, avoiding agricultural scams, or new courses designed to teach potential marriage migrants how to deal with a foreign spouse (Jintamas 2018). Thus, as I explore in more detail in subsequent chapters, engaging with an uncertain realm (such as migrant work) is a calculated act that brings into dialogue multiple actors—human, nonhuman, and inhuman (e.g., Takhian). One acquires what knowledge one can, and this knowledge can—and often does—include cultivating relationships with powerful individuals, physical or supernatural.

IMPERMANENCE AND POSSIBILITY

Thus, migrant work in the sense of going thiaw is an engagement with otherness and new possibilities—both within the self and without. Tui prepares for a radical change in his fortunes via continually engaging with lottery numbers even as he laments the loss of his family. Workers abroad imagine the transformations they will make to the land back home, and the pleasures of being abroad. Mon prepares for Fa's return, but also imagines a future in which she returns to Bangkok with or without him. Aek discusses the merits of raising Fern's son in Ban Beuk (with him) versus Europe (with the European husband). Ink describes the riches that will come when he is able to make his rubber orchard pay off, after the prices rise and Nong comes back from Bangkok. Jiap hopes to see her own potential via messages that Takhian might send to her.

These futures are speculative, just as the futures of Ban Beuk, the Mekong fisheries, Lo's factory, Aek's and Ink's rubber plantations, and Mon's riverside hotel are speculative. Each is dependent upon unknown qualities—sok, satta, rubber futures, the love of a foreigner—and each is fraught with the promise of future happiness or future calamity.

Further, like fishing, embarking on migrant work involves a particular kind of situated knowledge. One must interact with labor recruiters, foreigners, and potentially hostile spirits. But one must not only avoid these figures. Rather, the successful labor migrant must engage with them and win them to his or her side. One must secure the love of a foreign husband in order to succeed at marriage migration. One must appeal to Takhian's vanity via gifts of dresses, combs, or mirrors.

But such an engagement transforms the self. In my examples here, via Fa's life abroad, she becomes—even physically—a different person. Jiap, via asking a being that knows her better than she knows herself, finds a path toward self-transformation (i.e., making merit, seeking numbers, donating), even if she cannot know how she transforms. Tui's laments point toward the loss of his riverside life and the changes he sees in Ban Beuk (e.g., his "little fattie" is now "so skinny"). Mon's statement, "Fa and I will marry [hao si taengngan]" points to a future—indeed a "we" (hao) that may not come to be, and his statement, "Fa is my lover [hao pen faen kan]" points to a "we" that only exists within his mobile phone or once every few years when Fa returns from abroad. Additionally, the image of Fa that Mon treasures is not Fa today—one might say that the relationship that Mon holds with Fa is with the Fa that he remembers and imagines will return, not with the Fa that presently is. Similarly, Aek and Fern's fantasy about living together and raising her half-European son in a large Caucasian house ignores the existence of her spouse. As their lives have diverged, their life together shifts into the realm of fantasy.

Aek and Mon are in no way lost in this fantasy. Migrant work and intimate work pose risks of personal transformation, and, while Mon and others cling to a particular, deferred, moment of realization, as they wait, they make alternate plans, as Mon's local lover or Fern's arrangements for her son to adapt to life in Europe attest. For instance, Fern showed no interest in teaching her son Thai or Lao language but enthusiastically suggested he should be fluent in English. Fern's actions here contradict the end point that she mutually imagines with Aek—by not teaching her son Lao or Thai, she precluded the possibility of intimacy between Aek, who only spoke Lao and Thai, and a potential adopted son.

Aek alone, facing the collapse of local rubber prices and the collapse of fishing along the Mekong, seemed lost without his partner.

Carol Breckenridge et al. (2002), writing at the height of turn-of-the-twentieth-century fascination with globalization, transnationalism, and cosmopolitanism, remind us that our image of the globe-trotting artist or capitalist as the ideal cosmopolitan might in fact miss the point. Rather, they ask us to see "cosmopolitanism from below," meaning precisely those people like the travelers from Ban Beuk: refugees, migrant workers, and the like. These are people who, in W. E. B. Du Bois's (1994) terms, must acquire a "double consciousness" in order to navigate this world. One learns not only the rules of international migration, but when they should be bent or broken, and the many pitfalls that they hold. One also learns how to find and cultivate allies in that uncertain field, be they fellow migrants, foreigners, or, in Jiap's case, tree spirits. In other words, migrant workers are not simply pitiable bodies ("suffering subjects," as Joel Robbins [2013] might put it) shipped between countries to be exploited and used up, but adaptable individuals actively engaging in otherness and seeking to exploit it, even as they attempt to avoid exploitation themselves.

Migration, then, involves dwelling just as much as fishing does. Like the surface of the water, there is a veil beyond which the contents of the world (the heart of a foreigner, the intentions of a recruiter, one's own fate, the invisible occupant of a tree trunk) are unknowable. The future, the present, the qualities of one's self and of others—are all opaque. To engage beyond this veil involves adapting oneself to its changing present, whether that be by learning another language, modifying the landscape, or even altering one's own appearance.

From here, I return to Ban Beuk to look at more figures like Takhian—those other-than-human parts of the landscape that also find themselves changed in the currents of the present.

4

THE RIVER
GREW TIRED OF US

Previously, I have argued that the material qualities of the postdam Mekong lend themselves to uncertainty. New, unpredictable floods and ebbs render prior knowledge about the river obsolete, just as new biological hybrids cause fishermen to question what they think they know about what exists within the water and how they can exist with it.

Then, in chapter 3, I highlighted how the political economy of Ban Beuk is also dependent upon uncertainty. Villagers embrace the risk inherent in migrant labor, and, in the wake of catastrophes in the agricultural and fisheries sectors, migrant work remains an imagined source of prosperity, even if in practice it is dangerous and anything but reliable. But Ban Beuk relies upon migrants: distant people, like distant objects, like the dam, hold sway over the village. In this, they may not be physically present, but their effects—the futures that they enable, the way that they transform the everyday—are.

This characterization, that Ban Beuk is in the grip of things distant but still powerful, saw its most dramatic realization when people spoke of the ghostly lords of place (*jao*). Jao are, like Lady Mother Takhian, beings that hold sway over certain areas, and in doing so offer protection and good fortune to those that become their subjects. In this chapter, I show how, in the wake of the dam, just as the material and economic realms face a decline, other-than-human beings that were close at hand—in the river, in the village—had their potency reduced. But at the same time, those who moved, those with ties to Bangkok or even those who were said to have died and returned as a different form of the same being, reemerged with new links to new knowledge and ways of dwelling.

Here, "potency" resonates with notions of lordship in Southeast Asia as it has been analyzed in previous anthropological work. For scholars such as Benedict Anderson (1990), Clifford Geertz (1980), or Stanley Tambiah (1977), power is at the calm point in the midst of chaos, in actions not taken (but possible) and secrets not revealed (but extant). Thai kings were "world conqueror" but also "world renouncer" (Tambiah 1977), figures that balanced a separation from the world with the ability to cause change in it—compare the dualistic nature of power in the Thai idioms of *phra-khun* (charismatic power) and *phra-dej* (worldly power; see Johnson 2013). Similarly, as Anderson (1990) writes in the case of Java, and Geertz (1980) in his model of the Balinese "theater-state," potency is a feature of the still center, a ruler who draws upon hidden sources of power but who himself acts only sparingly. The Javanese king who retains a *halus* (placid, calm) composure despite the frenzied attack of his enemies, or the Buddha seated slightly smiling in the face of a demonic assault—these are the signs of potency in the world.

But in the tumultuous present, the focus of what is potent changes. New beings become potent in new ways as what was previously potent fails, and new sources of potency are identified, unreachable but nonetheless present. Thus, unknown or partially known things act upon us from a distance, not physically present, but with an influence that is felt everywhere.

Here, I trace this potency, first by exploring its relationship with concepts of lordship, and then by examining lordship in the context of the changed present.

LORDSHIP AND THE POWER OF THE STILL CENTER

Kai, an enthusiastic forty-something activist from a few provinces down the river, leaned close over a platter of grilled pork.[1] We were in a riverside restaurant on the bank of the Mekong and talking about both fish and those other inhabitants of the Mekong: nagas (*phaya nak*, mythical water dragons) and guardian spirits. As some of our dinner companions got up to refill their plates with meat, Kai spoke to me in a low but enthusiastic voice across the smoking barbecue grill. "There is one province that the [late] king [Bhumibol Adulyadej] has never visited. Can you guess where it is? And why he has never been?"

I thought for a moment, wondering what she meant and why she suddenly brought it up. Might she mean the restive southern provinces, where a long-standing insurgency and antipathetic Muslim majority would make the trip dangerous? Or—I thought—as the monarchy hadn't made a provincial trip in years, perhaps a northeastern border province like that near Ban Beuk, where the communist insurgency of the 1970s would have discouraged royal visits? But why bring up the king at all when the conversation had been about nagas?

"Yala," I guessed, naming one of the southern provinces. It was a dumb guess.

Kai smiled. "Mukdahan," she said, referring to a nearby province along the Mekong, one with neither of the political-historical conflicts that I'd guessed, being too far east for the heart of the communists and clear on the other side of the country from the Malay separatists. But I'd thought wrong—the problem wasn't insurgents; it was a problem of too many kings. "He cannot go. The guardian spirit will not allow it. The spirit [jao meuang] says that there can be only one lord [jao] of Mukdahan, and has forbidden any other [king] to enter."

Kai here refers to King Mungmeuang, the guardian spirit of the city of Mukdahan (and by extension the province). Here, I translate Mungmeuang's title "jao fa" as "king" although it is common among historical Shan or Lanna leaders and might also be translated as "prince." He is a part of a cult of guardian spirits in the province also including the Two Noble Sisters (jao mae song nang) that have parallels in urban centers across the Mekong region (for more on such guardian spirit cults, see Holt 2009; Rhum 1994; Tambiah 1970).

But what really intrigued me was Kai's comment, "There can only be one lord." Here, kings and spirits are one and the same—the divide between the political and the supernatural is blurred. In the way Kai speaks, kingship is an extension of popular religious practice surrounding lordship as well as a system of political control (cf. Anderson 1990; McCargo 2005).

The debate over how much myth and how much realpolitik drives Thai monarchism has gone back and forth for years (Gray 1986; Jackson 2010; McCargo 2005). Kai's comment settles decisively upon the former, as she rebukes the authority of the monarch to be a jao using the very same logic of lordship and divinity. Whereas the Thai royal cult promoted Bhumibol as an incipient Buddha (Gray 1992, 452), or as a Brahmin lord (cakkavattin, 31), Kai presents him in another form—not a Buddha at all, but an animist lord whose purview is not over the entire cosmos, but over a curtailed point in space and time. A jao, unlike the Hindu-Buddhist divine king to which Bhumibol was often compared (see Gray 1986), is limited.

Jao, in the sense that Kai and I were discussing, is a term that speaks to potency. If I say that I am the jao of a particular thing, it means that this thing follows my will, whether or not I am referring to a car (jao khong rot), a polity (jao meuang, a guardian spirit that looks after a city), or the sky itself (jao fa, a prince; here one must remember the link between monarchy and rain-making).

It refers at once to supernatural divinities, the Buddha, kings, or in a more mundane way to ownership. In Bangkok, if I were to refer to a jao without specifying, one might assume I was speaking of a member of the royal family. In older Thai chronicles, the term was synonymous with a king. Thus, the idea of jao articulates sovereign power. Via ownership of a subject person or thing, jao guide it toward prosperity and fortune and ensure that its actions and the beings within it progress (*jaroen*; see Johnson 2014). This sovereignty, as I define it here, has nothing to do with the official, Sanskrit-derived *athipathai* (independence) or *rathathipatai* (statehood, government), but instead the more colloquial *khwam pen jao* (lordship, godliness, the status of being a jao).

As such, we cannot transpose notions of sovereignty derived from Western sources onto notions of jao in Southeast Asia. Sovereignty means something more than kings, and khwam pen jao means something more than ownership. As this term suggests, in the case of the Mekong, there are jao other than the human owners of the map: jao more like Mingmeuang than Pong. These are guardian spirits, beings that John Clifford Holt describes in Durkheimian terms (in the case of Laos) as "a concept of power . . . intrinsic to a specific territory . . . or the very sense of social collectivity" (2009, 24). It is my case that, just as Pong finds fish through a combination of his knowledge, his technique, and an outside force, and just as Jiap finds fortune via the same combination, jao serve as this force that enables the realization of potential, a divine excess. Here, I seek to give some thought to these jao and, to do so, I must follow them through an analysis of animism.

The practice of Theravada Buddhism in the region has long been described by both local and international scholars as a blend of animism (Thai: *satsana phi* or *kan naptheu phi*, lit.: "spirit religion" or "spirit worship"), Buddhism, and folk Brahminism (Kirsch 1977; Shalardchai 1984; Tambiah 1977). In Myanmar (Burma), Melford Spiro's (1996) seminal study placed Buddhism and animism in a kind of productive tension, where the propitiation of the Burmese *nats* (a pantheon of divine spirits, similar to the Thai *thaewadda*) blended with Buddhism. Spiro (1996, 254) sought to understand how these two religious traditions were able to coexist, arguing that animism was irrelevant and subordinate to Buddhism (spirits can only harm the impious and aid the pious, so one is better off being a good Buddhist), but in practice animism was omnipresent. To resolve this tension, Spiro concluded that Buddhism and animism constitute two separate, parallel religions, each fulfilling different goals.

Spiro's notion of a supreme Buddhism and subordinate animism would certainly characterize the response to a casual question to my own interlocutors as well: "Which is higher, the Buddha or spirits?" would be answered with a confused "The Buddha, of course." Indeed, this view is shared by Thai scholars as well—Sit But-in (1980, 22), for instance, dismisses animism in northern Thailand as "not meaningful" in comparison with Buddhism.

As a counterpoint, more recent and less nationalistic observers have come up with more complicated pictures—for instance, Visisya Pinthongvijayakul (2015, 2018) argues that mediumship in Isan (Thailand's northeast) occupies a symbolically superior role to Buddhism, citing the appearance of Buddhist monks at mediumship rites and the monks' bowing to and taking blessings from the mediums.[2]

However, in positing a clearly split Buddhism and animism and asking which one is the superior, Spiro (and Sit) are asking the wrong questions. Here is not a binary division of worlds into pragmatic, money-oriented animism and otherworldly Buddhism. Instead, Justin McDaniel (2011, 16) argues that the way that these arguments are framed ends up reifying each pole and that the attempt to purify either folk animist religiosity or Buddhist theology is doomed to failure. Religious notions do not stay within their box: as a number of contemporary scholars point out, animism and Buddhism both adapt themselves to the needs and demands of forces as diverse as Thai politics, media, and economics (Jackson 1999; Morris 2000; Pattana 2007). The dynamism and variance of spirit practice leads Pattana Kitiarsa (2005) to reject claims of syncretism in favor of hybridity, by which he means that the two systems blend into a mix wherein one cannot separate an animist strand from a Buddhist way of thought. Rosalind Morris (2000), in her masterful *In the Place of Origins*, notes the virtuosic play upon media, politics, power, and modernity that undergirds Thai spirit mediumship.

With this in mind, in attempting to tease apart intertwined strains of ritual and religion, do we risk reifying a category of religion? That is to say: Is animism a religion in the same way that Buddhism is? And, on the converse side, do we also risk overlooking the profound impact of other nonreligious social factors upon conceptions of what is potent and efficacious in the world? Would not environmental change, migrant work, and shifting notions of politics affect the practice of Buddhism as much as animism might? And how might potency factor into the mix?

Here, I address the former first. In early anthropology, animism was one of the original categories of "primitive" thought. For early twentieth-century and late nineteenth-century writers, animism was a question of belief. E. B. Tylor ([1871] 2016) characterized animism as a belief in the persistence of the soul beyond the body, a soul that would naturally fix itself to objects (and other people). For Tylor, this belief would, once refined, lead itself to greater and greater abstractions and eventually become realized in its fullest form in world religions.

But in recent years, new approaches to anthropology have taken the notion of animism in new directions. This is especially relevant in light of ecological crises that prompt a reevaluation of nature and culture (Descola 2013).

For Philippe Descola, animism is one of the four basic ontological types. Animists, for Descola, perceive a fundamental unity behind the interiority of beings despite their exterior difference or, as Kaj Århem (1996, 188) puts it, a phenomenological difference masking a spiritual sameness. For instance, an animist in Descola's reading would say that animals are in some senses people, with social and interior lives that approximate human ones. While on the surface this may not seem terribly different from a Tylorian reading of animism (e.g., human souls fixed onto objects), ontological anthropology emphasizes not belief, but interaction and communication, placing the question of social personhood at the center of animism (Bird-David 1999; Willerslev 2007). Animists are animists because they interact with nonhumans in ways that mirror human interactions.

For instance, Rane Willerslev's (2007) *Soul Hunters* gives us a clear picture of an animist world: hunters hunt animals who have spirits that behave rather like humans. But in an animist world, one must interact. Willerslev points out how, in order to have a successful hunt, a hunter must seduce an animal spirit, convince it to give itself up and allow itself to be killed. Elsewhere, spirits are there to be "laugh[ed] with" (Willerslev 2012), not as sacred beings removed from the world.

In Southeast Asia, there is something immediately familiar to this notion of laughing with the spirits. Spirits are funny. Ban Beuk's guardian jao don (discussed elsewhere in this chapter) was fond of cracking ribald jokes about the physical attributes of female visitors. "Lord White," my guardian spirit interlocutor in Chiang Mai (see Johnson 2014), used to feed me giant gobs of fermented tea (*miang*) and cackle as I puked in the bushes. The humanness of such spirits can be jarring to those expecting a solemn rite. Cited in Mary Steedly's (1993, 16–17) *Hanging without a Rope*, the Dutch missionary J. H. Neumann, in a fictionalized diary attributed to one "Henk," gazes in a kind of horrified wonder at Batak (Sumatran) women falling into trance and possession in the middle of the night during a funeral. He watches in shocked and hushed silence and then, to his dismay, sees other villagers calmly smoking cigarettes, sleeping, or carrying on private conversations even as the otherworldly intrudes upon the present. But Willerslev (2012) points us to the answer here—spirits are not otherworldly for the Batak. They are, in Descola's notion of animism, beings with interiorities rather similar to those of humans and as such are not alarming guests at such an event, or at least not inherently so (in contrast, one can imagine the alarming entrance of a human enemy just as one might imagine the entrance of a supernatural one). Henk's shock is the realization that he is not an animist, but someone that expects an almost Christian sense of awe at the arrival of a god.

Indeed, notions of animism need to be adapted to the local context, and this is precisely what Guido Sprenger and Kaj Århem (2015) aim to do. In their volume, they argue for a particular Southeast Asian animism, one that reflects animists' long engagement in the region with states and world religions. Thus, here animism takes on a particular character of its own, distinct from the Amerindian or circumpolar characteristics that have defined it previously. Specifically, Sprenger (2015, 43) makes the case that Southeast Asian animism embraces a hierarchical world, one in which spirits become relevant at certain scales and world religions at others. As one result, animism here fails to be the engine of egalitarian social values that others have noted elsewhere in the world (Sprenger 2018), and also exists without conflict with long-established forces of Buddhism and Hinduism. But the hierarchy between the (in Redfield's [1956] terms) great tradition of Buddhism and the smaller tradition of animism informs, for Sprenger (2015, 42), all relations: humans and animals, humans and spirits. Indeed, lordship and subjection become key features of animism in Southeast Asia.

But I depart from Descola and a reading of animism that is too fixed on communities and collectivities, and simultaneously build upon the implications of Sprenger's suggestion that animism provides a lens through which to look at larger conceptions of hierarchy. Jao certainly embody the latter, and, like Sprenger's analysis, my own conception of jao is one that extends beyond politics (e.g., kings as jao) and ritual (e.g., spirits as jao) and looks toward broader mechanisms of conceiving of power. Here, I take a cue from Elizabeth Povinelli's (2016) work on "geontology," where she addresses the division between life and nonlife. Animism, for Povinelli, is one sort of division, one that erases the nonliving and ascribes life to all. But this is no radically alternative ontology, as it is in Descola's work. For Povinelli, the quintessential animist figure is not the spirit medium, but the capitalist, who sees stock rising and falling and capital moving as agents in themselves. There are animist qualities in us, as well as them.

And, indeed, there seems to be a link between the cult of capitalism and the cult of jao. Although Thai society occasionally goes through periods of moral panic surrounding *phutthapanich* (Buddhist commercialism), amulets containing images of famous monks, kings, Buddhas, or Hindu deities proliferate in Bangkok's markets, shopping malls, and post offices (Jackson 2016), and even around the necks of its prime ministers.[3] Peter Jackson (1999) and Pattana Kitiarsa (2005) both write in detail on the interpenetration of capitalism and the supernatural in these amulet markets and the market for other sources of the sacred power associated with jao (barami; see also Terweil 2012). As should be expected, the cult of the monarchy is one part of this revitalization of magic in public, as Thais collect royal paraphernalia, especially that surrounding the late Bhumibol (see Jackson 2009) or the Victorian-era Chulalongkorn (see Stengs 2009). Thus, the network of capitalism, monarchy, and jao is one that exceeds the narrow category of animism as the attribution of human qualities to nonhumans. Each, in this light, is an argument about potency.

Elsewhere, too, capitalism and religion seep into each other. John Comaroff and Jean Comaroff (1999) describe how the parallels between neoliberalism and the occult in turn generate new hopes and anxieties surrounding the transformations in South Africa at the end of apartheid. As liberation was to—in popular thought—make all South Africans prosperous, the answer to the question of why it did not in fact work for all quickly resolved as witchcraft. And in Singapore, small businesses similarly mobilize witchcraft against their competitors (see Johnson 2016a).

But here are the workings of similar spectral forces: capital and magic. Writers as long ago as Marx noted the "fetishism" of capitalism and the link between the two forces. A spirit, then, in an animist system, is one being among many, and models of spirits and spirit possession that rely too heavily upon Western or other sources of sovereignty and ontology fall short. J. Brent Crosson (2017), in a special edition of *Ethnos*, makes the compelling case that notions of spirit possession and sovereignty overemphasize ownership and bondage, and do not adequately take into consideration living with spirits as other beings. But we do not entirely understand those with whom we live: Crosson is entirely correct to note that spirits in many places are not just other *beings*, but *other* beings—they are not humans with different faces, but things with which coexistence is sometimes painful, annoying, or otherwise difficult.

As Crosson indicates, possession is not entirely ownership, despite the link between jao (lord) and *jao khong* (owner). Rather, it is the adoption of the appearance of a spirit (*song jao*) by a body intended to take particular forms (*rang song*). Mediums are not "intermediaries" (Thai: *khon klaang*), but—in Ban Beuk—are "artificial women" (*nang thiam*). Each of these terms is redolent with meaning. *Possession*, then, is the wrong word for song jao. To song jao or to become a nang thiam is not to be gripped by an outside force, but a more conscious adaptation of a body into another form with the assistance of an outside force (i.e., the spirit). It emphasizes the constructed effort on the part of the medium in becoming possessed (specifically, the medium takes on the form [song] of the spirit, thus becoming artificial [thiam]), even if—as we will see—she is occasionally compelled or coerced into it. We should recall here the role of migrant workers, who similarly become other to themselves in order to access foreign potency. Spirits in the sense of phi or jao are not always incorporeal, as the term also refers to very corporeal but nonetheless magical beings of the forest (Johnson 2017), or even individuals with strange powers (Toem 1987). Indeed, a plain inanimate corpse is also a phi in local parlance (as opposed to the more official term *sop*), as we have seen in the case of Ban Beuk's Corpse Rapid (kaeng phi).

But what relevance do these ideas have to Ban Beuk, especially to the persistence and problematic agency of jao along the Mekong? Here, I differentiate jao from a Descoladean definition of animism—it is not just that inanimate objects have souls and are coagents in the world; rather, it is that ownership exceeds the human. Just as Sprenger describes how animals can be eaten as they exist in a certain subordinate capacity, objects and features of the landscape are subject to their jao. Like the car over which I am sovereign (jao khong), places or beings within the river are subject to particular sovereign forces. In short, hierarchy extends in invisible networks from certain sources of potency and in turn animates other, subordinate sources: I, as jao of my car, enable it to function; the jao of the island enables fish catches in the river; the king, as jao of the land, produces prosperity. In short, jao enter into an assemblage in order to enable the potential of a thing to be fully realized: water gives fish, the sky gives rain, the kingdom prospers. This potential is that final addition to material, time, and technique that enables an action to bear fruit.

I have been speaking here of spirits; now I turn to kings. I continue to speak about jao. The word has both meanings. If, for Derrida, the sovereign is a beast, in Thailand, the sovereign is a ghost.

Kings

In many regions, the notion of outsider kingship often traced its legitimacy originally from the divine—indeed, the term of address for the current Thai monarchy is Rama, a reference to the incarnation of Vishnu in the Ramayana (Thai: *ramkhian*). But, as Graeber and Sahlins (2017) argue, such divine kingship is often blended with the trappings of neighboring sources of power and prestige. Additionally, kingship in Southeast Asia is a fractal affair. Rulers of smaller principalities (such as the sometimes-independent kingdom of Nan, northwest of Ban Beuk) often adopted elements of larger kingdoms nearby (such as Lanna, in Chiang Mai), who in turn adopted elements taken from Siamese or Chinese sources (Graeber and Sahlins 2017, 13). So smaller elements mirrored larger ones, while at the same time incorporating their own features, a process that Georges Condominas (1990) characterizes as *systems à emboîtement*, fractal-like formations where an ideal model of kingship comes to reflect relationships on smaller and smaller scales.

In recent years, scholars of the monarchy in Thailand have pointed out how the cult of the late Thai king Bhumibol Adulyadej blends both this connection with a divine source of power and legitimacy with bureaucratic power (see Gray 1986). Further, as Siam became surrounded by European colonies, the Siamese monarchy deliberately adopted Western court traditions and modes of dress as a means to claim European sources of legitimacy and power (see Peleggi 2002). Indeed, Bhumibol was a "would-be divinity" (*samuttithep*; Jackson 2010) as well as an internationally savvy man of leisure, a fan of jazz music, sailboats, and photography—the god-king was even a born American citizen, coming as he did from Massachusetts! Thus, cultivating an image as a Westernized as well as divinized individual meant not an adulteration of sacred royal power, but its intensification via mimesis.

This mimesis—in Graeber and Sahlins's (2017, 14) terms, "galactic mimesis"—is not simply a tool of propaganda. Rather, Graeber posits that ritual surrounding spirits and kings ("metapersons") "*are* the means of production . . . [as] they are known to be responsible for the success and failure of human work" (Graeber and Sahlins 2017, 16). Potency derived from sources outside the human is necessary for human techné to yield results.

This is a key point: along the Mekong, as in many other places, it is not simply the individual and his or her knowledge that leads to the power to effect change in the world. Indeed, Thanet Aphornsuvan (1998), in his historically focused study of the conception of freedom in Siam, points out that to be truly free, without either responsibilities to subordinates or superiors, is to be *theuan*, to be wild, uncontrolled, chaotic, bestial. It is the word that one uses for a state of anarchy or violence—a fight where machetes come out and blood is spilled is a theuan moment.[4] Instead, prosperity in Thai politics comes from being enmeshed in a network: having those above you who are responsible for you, and having those below you to whom you are responsible.

Here, I do not mean to become overly distracted with the specifics of kingship in Thailand. It is a powerful topic and one that, in the present reign of Rama X, raises a number of disturbing questions about autocracy and the military's influence upon the state—questions that are better answered elsewhere (Streckfuss 2010). As I found, it was also a topic about which my interlocutors were not terribly concerned. Some—especially Pla and other NGO-connected workers—occasionally expressed loyalty to the monarchy (in wearing purple, for instance, to honor the Crown Princess Maha Chakri Sirindhorn, or in wearing black in expressive displays of mourning upon the death of Bhumibol), others were neutral, and others were openly hostile to the monarchy (especially Bhumibol's successor, Vajiralongkorn, Rama X).

But simply because people do not think much about the throne in Bangkok does not mean that they do not think about lordship (khwam pen jao). Here, then, we must look at sacred kingship far from its putative source in Bangkok and as it enters the village.

The first thing one might suspect is that, as notions of lordship enter the village scale, the representative of the state in the village might be the substitute for the king's divine perfection (barami): recall the village head, Pong. Indeed, in Ban Beuk, Pong did strive for such a reserved, virtuous image (as I detail in chapter 1) to some extent. But no one would ever call him a jao or extend to him the quality of barami. Rather, the sacred body of the king moves to other sources, sources that share an implicit distance from humans and nonhuman animals alike—namely, spirits.

In the center of most villages and cities is a pillar, the *lak meuang*. This in Brahmanic terms is the shiva-lingam, but it has a history even within animist Thai Dam practice (the *seua meuang*, the spirit literally "covering the polity"). The spirit within the lak meuang is that which, like the sacred body of the king, controls and takes responsibility for the well-being of the city, managing prosperous features such as rainfall and health and defending against calamities such as epidemics and accidents (see Johnson 2014; Rhum 1994), much as a meritorious ruler would (see Jory 2016; Tambiah 1977). It is this conflict over who extends lordship over the city that kept Bhumibol out of Mukhdahan, at least in Kai's retelling. City pillars make cities cities, and there is a tremendous depth to which one might go in reading into a situation where urbanity is established via a divine phallus at the center of the city and wilderness is populated by often female spirits on the outskirts.

But lordship is not quite so binary. In Chiang Mai, for instance, the city is nurtured by different kinds of spirits: cannibal giants (*yak*) that, after being tamed by the power of the Buddha, provide coolness and prosperity to the city, and a benevolent spirit-lord (*jao luang kham daeng*) residing in an auspicious mountain cave (see Johnson 2014). In Tambiah's field site elsewhere in the northeast, the naga of a swamp exists in friendly opposition to urban spirits of the lak meuang and temple (see Tambiah 1970). This binary: nature and culture in concert, poses another challenge to Descola's assumption of an animism that inherently overcomes the dualism of nature and culture. But despite being dualistic, the opposition is productive: the raw power of the wilderness and the transcendent refinement of the human. One recalls that the lingam in the center of Cambodian cities had surrounding it a yoni—it is the combination of opposites that yields results.

Here, then, are the outlines of a Thai-Lao ontology of power. Lordship is a quality that all have in some quantity, but which really extends downward via a hierarchy of beings that can command barami, beings which may or may not be human. Additionally, this hierarchy is reinforced via devotion to those above and responsibility to those below. Recall the metaphor of a ladder of wisdom, where those above have a better (but not complete) vantage point upon the world. Here, those above also have an obligation to those below, to help them climb.

As I have outlined above, the ontological approach presupposes a system of relations—not belief, as Tylor would have it, which is the supposition of a bounded worldview (epistemology), but an extant world populated with particular beings, powers, and relationships between them. Ontological anthropology in turn (Holbraad and Pedersen 2017) suggests that we take this world seriously, not as a manifestation of culture but as an actually existing set of rhizomatic relations.

I support fully the idea of taking other worlds—or, to be more precise, world-making projects (see de la Cadena and Blaser 2018)—seriously. In this, I draw inspiration from new work on the agency of divine beings in regions where they have typically been excluded—namely, politics. Marisol de la Cadena (2015), in her study of "earth beings," argues that anthropologists must take seriously a politics where divine beings within the land (in de la Cadena: *tirakuna*) act politically. For de la Cadena, earth beings act; they are not simply manifestations of belief. They fight back against certain interests, thereby felicitously aligning themselves with the political rights of indigenous communities. De la Cadena's earth-being politics are therefore different from our own, but remain at the same time reconcilable as a contest of interested beings and identifiable parties (even if some of these are not human).

But I understand world-making projects in the context of change, of ontological worlds that are uncertain and in flux. As such, these projects do not exist entirely in the heads of a particular group of people, but rather via a give-and-take with other such projects: a world where certain forces that once worked do so no longer, and, where the land itself is transformed, new sources of potency come into being.

These linkages are more salient than we might think. In Australia, indigenous groups assumed that with the arrival of Australians, the flora and fauna of the land would itself change (Povinelli 2002). And, indeed, to some extent it did—think for a moment of the introduction of rabbits into rural Australia.

Separation between the social world, the spirit world, and the ecological world is nonexistent. With this in mind, how, then, can we think of the changing ontological worlds of people facing environmental disruption as an Anthropocenic animism? And should we?

In this, I support such a move. But, as I explore in this chapter and beyond, I find the ontological worlds of my interlocutors in Ban Beuk to be unstable and multiple. We (and they) exist at the nexus between multiple world-making projects, projects that are in themselves constantly changing. Jao, for instance, exist, according to most (but not all) of my interlocutors. But whether or not this or that jao exists is an open question (see also Stevenson 2014).

Do You Believe in Ghosts?

One night, while we played with his toddler, Mon asked me suddenly, "Do you believe in phi [spirits, including, in the local dialect, the category of jao]?" I was used to this question and responded with the quick "I don't believe, but I don't offend" that I knew usually brought a knowing laugh. But Mon had heard that answer from me before and wasn't having any of it. "Really, in your role as a professor who has been many places, do you believe [seua boh]?"

This was something new. I looked at Mon, wondering what he meant. He didn't have the half-joking glint in his eye that he normally did when he tested me, and the reference to my own profession and history stopped me for an instant. For a moment, I stepped out of the role of ethnographer, the Geertzean chronicler of Ban Beuk's ontological or conceptual world, and considered his question as he intended it: to me as a fellow being trying to make sense of a world that seems mysterious. He was asking not for ethnographic demurral or a verbal affirmation of his worldview, but for honesty. If I may rephrase what he asked of me, it is, "I am unsure about the ontological status of things in the world and I trust your judgment. Do phi exist?"

It is a problem that other anthropologists describe. Nils Bubandt (2014), for instance, sees Buli witches not as things existing in the world but as possible such beings, things that present a particular problem. In *The Empty Seashell*, he describes how modernity and Christianity fail to solve the problem of witches, as it is a fundamental problem of uncertainty. Witches are not representations of the problem; rather, they are a means toward dealing with it. Similarly, Sprenger also notes how animism is not a theology, but rather says, "Animist relationships emerge from permanent becoming and improvisation" (2015, 44).

Lisa Stevenson (2014) raises the point here of uncertainty. One of her interlocutors reported that some family members believed that a raven who had taken up residence in the backyard was actually his uncle. When Stevenson questioned him, he simply shrugged and responded, "It's still there." The raven, the uncle, the potential, in other words, was still there. Even if its ontological status is in doubt, something nonetheless exists.

Thus, back to Mon. Mon's question challenged me to improvise and think with him, to see the fishermen of Ban Beuk as individuals seeking sources of potency (and ruin, in the case of Bubandt's witches) and attempting a kind of bricolage with material, economic, and supernatural forces. Instead, just as he does when fishing, Mon presents possibilities—this or that jao, this or that cash crop, this or that catch. It caused me to ask myself not only what is a world where we take phi seriously, but also what is a world where we do not take phi seriously?

The doubt reflected by Mon here as well as in other such moments means that I cannot reflect upon ontology as something bounded (e.g., ontology as something shared within a closed cultural group, as I believe Viveiros de Castro [2015] intends), but rather an ontology as being in the world (in the Heideggerian sense) in the face of all of the uncertainty that this implies. Jao, here, provides one such suggestion for how things might be ordered, an explanation for how some things might contain hidden sources of potency, might be secretly manipulable, or the like. Jao is a way of seeing, of ordering the world: a technology, in Heidegger's terms, not in the sense of a world-destroying, hegemonic lens, but rather a way of allowing a potential world to come into being. A fisherman is not a fisherman (i.e., he cannot catch fish) unless a jao allows it.

Thus, in Ban Beuk, animism is neither a bounded set of beliefs nor a rhizomatic way of interconnecting humans with their environment, at least not entirely. Instead, it is the realization that certain things and places have an excess: something not entirely apparent, but which makes them surprisingly effective (or, alternately, harmful). An island that sends dreams, for instance, or a river that suddenly does not follow natural law are both examples of something in the grip of an outside force. On the converse, sometimes an island is just an island. Remember that, when I questioned Thip about my dream concerning Bird Island, she demurred—it might have a spirit. It never had one as far as she knew, but what did she know, really? It might be. If my dream was really a message. If I was reading it correctly. If the messenger was honest. If I could understand. She and I both concluded that the answer to at least one of these questions was likely "no."

While my own Bird Island deity was questionable, even more established jao had ontological statuses within the community in flux. But here I am getting ahead of myself. First, before we can address the spirits of the Anthropocene, we must address what exists within the cosmological landscape of Southeast

Asia. In northeastern Thailand, to speak of spirits and potency is to speak of lordship. Lordship is the possession of potency, and potency always exists in excess, lords hidden in seemingly innocuous things, like islands and river eddies and trees. But this potency is not always present. It can be lost. Here, I turn to these losses.

Spirits, Uncanny Beings, and Hidden Presences

Stanley Tambiah's (1970) *Buddhism and the Spirit Cults in North-East Thailand* is an encyclopedic look at religious life in a small town not far from Ban Beuk. It is a classic take on the village study model pioneered in post–World War II Thailand by Lauriston Sharp and Lucien Hanks (2018). Tambiah's study is far more nuanced than this earlier work, but it retains some features of Sharp's initial work: a rural town nonetheless close enough to a major urban center (Bangkok for Sharp, Udon Thani for Tambiah) for access to foreign researchers in the mid-twentieth century on one hand, and an attempt to get at cultural systems and dynamics without too much corruption from the forward motion of modernity on the other.

Like Ban Beuk, Tambiah's (1970, 340) Ban Muan Phran is a nexus in a number of different cosmological worlds. On one hand, there are malevolent ghosts (phi) that haunt the forest and cause afflictions. But other spirits (also phi) can be benevolent, such as a cluster of guardian spirits. These benevolent spirits, too, are neatly divided between those arising from nature (Tambiah's "swamp naga": *jao pho tong khyang*), from the temple (named *jao pho phra khao*), and from the human world in between (*tapubaan*, whose name simply means "village grandfather"). Further, humans themselves have a spirit essence (*khwan*) that can be manipulated in order to heal, and, finally, the power of the Buddha and the *devata* (Buddhist divinities; Thai: *thaewadda*) transcend all of the above.

These sources of potential in turn mobilize a variety of ritual complexes and specialized practitioners, from exorcists (*moh tham*) who provide defenses against malevolent phi, mediums (*cham, tiam*) who channel guardian spirits, diviners (*moh song*) and healers (*moh khwan*), and, of course, Buddhist monks. In Ban Beuk, a similar group might be found: a handful of thiam along with Bangkok-style mediums (*rang song*) and a few healers, as well as the omnipresent Buddhist monks.[5] Just as Tambiah describes, guardian spirit and temple-related rites come at particular points of the year, whereas exorcisms and healings occur when they are needed by the villagers.

Tambiah's (1970) is a carefully conducted and carefully balanced picture of village life. He links the cycle of rains and rice planting to Buddhist rituals

(154); monastic seclusion comes when rain is most needed (155); the village's largest celebration (*bun phra wet*) comes at harvest time. Rice and rain orient the calendar and the cosmological world.

But many things have changed in rural Isan since Tambiah's study. Indeed, as I drive to Ban Beuk from the regional capital of Udon Thani, I pass the district and, depending on the road I take, the very village where Tambiah worked. Ban Muan Phran is certainly not a remote town, at least not anymore, being just a short turn off Highway 2, a multilane monstrosity and a key pipeline for traffic heading to Bangkok from Lao PDR across the Friendship Bridge in Nong Khai. The village road that Tambiah maps in his account is now four lanes of blacktop lined with flags of the nation and monarchy. While rice fields still spread outside of Ban Muan Phran, there is also a military base in the direct center of the town. The forces I detail in previous chapters—the Central Thai army, migrant labor, cash crops, and so on—have not only come to Ban Muan Phran, they have taken over.

If Tambiah is correct in linking the cycle of the rice plant to the cycle of ritual, we should expect religious life to change with these new forces and, with it, the world of nonhuman and inhuman entities in the village. For instance, let us take just one factor into account—the paving of roads and the wide availability of cars and motorbikes. Ban Beuk got a permanent, sealed road in the 1980s, largely as an attempt to increase military access to the area in the face of communist insurgency. Now it is a twenty-minute drive to the district seat, and a one-hour drive to the city of Nong Khai. The religious life I detail below—trips to formerly remote forest monasteries (*wat pa*), the boom in social media–driven miraculous sites, and the spread of particular spirit cults—would not be possible without this road. In one move, the infrastructure of Ban Beuk suddenly enabled the use of a variety of sites of religious activity.

Here, then, is a problem for Durkheimians. If collective worship is worship of the collective, what do we make of a religious community when this collective scatters to very different kinds of places for ritual practice? As I detail below, Yai and Thip visit the local monk, but Mon seeks out famous charismatic monks from a few towns over. Tui and Aek turn toward animist ritual made popular via social media and linked to capitalism, and Pla turns toward nationally recognized divinities (see also Jackson 1999). Thus, the question: Just how much of a shared worldview is really shared? If I ask, along with Tambiah, "who is Uppakrut [the naga spirit of Ban Muan Phran]?," should I expect one, or multiple answers? While Tambiah anticipates this question, noting that "the villagers were by no means agreed as to who Uppakrut was" (1970, 169), his analysis treats the various responses as different lights shed upon a shared social structure.

Here, too, I think of Mon and Pong—the former denied the existence and power of the Lord of the Fish, and the latter scrupulously made appeals to him. I ask: What about change? Doubt? Uncertainty? What about the menace of new forces and the decline of old? What about the, as Susan Lepselter (2016) puts it, "resonance of unseen things": the feeling that something has gone wrong, but which one cannot identify? Here, I return to Ban Beuk and give a brief account, following Tambiah's, of the various religious institutions in the village and how they are used by some of the residents I have already introduced.

Village Sites of Potency

Within Ban Beuk, there are multiple different varieties of Buddhist temple, and different spirit shrines (*san jao*). Further, individuals often cultivate (*liang*) or worship (*naptheu*) deities and spirits individually. This leads to a wide array of sources of supernatural potency that make for a complicated mosaic—far more complicated than Tambiah's Ban Muan Phran.

Ban Beuk, like most small Thai towns, is built around a Theravada Buddhist temple (*wat*). In Ban Beuk's case, the village temple is named after the islands in the Mekong next to which it sits (figure 4.1). The temple is centrally located enough, and the town small enough, that, in the mornings just before dawn, the chanting of the handful of monks who live at the temple can be heard throughout most of the village.

Thip and Yai, Mon's sisters, go to this temple each week. On these days, Yai bangs on my window to wake me up (a feat made more or less difficult by whether or not Mon and the other fishermen had been drinking *lao khao* on the platform the night before). In the temple, they sit in their best clothes on the floor in front of a raised dais where the temple's monks chant in Pali.[6] As the monks chant, Yai and Thip pour water from a bottle into a cup, and as the water flows through the air into which the monks spoke the dharma, the water becomes something else (i.e., holy water). In turn, Thip and Yai take this water outside to pour at the roots of the temple's Bodhi tree (*Ficus religiosa*), a tree in which a benevolent spirit (phi) lives. The watering of the tree and the nourishing of the spirit with not simply water, but holy water, is, in Yai's words, a kind act that earns the women a certain stock of Buddhist merit (bun). Afterward, the women gather with the other attendees—mostly older women from Ban Beuk—and share food. Sometimes there are larger events: the ordination of a Buddha image in another temple nearby, for instance, where the abbot delivered a brief sermon in the local language and gave out amulets to the attendees. At these occasions, Yai made it a point to deploy elbows and shoulders in

Figure 4.1: Women on the riverbank, after morning prayers

order to collect as many amulets as she could as the monk threw them into
the crowd (and enlisted my help in grabbing more), so that she could proudly
distribute them once she returned to Mon's compound.

But the local village temple is only one kind of Theravada temple. Thailand's northeast is famous for its "forest temples" (wat pa; see Kamala 2003),
places that emphasize meditation on the extinguishing of the self, rather than
the role of the temple in village affairs. These temples also become a place where
political exiles or those falling out of favor in court politics are hidden away for
a time—in one such temple near Ban Beuk, for instance, a former lover of one
of the king's sisters was rumored to be hiding. At others, charismatic monks
said to be particularly efficacious set up schools of practice, and villagers might
seek them out on auspicious days or to obtain a particular charm.

Mon was such a person. On the days he did go to the temple—birthdays
and before taking a major trip—he did not take me to the local temple next
door to his compound where Thip and Yai went. This was for a variety of
reasons—significantly, this was the home of that abbot whom Nu had seen
reselling temple offerings. Additionally, this abbot was not from Isan, having
been sent to Ban Beuk from Bangkok. And, finally, Mon intimated other, less
savory rumors.[7] Instead, Mon took me to a forest temple thirty minutes' drive

away from his home. While the features of the ritual were similar to the weekly one that Yai and Thip attended—pouring water (my first year, I simply drank the water intended for pouring, and Mon looked at me as though I'd gone mad), listening to Pali, and sharing food—the temple was larger and brighter. At these times, too, Mon gave an orange plastic bucket filled with offerings to the monks as a means to make merit (bun) in anticipation of a risky journey.

But the story of religious life in Ban Beuk is not a story of Buddhism alone.[8] In addition, there are shrines to various animist spirits, including the guardian spirit of the town in the phallic lingam at its center. In addition, there are certain spirits nearby with larger, more elaborate shrines and more decentered cults: a shrine to a divine catfish (*jao pla beuk*); multiple shrines to nagas, divine serpents associated with the Mekong as well as caves; and divine island lords (jao don) that hold sway over particular sites in the river.

Pla, the Mekong rights activist from Nong Khai, made it a point to visit guardian spirit shrines up and down the river. She ran a Facebook page, in addition to her environmentally oriented one, dedicated to the *thep* (mythological angelic beings) of the Mekong. These actions were a part of her NGO work; indeed, as Daena Funahashi (2016) shows, models of NGO-based expertise that are secular elsewhere are often religiously inflected in Thailand. Significantly, just as Funahashi shows the monarchism of her NGO interlocutors in Bangkok, Pla was the most monarchically devout of any of my interlocutors and kept a collection of amulets devoted to the late kings Bhumibol and Chulalongkorn as well as divinities such as Ganesha, and various famous regional monks. She combined devotion to these with keeping a catalog of efficacious local spirits and mediums, a kind of portfolio of spiritual power. For Pla, such devotion was a part of her volunteer work, an attempt to maintain moral righteousness religiously and also in practice.

In addition to shrines to local deities, there are a handful of religious practitioners (in addition to Buddhist monks). There is a spirit medium (nang thiam) who operates out of a shrine to an island lord (jao don) in her home, another Bangkok-style medium (rang song) who lives in a cave at the back of a temple in Ban Thong (five minutes' drive from Ban Beuk), and a number of people who claim some degree of expertise in healing (*su khwan*).

Pho Khao, the rang song, was the newcomer. He had been in the district for the past five years, having moved to Ban Beuk from Kanchanaburi, a district in central Thailand on the Burmese border a few hours from Bangkok, where he had trained for a time with a senior medium.

He could not be more different from Mae Oi, the nang thiam. While in her ordinary life she went about her business like any other local woman, he lived the life of an ascetic. He always wore white linen clothing, always impeccably clean. His long, dyed-black hair was slicked back, and he wore a necklace of prayer beads around his neck. In short, he cultivated the manner of an ascetic and the image of a "ghost doctor" (*moh phi*) from popular Thai films. While Mae Oi's possession rituals were full of dancing, copious amounts of moonshine (lao khao), and shouting in the local dialect, Pho Khao spoke impeccable central Thai and often began his sessions with a Pali chant.

I met with him for my own consultation, once, as Pong had assured me that he was the most efficacious medium in the region—indeed, he at least looked the part. At the time, I was on the academic job market, and I had just given a lecture as a part of a job interview at the University of Washington–Seattle. I was asking for success in the position, and so Pong and I entered into negotiations. First of all, Pong and I sat down with Khao's assistant, a woman in her forties. She pulled out a spiral notebook and carefully wrote down all the things that I would offer the spirit were I to get my wish. She divided what I would offer the spirit, and what I would offer the medium: money, for the latter; goods and food offerings (a pig's head, for instance) for the former. I noted that other offerings were normally between 500 and 1,000 baht ($18–$26), and I, mindful of the need to act according to my perceived status, offered roughly twice this. I also included an immediate fee for the medium, which would be his regardless of success.

Pong and I then sat in front of the medium and gave him a low prostration. He in turn began to twitch as the spirit—a naga—descended. This did not include the loud retching noises that mediums in Chiang Mai often made, nor Mae Oi's constant reference to music and dance, but was a calm, internal affair. His eyes closed, he began to mutter in a high-pitched, Sanskrit-sounding language ("the language of nagas," his assistant told me), and then he opened his eyes again. He spoke to me in a tiny, quiet voice, with a benevolent smile. Here was a naga—a small one, a relative of the kind of being that I had been in a previous life (thus, the assistant told me, explaining my interest in the Mekong). Pong explained that I sought work "back home, in Washington, DC." I did not correct his mistake. The naga, then, informed me that, no, I would not get the job this month, but the next month I would hear back positively.

We thanked him and left. As it turned out, I was not offered the job in Seattle, but the following year was offered a position at Princeton University. I brought this up with Mon, who thought about it, then told me that my good fortune likely did not come from the naga. I wasn't required to pay back (*kae bon*) the boon. But it certainly came from somewhere, and as I hit a handful of roadblocks in my junior professorial position, I began to wonder more and more if I needed to correct this oversight. I asked Mon again, upon a return trip in 2019.

"Maybe," he replied.

Some residents, especially those that had spent time in Bangkok, gave offerings to other kinds of spirits: Hindu gods such as Ganesha or *asuras* (Thai: *asun*) like Rahu were popular figures among the more well-off in Ban Beuk. Still others brought the worship of particular spirits back from migrant labor stints in Bangkok and elsewhere: a relationship with a tree spirit, for instance, or a child spirit that they had cultivated (*kuman*; see Sinnott 2014).

While the temple is a site for everyday practices—merit making, weekly meditation, funeral rites—these shrines become locations for other kinds of practices: fortune-telling, the creation of contracts (*bon*) that might guarantee success in this or that venture. For a few residents, social media was a key place to follow news about new divinities being sighted or emerging elsewhere in Thailand, and they often shared videos and images of divine occurrences as well as guesses as to their import.

During my fieldwork, the Kham Chanot forest in Udon Thani became famous for just such a visitation. The forest became famous for being the home of the naga spirits Grandfather Srisutho and Grandmother Prathuma, where numbers revealed by dripping hot candle wax into holy water or the revelations of mediums of the "little naga" ended up being winners in the lottery, thus, according to Thai media, showing the sacred power (barami) of the naga couple.

Tui, in his role as a bricoleur of luck making, made the drive across two districts to seek numbers at Kham Chanot forest, where he scanned tree bark, the patterns made by wax in holy water, and the shapes of ash left by burning joss sticks for signs of numbers to be used in the lottery. He also made it a point to ask the spirits for help in his upcoming search for overseas labor—the very contract discussed in chapter 3.

Finally, there are other figures: the ghosts and other uncanny beings (phi) that come up in everyday discourse. For instance, a panic over an epidemic of cannibal ghosts (*phi pob*) made headlines in the papers, and, while few claimed to know of such spirits in Ban Beuk, many believed in their menace (see Baumann 2014). And there were other, less categorizable things: forest goblins (*phi kong koi*), forgotten guardian spirits, neglected ancestral ghosts, and the like.

Nu might have seen just such a forest goblin.[9] He had been walking in the forest in his home province of Phetchabun, near Nong Khai, when he came upon something standing in the middle of a stream. It looked like a person, but very small—no more than three feet tall, stark naked with gleaming white skin. Its hair would have dangled to its feet, but the ends were floating in the water. It stood staring into the water, arms poised and ready to snatch a fish should one pass. Stunned, Nu stopped and watched it hunt for a while until it wandered off. "It was a *phi kong koi* [liver-eating ghost]," Nu concluded, "but a real one."

Yai stopped him. "Phi kong koi aren't like that. They are short, yes, and look like people, but they have only one leg. They hop around the forest, and if they catch you, they will eat your liver."

Nu protested, "Yes, that's what they say, but phi kong koi are real! They are a kind of prehistoric human that lives in the deep forest. They don't eat liver— they eat fish from the stream. I saw it catching fish! And it had two legs, not one!" The young man, seeing Yai's doubt and glancing at me for help explaining his idea to Yai, looked for words. "It's not a ghost [phi]! It's a person [khon]! It has flesh! But it's a different kind of person."

Yai remained unconvinced. "Ghosts can be people," she concluded.

I asked her what she meant by that, and she expanded, "They can be tangible [*mi neua*]. It doesn't have to be like a spirit [*winyaan*]."

Yai's statement that "ghosts can be people" deserves some unpacking. She does not mean here the animist idea that ghosts are social beings that can be incorporated into the family. This concept is a common one around the world and especially in Southeast Asia: ghosts of dead kin remain social entities with whom one can communicate, or one might even adopt a ghostly child or be adopted by a ghostly mother (see Langford 2013; Johnson 2016b, respectively). Yai, slightly older than Nu and not having gone through the long periods of migrant work that Nu and other northeastern Thai men of his generation engage in, had a more nuanced view of what constituted a ghost. For her, *phi* meant something more like "uncanny being" (Baumann 2014) rather than the kinds of spectral presences indicated by the English terms *ghost* or *spirit*. For Yai, ghosts could be physical. They could, in the manner of the vampiric *phi phob*, be people that might occasionally turn malevolent. They could be guardian spirits. They could also be other kinds of humans that live in the forest (e.g., the term *phi tong leuang* for the Mlabri people of Phrae Province). In short, the term *ghost* indicates for Yai a presence from beyond the everyday, a horizon beyond which knowledge is incomplete. Whereas Nu attempts to categorize the physical, social, and spiritual worlds into tangible boxes (thus insisting that the phi kong koi was not a real phi because it was a person), Yai offers a variant of Hamlet's admonishment to Horatio: "There are more things in heaven and earth . . . than are dreamt of in your philosophy."

Here, then, is where my image of religious life in Thailand's northeast differs from Tambiah's—individuals in Ban Beuk saw the supernatural world as a part of the physical and social (e.g., the idea that ghosts can be people), but with portions that are removed from direct human perception. As Sprenger (2018) notes in Laos, strangers and spirits are both outsiders of a sort. But while they can be threatening, they are also full of potential—the world of jao and phi is paradoxically a place where one can find greater knowledge but also a place where one's own judgment is less effective. While the laws of merit and karma are nearly universally accepted (although propitiation of spirits such as Takhian allows one to manipulate their currents somewhat), it is difficult for humans to understand them, and, while potency exists, it is subject to change and doubt. For instance, as I sit in New Jersey writing this chapter, I wonder about my own potential for tenure. I wonder if I did the right thing in dismissing the bon that I took out with Pho Khao, and as my doubts grow, I feel the possibility of the presence of an outside force ruling over parts of my academic future. Or, rather, maybe I feel it.

Just like us, these phi are also in a state of flux. They have their own angers, journeys, likes, and dislikes. They die and, sometimes, they come back.

THE RETURN OF THE NAGA

Mon knew something was wrong. The surface of the water, just where the bank sloped down behind the Buddhist temple, had begun to froth and bubble, as though there were something big underneath, thrashing around. Mon and his two sisters stared into the foaming water to see what was causing the disturbance, but the water was opaque, reddened with silt. They could make nothing of the froth.

The disturbance lay right where the village government had brought in heavy machinery in order to fortify the banks of the Mekong with concrete. This was an attempt to stave off erosion caused by the river's new flow in the wake of water releases from Jinghong; instead of a rise and gradual fall over the course of months, the water rushed by in a steady current.

Later, Mon told me, "There was a cave there [behind the temple], a place where a naga lived. [In the past] my sister saw one sunning itself right there [on the bank]. And then, when the district began construction, all the activity must have blocked the mouth of the cave. This [disturbance] is [evidence of] the naga trying to get out." Mon speculated that the great serpent had died, trapped in its collapsed lair.

Nagas are everywhere in Ban Beuk. In addition to Pho Khao, the medium in the cave behind Ban Thong, there is a large naga shrine at the mouth of a river just south of the district head. Elsewhere in the district, there is a shrine to the king of nagas associated with a cave (and, at the end of a long and narrow tunnel, a shrine in the depths of the cave for more serious devotees).

As in Tambiah's study, nagas are important—Tambiah's (1970, 169) Uppakrut was a being that was born when the Buddha cast his semen into a pool, where it was swallowed by a mermaid. For the villagers in Tambiah's study, calling forth the naga and chanting a Pali blessing over it is a key feature in the yearly cycle of ritual (171), calling the naga forth to defeat the powers of death (personified by the Buddhist demon Mara).

This particular naga was not the great lord whose shrine graced the top of Ban Thong. Nor was it metaphorical. Rather, it was one that many had seen—physically—in the water just outside the temple. In addition to Thip, who saw it on the banks, Nu had been on the river when the naga emerged momentarily from the water just near his boat. Mon, too, had seen the naga spit fireballs (*bang fai phaya nak*) into the air late one night. The naga was (thought to be) a physical, extant being—indeed, in speaking about nagas in Ban Beuk I was reminded of an exchange during earlier fieldwork in Chiang Mai (Johnson 2014): when I mentioned that I liked naga statues out of an earlier fascination with dinosaurs when I was a child, my interlocutor responded, "Nobody's ever seen a dinosaur. People see nagas all the time."

In Ban Beuk, though, the collapse of the cave and death of the physical naga is no disappearance of the enchanted old to make way for the concrete new. Instead, the naga reemerged as a ghost of its former self. The site of the collapsed bank—this site of death—now allowed Mon and his sisters to communicate with the naga in a new way. Rather than go through Pho Khao, they set up an impromptu shrine on the side of the road, in the same way as northeastern migrants do for the spirits of uprooted trees in Bangkok (see Johnson 2012). Rather than using a Pali chant, they brought down incense sticks, sweetened coffee, or Fanta soda and fruits to place on the sand, and they asked the dead naga not for fish, but for better rubber harvest prices, lottery numbers, a new job, and so on.

Many in the village saw the naga's disappearance as the latest in an exodus of magical beings. Pong, on the subject of nagas, related, "Nagas used to come up out of the river. They would come into town, put on human clothes, and come to the temple to listen to the Buddhist chanting. Sometimes they would even marry women from the village. Then they stopped."[10]

He paused. I pressed him: "Why did they stop?"

He responded simply, "They grew tired of us."

That which is present fades in importance. It dies or grows tired, and as it does so, it changes. Rather than fading away, beings like nagas become more and more like the naga of Kham Chanot forest or the ghosts of bad death (Johnson 2014), dealing out lottery numbers and quick fortune (*chok lab*). But what about those who refuse to undergo such alterations? What of those that remain in place despite the currents of change flowing around them? Here, I turn to the story of Mae Oi, the last remaining female medium—nang thiam—in Ban Beuk. As I show here, the answers that Mae Oi gave (and the ways in which these answers were interpreted by those seated around her) do not point toward a clear resolution. For some, Mae Oi's answers confirmed her status as a crazy old lady, while others found mild encouragement in them, and still others sought hidden and unarticulated truths within them. And all of these hinged on the river.

The Island King Fails

Mae Oi sat with her eyes tightly shut, her hand to her mouth. Around her head she had wrapped a bright pink polyester turban, and she had put on a pink and purple Hawaiian shirt to match it, marking her as being possessed by a spirit. In this case, she was possessed by the jao don, the spirit of an island in the middle of the Mekong, a spirit that had been the guardian of riverside villages on either bank for longer than anyone I spoke with remembered. Mae Oi was the latest—and last—person to be a thiam for him.

I knew Mae Oi and had spent many afternoons in her concrete shrine down an alley off a rural lane in Ban Nong. There, she was supported by one daughter who lived across the lane, and another sending remittances from Bangkok. Her career as a medium had begun in her fifties, when her son suddenly died of some unexplained gastric ailment. She was distraught, and her emotional torment quickly turned into a stomach pain, something persistent, and something that she was sure was a sign that she, too, was destined to die like her son. As is common among nascent spirit mediums in Thailand and Laos (see Morris 2000), she went first to the hospital, where the attending doctor told her (as she related to me) that he could not identify the illness, but that it could well be fatal. Relief came upon the intervention of a medium (also thiam), an older woman living in the next village inland, who took Mae Oi on as her apprentice medium. Once the spirit was correctly identified and named, the illness vanished, and Mae Oi became the village's medium. She channeled three different spirits: the first to appear was her son, but his spirit came less and less in current years; the second was the jao don, the island king; and the third was a prosperity god of uncertain provenance, an august, reserved spirit who lacked the fiery temperament of the jao don.

It was the jao speaking that day. Nearly all of my interlocutors identified the island he was said to inhabit: a tall, steep-sided, forested hill rising up out of the river. While most propitiation of the jao took place on the bank, or in the shrine of Mae Oi, some devotees drove their boats out to the island to make offerings. Older fishermen described how the spirit had kept the village safe from drowning: whereas villages up and down the river had occasional deaths, and while bodies sometimes floated downstream (e.g., in *kaeng phi*), Ban Beuk never seemed to lose one of their own to the river. Pong described to me the village's loyalty to the jao during a border war with Laos during the 1980s: Lao soldiers had set up camp on the island and were shooting any Thais that approached, but Thais braved the bullets to make offerings to him, occasionally in secret.

The ceremony began in the early morning in a glade behind the temple at Ban Nong. I arrived along with Kai, Pla, and a group of local high school students that they had brought along. When we arrived, only a few of the villagers from Ban Nong were there, including Lert. They were busy in the back of the clearing getting a fire going and clearing out a spot to begin cooking. One of them had a squealing pig in a sack and, once the area was cleared, struck the pig unconscious with a single blow from a thick bamboo stick. The others began to prepare the day's dish: a light, sour *larb* of raw pork, chili, roasted rice, mint, and green onion. More harm than help in such matters, I sat on a spread plastic mat and waited for the morning's chill to burn off.

As people arrived, they separated into distinct groups. Pla, the students, Kai, and the village women sat around a large wooden spirit house (san jao, lit.: "the court of the king"), where Mae Oi was to set up her session. The men, cooking now done, ate seated on fallen logs in the back of the clearing and drank rice wine out of glass bottles. Through the day, I moved between a spot next to Lert where I was more welcome, and a spot in the front next to Mae Oi, where I'd set up my recording equipment.

Mae Oi arrived not long afterward and busied herself in front of the spirit house. Eventually, as the clearing filled up, she sat in front of it and closed her eyes in preparation. She sat still like this for a while, as the rest of us talked, joked, and started to eat. Then, as an older man began to play the bamboo saxophone (*khaen*), Mae Oi rose and started to dance, eyes still firmly shut. She bobbed along with the hypnotic drone, and Kai leaped up to dance with her, forming a kind of multigendered duo, two bodies between feminine and masculine: Kai being *tom*, a gender category akin to "butch" (see Sinnott 2004), and Mae Oi, possessed by a masculine spirit in a female body.

Mae Oi's hands began to move, making the shapes of numbers. Here he held up three fingers, there she made a circle with her thumb and forefinger as if she were making a nine.[11] As people began to shout out to her, asking for definitive numbers, the jao gave an enigmatic smile and kept dancing.

The jao then fully emerged, and Mae Oi's body, still with eyes closed, sat back down. The jao demanded a drink.

As the morning passed, the jao alternated between ruling on local matters and showy demonstrations of prowess. For instance, one woman asked about a dispute over a buffalo. A neighbor had claimed that her buffalo was in fact his, and the two had been fighting for years over it. The jao, in response, gave a long litany of complaints about the selfishness of people before announcing his support for the woman and threatening dire consequences should the neighbor refuse to give up his claim to the animal.

Then, the jao demanded another drink. When the devotee with the contested buffalo had poured a splash of whisky into the jao's glass, he scoffed, "That's it!? More!" The woman poured until she had put a pint of whisky into the glass, after which the jao, without hesitating, gulped it down (figure 4.2). Those crowded around the jao murmured, impressed by his fortitude, and Mae Oi's body swayed slightly as he put the glass down. At another point, he lit a homemade cigar, where harsh Lao tobacco had been blended with chili pepper, and, although Mae Oi's body seemed unaffected by the acrid smoke, others in the crowd coughed and backed away.

Then, Kai asked her something specific. She leaned in and asked, "Grandfather. Your children want to ask you [about] this Sayaburi Dam. They are building [the dam] just a few kilometers north of Chiang Khan in our Thailand. If they build this, it will make your children in Ban Beuk suffer in trying to find something to eat. They are making it now, grandfather. Can you help us?"

The jao listened, eyes closed, nodding his understanding. He then lifted one of Mae Oi's hands to her ear, as if he had a hidden mobile phone in it. "I'm calling Laos," he announced. "I'm calling the jao don in Laos."

"Hello? Hello?" the jao shouted into the phone in a loud voice. "One two three hello? Laos is coming. Laos is coming. Hello? One two three? Laos is coming! We're talking."

At the mention of numbers, some who had been drowsing perked up. "One, two, three?" asked one of the students, clearly wondering if the jao had, like his Kham Chanot counterpart, started to give out lottery numbers again. But some of the men, now drunk, began to shout back at the jao. "Your phone number is one, two, three?" called one, while another said, "That number is too short! It can't be just one, two, three!" Finally, Lert shouted, "You need the international calling code if you're going to call Laos." Each time, there were gales of laughter, and at this last one, the jao shouted back, "I am older

Figure 4.2: Mae Oi, possessed

and greater than you! I don't need a fucking international code!" Lert laughed back at him and, turning to me, loudly asked me, "Hey, Professor, do you really believe this stuff?" At this, three women close to Mae Oi shouted at him and he quieted down. I didn't respond, wanting to alienate neither Lert nor the jao.

The jao returned to his phone call. "Laos is coming. I'm [*ku*] asking you [*meung*]. Can you help me? If you make this [dam], then the citizens [*ratsadon*] will die. I will suffer! Do you understand? Do you understand? I will suffer! I'm calling upon you to put a hole in [the dam]. Can you put a hole in it? You can? Yes, that's what we want! They are worried that if you build it, then the citizens will die."[12] The jao nodded his head, obviously approaching satisfaction that promises of a hole might fix the concerns of his devotees.

But in this, he was wrong. As he looked to finish his call, many of the men began to shout, "Don't let them build it! Don't let them build it at all! It will flood us!"

The jao, only partially hearing, turned back to the call and relayed his disapproval. "It cannot be. It cannot be. You have to puncture it. Do you understand? [The water has been going] up, down, up, down! It cannot be! You have to puncture it! Is such an agreement OK for your village?"

Eventually, the jao and his hidden interlocutor arrived at the same conclusion as before: "If it has a hole, then downstream won't be so dry." He reported back to the crowd, "I think he can make sure that there is a hole."

One of the men behind me blurted out, "But we don't want it built at all. If they build it, we cannot find fish. We cannot find anything."

The jao, frustrated, hung up his phone and responded back to Lert, "You cannot forbid [Laos from making the dam]. They want development for their own village. They can only make a small hole. That's all they can do."[13]

For the men—all ex-migrant laborers—with whom I was sitting, having one's suffering brushed off by a distant bureaucrat was a situation that resonated (see also Sopranzetti 2017b). The island king's response echoed the stony resistance that Maersk had put up to Lert's complaints about exorbitant recruitment fees, resistance founded upon meaningless platitudes such as "this is what is required"—indeed, in relating the story to me, Lert had used the exact words that the island king later used regarding the dam. The men's disdain, then, is one of recognition. The river's island lord had proved to be just as ineffectual against red tape as the river folk. His own accessibility and proximity to the village indicated his lack of potency.

Here, the island king is tricked just as an unsavvy villager is tricked—those in power (here, the Lao lord) have brushed off a righteous complaint with bureaucratic finality. Unlike Mon's naga, and unlike Lert himself, this particular river being has not yet learned to adapt to the new ways that hostile international entities act.

In a migrant world, those who can successfully enter the flow hold potency. Those that are potent are adaptable, distant, mobile, just as spectral as capital and the market itself. Those who stay put and stay material have their potency slowly eroded, just as the island king's own island is slowly eroded by the newly changed Mekong.

POTENCY AND EROSION

Writing about Burmese spirit worship, Spiro (1996, 255) tells us:

> According to Buddhism, there can be no nonmaterial entities, for every-thing is compounded of four physical elements—earth, air, fire, and water. Hence, if the nats are nonmaterial, they cannot exist; conversely, if they do exist, they must be material. Now from a worldly (lokika) point of view, since they give the appearance of being material—they have been seen, touched, heard, etc.—they exist. In reality (lokuttara), however, their materiality is an illusion. . . . The existence of the nats is only apparent, not real; but since one must live in the world of appearance, it is expedient to act as if they existed.

Burmese nats—a category in some ways comparable with jao—present an ontological problem to Spiro and, in his writing, to Buddhists.[14] They exist because people see and interact with them, but, for Spiro's imagined Buddhist, they are nonmaterial, so they cannot exist. Thus, the Buddhist throws up his or her hands and says, "I know this is not real, yet I must act as though it is." Spiro presents this as a problem. I argue that this may be the case only for Spiro—where he sees a contradiction to be resolved, I see ambiguity to be lived with, and an acknowledgment that some extant aspects of the world are beyond human comprehension—the potency that underlies acts and renders them efficacious or not, that makes seeds take root and gambles succeed. Jao is just such a thing, hence the connection between jao and rain, fertility, the lottery, gambling, marriage, love, fishing, and everything else that requires the seem-ingly barren to bear fruit. For Spiro's frustrated Buddhist, the world has been revealed to be beyond comprehension—but that, I argue, is just how worlds are.

Here, too, there is a resonance with other animist world-making processes. Lisa Stevenson's (2014) raven who might be an ancestor (or might just be a raven) is a perfect such example. It may be a raven. It may be a relative. But nonetheless, as her interlocutor says, it's still there.

But, as much as we might relegate them to the religious sphere, they refuse to stay there. On the Mekong, the workings of spirits are both the cause of and caused by environmental change—just as the river lord claimed to be able to affect the dam construction, the naga in turn is profoundly affected by it. Lordship is one node in the ecology of the Mekong, not a cultural veil put over the environment in order to explain its possibilities.

Lordship, then, is an explanation for why certain places and people are exemplary, and others are not. Lordship is bound to these people and places. It is an excess that actualizes the potential of a place, enabling peace, protection, and prosperity. It is my argument here that those spirits that inhere in a place and render it efficacious, dangerous, or otherwise exemplary—the jao— are neither wholly an epistemological concept to be understood rationally nor an ontological being with which to interact. In the first case, ideas might differ (as with Yai and Nu) and one might run up to the limits of what is knowable by a person (as is Thip's case in questioning the existence of the island spirit). In the second case, spirits often exist behind a veil. One is never exactly sure what one is dealing with, or what exists—as evinced by Mon's question to me. Spirits are a possibility. They exist in a hauntological middle ground—relations continually influenced by that which is not present. And, just as lordship is capable of being identified, it is capable of being overturned.

The two ethnographic vignettes that I provide here each revolve around erosion. In the case of Mon's naga, erosion caused by the irregular flow of the Mekong provokes a crisis in the notion of sovereignty and place: one lord of a particular place in the river finds himself unable to adapt to the physical erosion of his home, while the other finds his authority eroded both within the community and without. While these proximate places—places known and frequented by those living nearby—become stripped of divine authority and lordship, other places, farther away, gain such power: the dam controller who regulates the floods, the Lao river lord who approves the Lao dam. Just as erosion is not the annihilation of land, but rather its movement and deposit elsewhere, here power is not removed from the world, but displaced.

Lert, that skeptic of the jao don, and I sat at the lookout over the deep pool where until recently one could find beuk. "They believed that the fish was a god [jao thi], that it was an angelic being [thep]. Or that there was a god who looked after the fish. But now maybe it's gone. Or maybe we can't find it [ha boh joe]. Or we don't know." I turn in my conclusion to this uncertainty in the face of a changed world, the productive power of *maybe*, and that divine excess that remains beyond human perception.

5

HUMAN AND
INHUMAN WORLDS

It is my argument in this book that, along the new Mekong, destructive and productive world-making projects depend upon the presence of a potential that is beyond human perception, but which comes to bear upon us. Despite—and, as I argue, because of—its physical or epistemological distance from us, this potential is also a point of desire, an influence incorporated into how individuals dwell along the great river.

This is something not unheard of in Continental philosophy. Henri Bergson suggests that the unknown "implies many orders, many existences, and a spirit [jeu d'esprit] that juggles unconsciously with them" (1930, 62), thus exceeding the real. On the Mekong, it is my argument that my interlocutors, especially in the face of radical change in the world, seek to appeal to those entities that live in that possible realm and to coax some of that outer potential into the real. Fields of *maybe* become points where new vistas on potential come into being, new opportunities to find entities with which one can find favor. As such, many moments are intimately tied to moments of change—moments like the present—and require reconfigurations of one's ability to dwell in these changed worlds.

In the height of Isan's hot and dry season, I was sitting in the cool dark of Mae Oi's home shrine, waiting for the jao don to come down into her body. She sat with her back to me, eyes tightly shut and facing the line of sacred objects that she had collected: crystals, pictures of snakes ("really" nagas in snake form), statuettes, and the like. Indeed, it was the value of these objects and not the sacrality of possession that had made her forbid me from taking pictures—she was worried that someone might see a picture of her crystals in my book and try to steal them.

She began to mutter in the voice of the island king, so low that I could not hear her. Occasionally, though, she burst out with a wild proclamation: "I am from this time! You have said I'm from the past! I'm not!" she shouted at me. This seemed confrontational, but I hesitated. Spirits were like that, sometimes. Then, another: "There are only three pa beuk left!"

Then, another: "You cannot make Siam give back the Emerald Buddha!"

Then, another: "You cannot make the dam—[the one that is] in progress—stop!"

Then, another: "You do not believe in me [*meung bo seua leuang pu*]!"

Mae Oi was shouting one side of a conversation. She was giving voice to the jao, but we did not know or hear to whom the jao spoke.

Here, then, are three different levels of removal. I am watching Mae Oi. But her voice is not her own; rather, it is that of the island king. Further, that island king is in communication with some fourth party, something beyond anyone's perception.

What the island king and his interlocutor speak of are claims to knowledge about the materiality of the river ("there are only three pa beuk left"), power and historical relations ("you cannot make Siam give back the Phra Kaew"), present-day catastrophes ("you cannot make the dam in progress stop"), and at the same time doubt over his own authority ("you have said I'm from the past" and "you do not believe in me").

As the island king wrestles with this fourth figure, he negotiates the question of potency and its disappearance. So much has vanished from the river: its fish, its Buddhist artifacts, its flow, and now the power of its jao. Here, too, the island king exposes a fundamental uncertainty in the river, the lives of people alongside it, the beings that haunt it, and our own position vis-à-vis an unknowable world. To expand upon Heidegger, our dwelling involves not just those known, productive, preservative forces around us, but also linkages that extend off into the realm of the unknown, potentially hazardous (and potentially beneficial). This uncertainty is a part of our dwelling; it is a source of potency that lingers in our intertwining with the world around us. Whereas other analyses of uncertainty (Bubandt 2014) speak of the horrific and uncanny aspects of these moments of ontological uncertainty, I have shown how this opacity offers a sense of potential. For those working in the unpredictable worlds of the Mekong—with its newly unstable hydrology, newly uncertain biota, and volatile economy—such barriers to knowledge provide a threat, but also a promise that the world might be otherwise.

Such a notion—a world that lies beyond our apprehension but which nonetheless affects us—is central to the notion of the unconscious. Both for Freud and for Deleuze and Guattari (in very different ways), the unconscious is an unknowable part of ourselves. It communicates with us in mysterious, hidden ways—a compulsion, a fixation, a dream. Especially in the Deleuzean unconscious, it is always already infected by outside influences—the individual, here, is a momentary production. Living with the unconscious, then, involves living in a system of irruptions and changes, where something that is fundamentally unknowable in total (as with Buddhist notions of dharma) emerges and contains entities with which one can engage. As this unknowable whole changes, it alters who "we" are. Indeed, building upon Buddhist notions of dharma just as upon Lovecraftian notions of the weird, this unknowability is in fact the world as it really is, that we see only in fragments. In other words, as the world changes, our unconscious apprehension of it changes along with it, and as it does, so do we.

This inhuman world, then, like the world of weird fiction, is already within us. We are, like Lovecraft's protagonists, already other to ourselves. We are motivated by things beyond our control. But this lack of control does not have to be horrific. We are borne upon its flow just as Mon's boat is borne upon the river.

In portraying a weird world populated by hostile beings that have—often—already become a part of us, Lovecraft's point is to render the world uncanny (in Freud's sense, not Todorov's). His work, coming as it did in the 1920s and '30s, pointed to the disquiet presented by a new, more "real" world unveiling itself in futurist art, mass immigration, and new technologies of warfare (i.e., World War I). Lovecraft's doomed protagonists are often scientists, folklorists, artists, or writers who reveal a horrific synergy between these fields.

Like the unconscious, inhuman beings are knowable only by their actions, but they are not reducible to them. Whereas Lady Mother Takhian speaks to us only in numbers, swirls on bark, and dreams, none of my interlocutors would make the argument that this is all that she is capable of doing. For those who slighted her, she caused car crashes and sudden diseases or legal troubles. Indeed, for many of these inhuman beings, action occurs not through their own direct action, but via the influence of their potency upon another. Fern's European husband acts, in Ban Beuk, through Aek's rubber orchard. The Lord of the Fish acts via fishermen who draw in a beuk. Takhian acts via the lottery.

But are the beings that I describe here uncanny? Freud's uncanny is that of middle-class moderns who believe themselves to have surpassed a haunted world (see also Morris 2008). The Freudian uncanny emerges when a thing thought to be overcome is in fact revealed to be still present. This is certainly the case in middle-class circles in Thailand, who escape to high-modern housing developments only to discover that village ghosts have followed them (see Johnson 2014). But, as Rosalind Morris (2008) notes, in a world saturated by ghosts, is there room for the uncanny?

Morris is correct in noting the uncanny's unsuitability to Ban Beuk. But otherworldly does not mean uncanny. Yes, there is an aura of the unknown that lingers upon those beings that are connections to the unknown or the uncertain, upon nagas as well as dams. One is reminded in the presence of such beings that one is subject to powers that are not able to be fully understood. But these beings might evoke other emotions: awe in addition to fear, curiosity and amusement in addition to unsettlement. These are feelings that invite desire just as often as they provoke panic. Recall Lert's anxiety over his vision of a distant, collapsing dam juxtaposed with Thip's curiosity over the possibility of a spirit living next door to her. Dread and awe are two sides of the inhuman.

Ban Beuk, for all of its marginality vis-à-vis Bangkok, Beijing, and other seats of government, is caught at the nexus of different sources of hidden power. Indeed, one can argue that it is because of its marginality that it is so. The possibility of the border is one such veil hiding these sources of power, enabling as it does alternate ways of envisioning the state, new kinds of people (potential workers, lovers, or dangers), or the potential the border holds as a resource in itself. But there are other borders—ones that separate not only nations, but people from people, other-than-human entities from us, and us from aspects of ourselves. Foreign factories and foreign lovers hold their own sources of potential risk and profit as well as new dreams. New cash crops and farming techniques hold new possibilities if one can manipulate the foreign powers within them properly. Our own sleeping minds might open a channel to powerful patrons that we cannot see in waking life. Finally, the river itself is a source of potency: the new biota within it, the spirits that control it, and, of course, its flow.

Such sources of potency enable actions to yield profit when ordinarily they do not. An ordinary migrant worker like Jiap without a grand fate (sata-kam) might not be able to make much money in Bangkok, between everyday exploitation and low wages, but if she can charm Lady Mother Takhian into sending a message (and then properly read it), she might just be able to catch a lucky break. Aek cannot buy a rubber plantation on his own, but using the money Fern gets from having successfully wooed a foreign spouse, he can—providing that he is able to maintain Fern's interest. While Mon's naga is dead, its return as a phi (ghost) provides new sources of cash instead of fish. A visiting foreign researcher might suddenly awaken the interest of a previously dormant jao in an island nearby.

At the present moment, as at other moments of flux in Isan history, established sources of power are open to challenge. Fish and their divine lords wane as cash and its new gods rise. Where this leaves the residents of Ban Beuk is in a search to discover the means to access new sources of potential and the means to avoid their dangers. In preserving the response, "maybe," one preserves its power. But one can dwell with this "maybe" in new ways. A changed material and potential world involves new techniques—the hermit Pho Khao, for instance, in lieu of Mae Oi, or the car battery in lieu of a failing luang mong.

Infrastructure is not exempt from this world. Christina Schwenkel (2017) argues that the "haunted infrastructures" of Vietnam act as conduits for collective resistance against development projects, allowing for critiques of discourses that are otherwise hegemonic (see Harms 2012). In Thailand, too, spirits in infrastructure (airports, for instance; see Ferguson 2014) showcase anxieties that are at the same time political and religious. In my previous work (Johnson 2013), I have taken a similar perspective upon the uncanny presence of ghosts in high-modern architecture in Chiang Mai.

Here, I take a slightly different tack. The Jinghong Dam, for Lert, is not haunted. Rather, it is that which haunts. Similarly, the discovery of ancient tree trunks under the city does not provide resistance to development; rather, they hold an opportunity to acquire a bit of magic oneself. Hirokazu Miyazaki (2004), building upon Ernst Bloch, describes hope as discovering that reality is in a state of "not-yet," and a hopeful moment as that time when we feel like we may still influence this potentiality—here, then, my interlocutors find those who see and can act upon this state of being.

How, then, to think about beings with which we live—the naga, the foreign husband, the dam—but which hide behind particular barriers to knowledge, perception, or access? Here are not just human and nonhuman worlds, but ones that rely upon this distance for their power. Are these, too, nonhumans?

We must find a better word for these things than "nonhuman" or "other-than-human." As the literature on the "nonhuman turn" (Grusin 2015; Haraway 2016; Tsing 2015) would seem to indicate, such beings are rarely mentioned (Bubandt 2017 is an exception). Indeed, speaking of the nonhuman places a particular frame atop the lived worlds of my interlocutors, one where liver flukes exist and nagas do not. It, in short, silences the otherness of Mekong worlds.

But there are other silencings. If we accept the ontological world of my interlocutors as a world, and paint a portrait where nagas roil beneath the surface of the river and certain islands have ghostly kings, we silence its uncertainty, and cordon it off to some Thai-Lao reality that is not ours. At worst, we patronize our interlocutors and assume that they believe certain realities that we know are otherwise. We assume that Mon does not mean it when he replies, "Maybe." We reach an impasse when Pla hangs on every word from the island king and Lert mocks. While de la Cadena and Blaser (2018) propose a "pluriverse," where some actors are present to some other actors but not to all (e.g., a political project that holds within it mountain spirits that only some within the project accept as ontologically real), what of those beings that are sometimes real, but not always, to a particular person? What of my own possible jao of Bird Island (or, perhaps, its tree)? What of those things that might be one thing, might be another, but, regardless, are still there? What of doubt, or a world irreducible to our perceptions of it?

Scholarship on animism has long explored the boundaries of personhood, and how nonhumans can readily be given such status. Guido Sprenger (2018) as well as Naveh and Bird-David (2014) have explored how animist notions of personhood, previously self-evident when applied to nonhumans, become complicated when these nonhumans also become enmeshed in market relations. For instance, for Sprenger (2018, 281), Jru' (upland Lao) rituals that confer personhood on land fall out of use when cash crops enter the market.

Sprenger rightfully focuses upon the rituals undertaken to open lines of communication between distant spirits and the Jru' (and not Jru' suppositions of the interiority of spirits). But here, the notions of "nonhuman" and "person" seem deficient. The subject positions and the very identities of the beings that I describe here are not only unknown, they are unknowable. Thip cannot inhabit the subject position of the island that sends me dreams, and only offers tentative suppositions as to its desires and identity. Indeed, she guesses that it might not even exist in the way that she thinks. Similarly, Pong has no way of knowing the Chinese dam controller's intentions regarding the weekly release of water from Jinghong, and Aek must guess at the attentions and appeal of Fern's foreign husband. To do so would be impossible.

Here, then, there is something unassimilable. In this, I take inspiration from the work of James Siegel. In his essay "The Hypnotist," Siegel (2011) points to the emergence of new uncanny figures in the wake of the 2004 tsunami in Aceh. Of these, one is the hypnotist, a being that entrances people on the street and takes their jewels, but is forgotten by the victims afterward and is never actually seen. For Siegel, the hypnotist is significant because he is known "only by his effects and never through experience as it is remembered" (2011, 113), a description that lines up neatly with Agrippa's "occult."

But compare for a moment the hypnotist as a postdisaster being with Anna Tsing's (2015) now-famous example of the matsutake growing out of "blasted landscapes," or the hybrid species that she, Gan, Bubandt, and Swanson term "ghosts and monsters of the Anthropocene" (Tsing et al. 2017). In these examples, new biota emerge into new landscapes, and individuals forge new rhizomatic ways of dealing with (and in the case of the matsutake, prospering from) it. The hypnotist here, as with Mon's naga, is something a little different. While it also emerges from disaster, it is by definition unable to be clearly witnessed—it is, like one of the great whirlpools that sometimes form on the surface of the Mekong, an effect in its motion but at its heart an absence. Yet despite this absence, individuals seek it out for the very potency that such an absence provides.

My point here is that an examination of nonhuman agency must bring to bear the nonhuman and inhuman world in which our interlocutors live. And this involves an everyday interaction with beings who, like Wittgenstein's famous lion, are uninhabitable. One cannot guess what they are thinking, although one can try to divine what they will do.

I have proposed *the inhuman* as a term to refer to these beings whose subject position is beyond human perception or imagination. The dam, the foreigner, the spirit, even the depths of the river here seem to fit this description. This is not, of course, to be taken too literally—poor Fern's cuckolded husband is certainly human from his own point of view—but rather to highlight how Fern, Aek, Ink, and Nong saw his thoughts as inscrutable, and only his actions as interpretable.

The inhuman presents a counterpoint to a materialist turn in anthropology that, while it readily embraces the uncertain (Rojas n.d.; Whitington 2018) in ecological systems, has downplayed the cosmological, the supernatural, the uncanny, and others. I have made the argument here that, for my interlocutors, the natural, the economic, and the supernatural blend. Bait and spells, for Pong, are variations on how one gets fish into a net, and the unpredictability of rubber prices and the love of foreign husbands are both complications on the theme of waiting for Fern and Aek.

The word is not perfect. *Inhuman* too quickly conjures *inhumane*, a moral valence that I do not seek to import here. I do not mean to represent, for instance, the inhumanity of militaries (like the Thai military) that treat their citizens as targets for repression or torture, but rather to recognize the fundamental unknowability of certain actors.

The inhuman, too, allows for the recognition of fuzzy boundaries to ontological worlds. It complicates claims to a Thai or Lao ontology that features certain beings as possibilities and not others. Instead, the things that exist in the world might be in doubt, in flux, or both. Inhuman things are, like Stevenson's raven, "there," but what they really are is unclear. Thip suggests something speaks to me, but she knows not what. While Pong and Lert make offerings to the Lord of the Fish, Mon scoffs. At the same time, Mon suggests that "maybe" Pho Khao has blessed my job search.

"YOU DO NOT BELIEVE IN ME"

Here, I return to the island king's words as he lays out his own knowledge and his own failings vis-à-vis the river, history, infrastructure, and epistemology. In each of these realms, something about Ban Beuk has changed. The region remains politically subordinate to Bangkok, a fact underlined by the repression of Red Shirt protestors in 2010, individuals largely drawn from the northeast. The river's fisheries have withered. Dam construction continues apace, despite its deleterious effects upon downstream communities. The island king's shouts are angry retorts to a world that is in flux, one where he faces his own withdrawal.

But to whom is the island king speaking? His interlocutor is silent. Mae Oi's head is bowed, her eyes shut tight. The island king, already a source of potency that lies beyond immediate perception, speaks to something even more distant. One could speculate that he speaks to the world that is coming, but I do not know. Here, from anthropologist to medium, medium to island king, island king to unknown outer interlocutor, is a chain stretching past the limits of my sight just as much as Mae Oi's. You, the reader of this book, are one more link further removed from whatever spoke that day.

Mekong worlds speak to the necessity of a particular kind of excess—a distant potency that enables present techniques to function (e.g., fish to come into a net), or disasters to appear (e.g., a distant dam creates a flood). But this is not simply a revisitation of Malinowski's ([1935] 1978) garden magic, where magic becomes an extra insurance when an activity is fraught with uncertainty. Rather, this distant potency must hold within it something beyond the boundaries of the known, something that contains within it a kernel of the unknown and unknowable.

Like Siegel's witch (2005), the inhuman elides complete capture in a name or personality. While we may identify Lady Mother Takhian, for instance, we do not completely know what she is capable of, or if we are correct in addressing her as Lady Mother Takhian at all. Thus, a shadow hangs over the Mekong, a shadow of both the messianic and apocalyptic potency of distant forces: the dam, China, foreign capital, new divinities. But this shadow proves inescapable, just as tracing the contours of the place from where exactly it is cast proves impossible. But, for my interlocutors as for us, this is not an end to action. One must live with the unknowable, harness it, and learn how to dwell with it even as it in turn slips from our grasp.

INTRODUCTION: THROUGH A GLASS, DARKLY

1   I transcribe what Lert said here as he said it. Three dialects were spoken in the area where I conducted fieldwork. Central Thai remains hegemonic and is the language of education and administration, while most residents spoke either Northern Lao or Vientiane Lao. I am fluent in all three, although much more comfortable in Central Thai. I spoke Vientiane Lao—heavily interspersed with Central Thai terms—with Lert.

2   All names are pseudonyms. When I refer to municipal zones, I am translating from the Thai terms. Here, *town* refers to a *baan*, *subdistrict* refers to *tambol*, *district* refers to *amphoe*, and *province* to *jangwat*. I am specific only to the jangwat level (Nong Khai). Here, *thammasat* is a Lao pronunciation of what in Central Thai would be *thammachat*. It has nothing to do with the term for Dharmic law, also pronounced *thammasat*.

3   The choice here to use *world* at times and *world-making project* at others is deliberate. As I argue in this book, a Buddhist world (and a "weird" world) is one that exists, but which is inaccessible in its entirety. Thus, a world-making project refers to the actions that reveal portions of the world, and *world* refers to the reality that is (dharma) both inside and outside of human action.

4   While climate change and the unpredictability of the monsoon are issues for the Mekong, the dam is a far more proximate and influential force. The Anthropocene, indicating as it does a world in which human forces are inseparable from nonhuman forces, encapsulates both carbon spat into the air and concrete slung across rivers—both are environment-changing human actions.

5   Each of these words is identically romanized in the two languages (Lao and Thai) used in my fieldwork, although tone, unmarked in romanization, differs.

6   Yai is, of course, not entirely correct. The Mekong has its headwaters in Tibet, certainly near snow-covered mountains but far from the England that she often assumed was my birthplace (however, I was born in the Norfolk in Virginia, not the UK). I could not be American, Yai suggested, as I was too thin and small to have grown up on pizza and hamburgers. As another example of Yai's understanding of geography, she became convinced that I had died during an earthquake in Nepal in 2015, as the Himalayas were, for her, next to meuang farang.

7   Thai and Lao nicknames—used far more often than real names—are often very different from official names, and often are drawn from pop culture. Yai's son's nickname was Superman, shortened to Man. She had named her children after the cartoons she watched while pregnant.

8   *Gypsy* and *Lapp* are offensive terms. I reproduce them here because Mauss used them and because more readers would recognize these terms than *Roma* or *Saami*.

9   Benjamin Baumann chooses just this word—*numinal*—to describe the Thai concept of *phi* (ghost, spirit). I use it here to underscore the idea of a being in touch with something beyond individual ken.

10 Dan Lusthaus (2002) describes a "Buddhist phenomenology" in a rather different manner than I do here, via a deep reading of Mahayana texts.

11 I transliterate the term *charoen* in accordance with the Royal Thai system (Johnson 2014). However, this does an injustice to the consonant *j*, which is an unaspirated *ch*. It is neither the full *ch* as in English (e.g., *char*) nor the voiced *j* (e.g., *jar*), but something in between the two.

12 "Buddha" is not a name but a title for one who has achieved this status. In Theravada tradition, only Siddhartha Gautama has achieved Buddha status, roughly 2,562 years ago.

13 In her analysis of medical health professionals in Thailand, Daena Aki Funahashi (2016) discusses the use of the term *panya*, "wisdom." For Funahashi, invocations of these differential levels of panya by Thai experts was a way to legitimate a hierarchical form of governance. Indeed, this is the implication of such a system. But here I seek to look at the differential invocation of wisdom and knowledge on a more personal level.

14 I am indebted to Daena Funahashi for this term.

15 Haraway also mentions Lovecraft's racism and rejects it as a symbol of xenophobia, while at the same time appropriating the word *Cthulhu* in her own way.

16 Here I am using a romanization of the Thai term for the place. A Lao romanization would be Sainyabuli or Xayabuli.

17 American readers might imagine Smithfield, Springfield, and the slightly more exotic Catfishfield.

18 See Sopranzetti (2012; 2017b) for more detail.

19 I do not name the district seat (amphoe) for confidentiality purposes. It is a town of about three thousand people (i.e., everything within the central tambol), about thirty minutes' drive from Ban Beuk. Here, I refer to it simply as "the district head" or "the district seat."

20 The Chinese *Lancang* may have a relationship with the Lao *Lanxang* or Thai *Lanchang*, "One Million Elephants," the name of the historical Lao kingdom centered on the banks of the Mekong. Such a Tai-langauge link would be unsurprising, as Xisuangbanna, where the Mekong flows last before it enters Southeast Asia, is dominated by Lue speakers, a language close to Lao. Indeed, *Xisuangbanna* is a sinification of *Sip-song panna* (twelve principalities).

21 Indeed, the wealthiest man in the village, Pong, had worked for a time as unskilled labor in Taiwan. To find villagers who were too wealthy for migrant work, one had to go to the district seat.

1 Also relevant here is how such barriers enable things—Anna Tsing's (2005) "friction."

2 I do not mean to make too much of this characterization of Hindu/Buddhist Thailand and animist Laos (although see Holt 2009). Certainly Lao kings also drew from the same Indic well as did Thai ones; the difference being that non-Buddhist populations were closer at hand for Lao lords.

3 I do not mean to downplay political economy here. While in theory the divine presence enabled the loyalty of subjects, in practice things could differ.

4 Readers should note the difference between Taksin, the king, and Thaksin, the politician. The names differ in terms of aspiration and initial vowel length, although some, noting the similarities (see Wassana 2009), suggest that Thaksin's own conflicts with the monarchy might be a form of retribution on behalf of a karmic ancestor.

5 Taksin was deposed soon after by another military leader, the ancestor of the present-day Chakri dynasty, who moved the capital to its present location and began the process of naming monarchs for Vishnu's avatar, Rama.

6 Sukhothai, of course, existed. It was a thirteen-century northern Thai polity and later competitor with Ayutthaya. But much of its history was manufactured along nationalist lines during the nineteenth century, and certain artifacts from that era (e.g., the Ramkhamhaeng stele) are of dubious lineage. For Thai monarchists, Sukhothai emblematized a benevolent paternal despotism, and for Thai leftists (cf. Jit Phumisak), Sukhothai offered a harbor from Angkorean slavery.

7 *Tai* refers to the linguistic family, *Thai* refers to the nation-state.

8 Jin Haw refers to Yunnanese Muslims that had long been traders in the north. But following the Taiping Rebellion in the mid-nineteenth century, a defeated Chinese army fled south, pillaging as it went, and when they reached Laos, the Lao referred to them also as *jin haw*, and to the wars that followed as the "suppression of the haw."

9 Theravada Buddhism holds that only Siddhartha Gautama achieved Buddha status. However, in Theravada millenarianism, a new Buddha, Maitreya, will come to rescue humanity from a dark age.

10 To be fair to Walker, here he discusses not the Holy Man revolts of 1901 Isan, but the Phrae uprising a few provinces away in the same year.

11 *Haw* is a misnomer. The *jin haw* were a group of Yunnanese Muslims that operated trading caravans through the region. When the Taiping Black Flag rebels escaped the Chinese crackdown, Lao and Thai observers lumped these newcomers in with the preexisting Haw.

12 Naturally, opium warlords such as Khun Sa or the remnants of the Kuomintang resident in Thailand were also globally and regionally interconnected: the former was a Burmese Shan warlord resident in Thailand, and the latter were right-wing revolutionaries from China who escaped to Thailand after the revolution and began dealing in heroin as a means to purchase arms.

13 Elections in 2019 were disputed. The military-aligned party had arranged 250 votes by appointed "good people," thus giving them a significant advantage. They won,

thus technically ending military rule, but foreign observers cast doubt on the election's legitimacy.

14   The Sayaburi Hydroelectric Power Project estimates its own production at 7,370 GWh annually.

15   Mon and others found this word amusing. The term *khreuang* in Thai refers to heavy machinery: engines, airplanes, and so on. While in their version of Lao, Ban Beuk residents had adopted the Thai meaning, on the other bank *khreuang* just means "stuff," a meaning preserved in some Thai usage: *khreuang tom yam* indicates a preassembled bag for making tom yam soup stock.

16   Here, I have juxtaposed Sulak with those arguing against lèse-majesté. In fact, Sulak himself, a self-avowed royalist, has repeatedly run afoul of the lèse-majesté laws in his blunt talk on history and politics and his opposition to knee-jerk nationalism and royalism. I hope that the savvy reader of Thai politics will excuse my having lumped Sulak on the side of apologists for lèse-majesté; I quote Sulak here as his is the most thoughtful and articulate defense of a morally founded system of governance.

17   There are a few jokes here. First of all, the platform is hardly luxurious, so hardly a resort. Second, Lao does not have the heavily rolled *r* of Thai—indeed, being able to roll one's *rs* is a hallmark of Bangkokian upper-class speech. Lao replaces most *rs* in Thai words with *h* or *l* sounds. Thus, for Lao speakers (including the vast majority of Ban Beuk's residents), *resort* would be pronounced "lisort." The chief inspector, although he is originally from southern Isan, is perfectly capable of speaking Central Thai with a Bangkokian accent, but using the stigmatized local dialect was a marker of cultural intimacy.

18   I could never evaluate the chief inspector's English proficiency. Once, he called me over and said to me in a deep, menacing voice, in Thai, "Andrew. I know what you are doing. I know what you intend to do here." "What?" I responded, terrified. "You are doing, [in English] *qualitative research*. Is that correct?"

19   I never saw them, if they exist.

CHAPTER TWO: RIVER BEINGS

1   *Watermen* denotes working-class, generally white men who make a livelihood on the water. Mon, were he to live on the Chesapeake, would be a waterman.

2   *Phi* means "ghost" in Thai, but it also (in this context) refers to a corpse.

3   *Phi* here, being both "spirit" and "corpse," complicates a Western notion of a split between spirit and materiality. In chapter 5, I go into more detail.

4   Read further for this story.

5   Four years later, on a subsequent visit in 2019, Mon still referred to me as "the guy who throws back perfectly good fish."

6   In a rare public display of sibling rivalry, Mon's younger brother Nai posted on Facebook a video of Mon fishing. Mon is drawing up his net, all the while saying, "There's something big in here. I can feel it. I've got something big. A fish, for sure. A big fish." When Mon pulls the net aboard, a large rotten stick is caught in the net. Nai breaks into peals of laughter and announces, "Ban Beuk: come and catch a stick here!"

7　A naga would be larger, (super)naturally.

8　For obvious reasons, I keep any identifying information out of this section.

9　This is a reference to the 2006 novel *The Road*, which depicts a hopeless postnuclear landscape.

CHAPTER THREE: DWELLING UNDER DISTANT SUNS

1　This is Central Thai, and I leave it as such as the position is explicitly a Bangkok-oriented one. Assistants (phu chuai) were the lowest rung on the provincial hierarchy, but some assistants such as Mon would leverage their status in the village to—eventually—rise as far as subdistrict head (*kamnan*).

2　At the time of writing (mid-2019), he is still in Korea.

3　While Thailand, in comparison with many countries worldwide, appears quite tolerant of homosexuality and third genders, migrant labor circles seem to be among the most homophobic. Dress or behavior that was seen as overly feminine or that might indicate homosexuality was routinely mocked. For instance, once I wore a flowery shirt, a gift from Yai, and spent the afternoon having men (Lo, for one) plucking at my shirt and muttering *kathoey* (a term for Thailand's third gender, but here used in a derogatory and homophobic fashion).

4　The conflict may have been regional. Especially in Thailand's north and northeast, menstruation is considered spiritually polluting in ways not shared by central, southern, or Sino-Thai communities (see Johnson [2014] for a northern Thai example). All at the drinking table (men and women alike) agreed that cleaning another person's menses-stained underwear was far worse than cleaning underwear stained with feces.

5　Johan Lindquist (2010) raises the entirely appropriate point that research has too often focused on laborers and ignored the vital role that recruiters play in this interstitial space. He is correct in this, and my characterization of recruiters as potential con artists does nothing to fill this lacuna. I simply note here that I am representing recruiters just as Lert and others in Ban Beuk did.

6　This aside is significant. Lert sees his experience abroad as something that brings him closer to me. We are both cosmopolitans, in Lert's characterization, and he should be able to communicate with me in my own language.

7　Lert's geopolitical analysis is completely correct. Chinese belt-and-road initiatives often use unfair trade deals as penalties for those defaulting on infrastructure loans (see Doig 2018).

8　Prices recovered somewhat in 2019.

9　The word is Indonesian, not Thai.

10　While Ban Beuk farmers saw this as a clear example of a scam, it is typical agribusiness practice in the United States.

11　An epicanthic fold is a part of the eyelid present in some populations, primarily in East Asia. While in East Asia (and among upper-class Thais) many women and some men undergo plastic surgery to remove the fold by making a higher nasal bridge, among many in Thailand the presence of an epicanthic fold indicated East Asian ancestry and was therefore attractive.

12 The word *faen*, derived from the English "girlfriend/boyfriend," can mean anything ranging from *lover* to *spouse*. I translate it here as *fiancée* owing to Mon's future plans. Because of the diversity of English terms for a romantic partner, I stick to the Thai here.

13 Mon uses the more polite term *Arab* rather than the usual term *khaek*.

14 Here, I am being deliberately vague owing not to political or legal concerns, but to personal sensibilities. Given the sensitivity of the topic discussed, I refer only to general regions (e.g., the Gulf or Europe) to add a further layer of anonymity for my—already pseudonymous—interlocutors. Aek and Fern as I present them here could be one of any number of similar couples across Isan.

15 Here, Fern is speaking Central Thai to me, although Fern spoke with Aek in Lao, the local language in Ban Beuk. For "work," *thamngaan,* the Lao would be *het wiak.* Fern, more than any other Ban Beuk resident, addressed me in Central Thai.

16 Tourism in general remained a bright spot for the Thai economy owing to the meteoric rise in Chinese tourists. Large Chinese tours, though, never came through Ban Beuk.

17 Another significant oversight in many of the aforementioned studies is an excessive attention to international sex work, rather than to a domestic clientele. Here, my data do not help, as Fa and Nong worked in internationally oriented circuits. Among my male informants in Ban Beuk, some visited brothels run and staffed by Laotian syndicates, on both the Thai and Lao sides of the border.

18 One limitation of my data lies in the fact that my interactions were primarily with the male partners: Mon, Ink, and Aek. While I met and spoke with Fa, Nong, and Fern, I never did so alone and cannot claim to speak for their aspirations unfiltered by the presence of their partner or my own role as friend of their partner. Further, to demand to speak with them alone would have been methodologically problematic for a male researcher of a similar age.

19 I do not mean to imply that all or even most marriages to foreign spouses in Isan or Ban Beuk began in a commercial manner (see Esara 2009, 420).

20 Here, politeness forbade me from asking "and your husband?" as at the time Fern was leaning on Aek's arm and discussing how nice the house would be in terms that implied they would be in the space together.

21 I am grateful to Daena Funahashi for this turn of phrase.

22 I highlight this caution to bring to light potentially distracting slips we may make in looking at the excess of Fern's return. The first is to side with community gatekeepers like Pong or Pla (who was not even from Ban Beuk), who told me that Fern's party, with its violence and alcohol abuse, was somehow pathological or not typical of Songkran homecomings. Underlying this view is an urge to present Ban Beuk in a positive light versus the economic, social, and environmental disruption the community faces, and to combat the too-pervasive stereotypes in the Thai press of Isan villagers as uncouth peasants. From an academic angle, those seeking to present models of rural community cohesion and solidarity (Chatthip 1999) might also see a focus on violence and alcohol abuse as emphasizing undesirable or pathological elements (sometimes classed as foreign or capitalist) rather than positive ones.

23 Everyday Thai racial categories erase a lot of geographical and historical nuance. *Farang* refers to Caucasian-appearing people, who are assumed to be Christian. Most residents of the United States, Europe, and Australia are assumed to be farang (with the exception of African Americans). The term is originally Persian, meaning "French." Farang are assumed to be uncaring and greedy, but fashionable and technologically savvy. *Khaek*, literally "guest," refers to South Asians and Muslims more broadly—the line between Hindu and Muslim here is blurred. In Ban Beuk, residents displayed a great deal of antipathy toward khaek and Muslims in particular. Africans and African Americans are often termed *nikro*, a loan of the English *Negro*, and a few of my interlocutors had unknowingly borrowed racist slurs from popular American music that they, to my embarrassment, deployed frequently. East Asians and other Southeast Asians were referred to by country of origin: for example, *jiin* (Chinese), *kao-li* (Korean), *yiiphun* (Japanese). Concepts such as "Japanese American" were hard to convey.

24 Normally, men do this at one point in their lives, often on the occasion of the father's death.

25 In Thai (*khae khwam cheua*), this is not as dismissive as it sounds, although it is a way of ending the conversation.

CHAPTER FOUR: THE RIVER GREW TIRED OF US

1 Part of this section has been published as "Land and Lordship: Royal Devotion, Spirit Cults, and the Geo-body" (Johnson 2017).

2 Indeed, Visisya notes that the (female) mediums would touch the (male) monks' heads in blessing, a move that is in radical departure from normal rules of comportment for Buddhist monks.

3 I take Justin McDaniel's (2013) admonition that Narai (Vishnu), Phraphikanet (Ganesha), and other Hindu deities in Thailand are as Buddhist as Jehovah is Christian, and scholars rightfully should avoid the label "Hindu" when speaking of them. But here, I ask his indulgence to use the term. In addressing an audience perhaps unfamiliar with Theravada Buddhism, I seek to conjure the correct image and note Theravada's closer ties with Hindu iconography than, say, the Mahayana Buddhism of China, Japan, Vietnam, and Korea.

4 The closest term in English might be *outlaw* (see Fiskesjö 2012).

5 Tambiah writes *tiam* with an unaspirated *t*, whereas I use *thiam* to note the word's aspiration.

6 Pali is the sacred language of Theravada Buddhism. It is the language of the Theravada texts and is normally written in a Cambodian-derived script. For those more familiar with Western religions, one might imagine the role of Latin in the older Catholic Church.

7 Bluntly, the monk made sexual advances toward young men. When I visited him, he would comment on how handsome I was (a relatively standard thing to do in Thai conversation, providing that one is handsome) and, once, made me sit next to him, out of sight of windows or doors, and placed his hand high on my knee, only to move it swiftly when another monk suddenly came in. He later invited me to

stay at the temple overnight. It is true that physical contact between men is much more accepted in Thailand than in my native (white, Scandinavian American, middle-class) United States, but given the monk's reputation, everyone I spoke with agreed that this was suspicious behavior.

8   There is a small Christian community in the district seat that I do not mention here, as none of my interlocutors were Christian and I did not know of any Christians in Ban Beuk. I met missionaries only once—a Finnish man who approached me while I was eating at the district seat. He had been having a hard time finding people who spoke English (he spoke neither Thai nor Lao). "Have you heard of Jesus?" he asked me, to which I replied that I was familiar with the name. "Well," the missionary announced, "he's coming back."

9   This snippet was previously published in November 2016 as "Ghosts Can Be People: Physicality and Spirits in Thailand's Northeast," in *Global Modernities and the (Re-)emergence of Ghosts—Voices from around the World*, Global South Studies Center, University of Cologne, Germany, http://voices.uni-koeln.de/2016-2/ghostscanbepeople.

10 River beings and their human marriages feature in many Southeast Asian stories, ancient and present-day. For instance, thirteenth-century Chinese traveler Zhou Daguan reported that the Angkorean (ancient Cambodian) king had a naga queen (see Zhou 2007). Similarly, surrealist Mekong region–born director Apichatpong Weerasethakul (2010) depicts a union between an Isan princess and an amorous catfish in his *Uncle Boonmee Who Can Recall His Past Lives*.

11 My prounouns switch here. As the island king is masculine and Mae Oi feminine, I assign *he/his/him* to those actions attributed to the king, and *she/her* to features of Mae Oi's body. Lao has no such gendered distinctions, although one's pronouns change with status.

12 The jao here is using extremely familiar—to the point of rudeness—terms of address. Imagine a rough old warrior-king, a Lao version of a Viking chief, and it will conjure the right image. Also, *ratsadon* is an unusual word here—the expected word might be *children*, as in "my subjects."

13 Here, "village" (*baan*) could be interpreted as village, nation, or community.

14 Naturally, there are stark differences between nat and jao. Whereas jao are innumerable, there is a specific number of nat. Whereas *jao* refers to humans as well as spirits, *nat* refers only to angelic spirits.

REFERENCES

Agrippa, Henrich Cornelius. 2018. *Three Books of Occult Philosophy or Magic.* New York: CreateSpace.

Allison, Anne. 2013. *Precarious Japan.* Durham, NC: Duke University Press.

Alpern, Stephen I. 1975. "Insurgency in Northeast Thailand: A New Cause for Alarm." *Asian Survey* 15, no. 8: 684–92.

Anan Ganjanapan. 1984. "The Idiom of Phii Ka': Peasant Conception of Class Differentiation in Northern Thailand. *Australian Journal of Anthropology* 14, no. 4: 325–29.

Anand, Nikhil, Akhil Gupta, and Hannah Appel. 2018. *The Promise of Infrastructure.* Durham, NC: Duke University Press.

Anderson, Benedict. 1990. "The Idea of Power in Javanese Culture." In *Language and Power: Exploring Political Cultures in Indonesia,* 17–77. Ithaca, NY: Cornell University Press.

Anderson, Benedict. 2016. *Imagined Communities: Reflections on the Origin and Spread of Nationalism.* Rev. ed. New York: Verso.

Apichatpong Weerasethakul, dir. 2010. *Uncle Boonmee Who Can Recall His Past Lives* [film]. Kick the Machine. 114 minutes.

Århem, Kaj. 2015. "Southeast Asian Animism: A Dialogue with Amerindian Perspectivism." In *Animism in Southeast Asia,* edited by Kaj Århem and Guido Sprenger, 279–301. London: Routledge.

Arias, M. E., T. A. Cochrane, D. Norton, T. J. Killeen, and P. Khon. 2013. "The Flood Pulse as the Underlying Driver of Vegetation in the Largest Wetland and Fishery of the Mekong Basin." *Ambio* 42, no. 7: 864–76.

Asaree Thaitrakulpanich. 2017. "Thais Working in Korea Are Dying in Droves." *Khao Sod English,* December 13.

Bachelard, Gaston. 1999. *Water and Dreams: An Essay on the Imagination of Matter.* 3rd ed. Translated by Edith R. Farrell. Dallas: Dallas Institute of Humanities and Culture.

Baird, Ian. 2013. "Millenarian Movements in Southern Laos and Northeastern Siam (Thailand) at the Turn of the Twentieth Century: Reconsidering the Involvement of the Champassak Royal House." *South East Asia Research* 21, no. 2: 257–79.

Baird, Ian. 2017. "Biography and Borderlands: Chao Sone Bouttarobol, A Champassak Royal, and Thailand, Laos, and Cambodia." *TRaNS: Trans-Regional and -National Studies of Southeast Asia* 5, no. 2: 269–95.

Baird, Ian, and W. Nathan Green. 2016. "Capitalizing on Compensation: Hydropower, Resettlement and the Commodification and Decommodification of Nature-Society Relations in Southern Laos." *Annals of the American Association of Geographers* 106: 1–21.

Bakker, Karen. 2004. *An Uncooperative Commodity: Privatizing Water in England and Wales*. Oxford: Oxford Geographical and Environmental Studies.

Banchob Sripa, Paul Brindley, Jason Mulvenna, Thewarach Laha, Michael Smout, Eimorn Mairiang, Jeffrey Bethony, and Alex Loukas. 2012. "The Tumorigenic Liver Fluke *Opisthorchis viverrini*: Multiple Pathways to Cancer." *Trends in Parasitology* 28, no. 10: 395–407.

Baran, Eric, Eric Guerin, and Joshua Nasielski. 2015. *Fish, Sediment and Dams in the Mekong*. Penang: WorldFish and CGIAR Research Program on Water, Land, and Ecosystems.

Baumann, Benjamin. 2014. "From Filth-Ghost to Khmer-Witch: Phi Krasue's Changing Cinematic Construction and Its Symbolism." *Horror Studies* 5, no. 2: 183–96.

BBC News. 2018. "Laos Hydroelectric Power Ambitions under Scrutiny." July 24. https://www.bbc.com/news/world-asia-44936378.

Bear, Laura. 2014. "Doubt, Conflict, Mediation: The Anthropology of Modern Time." *Journal of the Royal Anthropological Institute*, April 14, 3–30.

Bennett, Jane. 2010. *Vibrant Matter: A Political Ecology of Things*. Durham, NC: Duke University Press.

Bergson, Henri. 1930. "Le possible et le réel." In *La pensée et le mouvant: Essais et conférences*, 99–116. Paris: Les Presses universitaires de France.

Billé, Franck. 2018. "Skinworlds: Borders, Haptics, Topologies." *Environment and Planning D: Society and Space* 36, no. 1. https://doi.org/10.1177/0263775817735106.

Bird-David, Nurit. 1999. "'Animism' Revisited: Personhood, Environment, and Relational Epistemology." *Current Anthropology* 40, no. S1: S67–S91.

Bishop, Ryan, and Lillian S. Robinson. 1998. *Night Market: Sexual Cultures and the Thai Economic Miracle*. New York: Routledge.

Bowie, Katherine. 2014. "The Saint with Indra's Sword: Kruubaa Srivichai and Buddhist Millenarianism in Northern Thailand." *Comparative Studies in Society and History* 56, no. 3, 681–713.

Breckenridge, Carol A., Sheldon Pollock, Homi K. Bhabha, and Dipesh Chakrabarty. 2002. *Cosmopolitanism*. Durham, NC: Duke University Press.

Breiner, Josh. 2018. "Thai Workers in Israeli Border Communities Traumatized after Gaza Violence." *Haaretz*, August 13. https://www.haaretz.com/israel-news/.premium-thai-workers-in-border-communities-traumatized-after-gaza-violence-1.6365738. Accessed December 26, 2019.

Bubandt, Nils. 2014. *The Empty Seashell: Witchcraft and Doubt on an Indonesian Island*. Ithaca, NY: Cornell University Press.

Bubandt, Nils. 2017. "Haunted Geologies: Spirits, Stones, and the Necropolitics of the Anthropocene." In *Arts of Living on a Damaged Planet*, edited by Anna L. Tsing, Heather Anne Swanson, Elaine Gan, and Nils Bubandt, G121–42. Minneapolis: University of Minnesota Press.

Campbell, Stephen. 2018. *Border Capitalism, Disrupted: Precarity and Struggle in a Southeast Asian Industrial Zone*. Ithaca, NY: Cornell ILR Press.

Cao Yin and Ma Danning. 2016. "China Releases Water from Dam to Alleviate SE Asia Drought." *China Daily*, March 16. http://www.chinadaily.com.cn/china/2016-03/16/content_23891709.htm.

Cassaniti, Julia. 2006. "Richard G. Condon Prize: Toward a Cultural Psychology of Impermanence in Thailand." *Ethos* 34, no. 1: 58–88.

Cassaniti, Julia. 2014. *Living Buddhism: Mind, Self and Emotion in a Thai Community.* Ithaca, NY: Cornell University Press.

Castaneda, Carlos. 1968. *The Teachings of Don Juan: A Yaqui Way of Knowledge.* Berkeley: University of California Press.

Chatthip Nartsupha. 1984. "The Ideology of Holy Men Revolts." In *History and Peasant Consciousness in South East Asia,* edited by Andrew Turton and Shigeharu Tanabe, 111–34. Osaka: National Museum of Ethnology Senri Ethnological Studies.

Chatthip Nartsupha. 1999. *The Thai Village Economy in the Past.* Translated by Chris Baker and Pasuk Phongpaichit. Chiang Mai: Silkworm Book.

Cochrane, Liam. 2017. "China Wants to Dynamite the Mekong River to Increase Trade." Australian Broadcasting Corporation, May 15. https://www.abc.net.au/news/2017-05-15/china-wants-to-dynamite-the-mekong-river-to-increase-trade/8524008.

Cohen, Erik. 1982. "Thai Girls and Farang Men: The Edge of Ambiguity." *Annals of Tourism Research* 9: 403–28.

Cohen, Erik. 1986. "Lovelorn Farangs: The Correspondence between Foreign Men and Thai Girls." *Anthropological Quarterly* 59, no. 3: 115–27.

Cohen, Erik. 1993. "Open-Ended Prostitution as a Skillful Game of Luck: Opportunities, Risk and Security among Tourist-Oriented Prostitutes in a Bangkok Soi." In *Tourism in South East Asia,* edited by M. Hitchcock, Victor T. King, and Michael J. G. Parnwell, 155–78. London: Routledge.

Cole, Jennifer. 2014. "Producing Value among Malagasy Marriage Migrants in France: Managing Horizons of Expectation." *Current Anthropology* 55, no. S9: S85–S94.

Comaroff, Jean, and John Comaroff. 1999. "Occult Economies and the Violence of Abstraction: Notes from the South African Postcolony." *American Ethnologist* 26, no. 2: 279–303.

Comaroff, John, and Jean Comaroff, eds. 2001. *Millenial Capitalism and the Culture of Neoliberalism.* Durham, NC: Duke University Press.

Condominas, George. 1990. *From Lawa to Mon, from Saa' to Thai: Historical and Anthropological Aspects of Southeast Asian Social Spaces.* Canberra: Australian National University.

Constable, Nicole. 2009. "The Commodification of Intimacy: Marriage, Sex and Reproductive Labor." *Annual Review of Anthropology* 38: 49–64.

Crapanzano, Vincent. 2004. *Imaginative Horizons: An Essay in Literary-Philosophical Anthropology.* Chicago: University of Chicago Press.

Crosson, J. Brent. 2017. "What Possessed You? Spirits, Property, and Political Sovereignty at the Limits of 'Possession.'" *Ethnos* 84: 546–56. https://doi.org/10.1080/00141844.2017.1401704.

Cruikshank, Julie. 2005. *Do Glaciers Listen? Local Knowledge, Colonial Encounters, and Social Imagination.* Seattle: University of Washington Press.

Daniel, Rajesh, and Songphonsak Ratanawilailak. 2011. "Local Institutions and the Politics of Water Management in the Uplands of Northern Thailand." In *Water Rights and Social Justice in the Mekong Region,* edited by Kate Lazarus, 93–111. London: Earthscan.

de la Cadena, Marisol. 2015. *Earth Beings: Ecologies of Practice across Andean Worlds.* Durham, NC: Duke University Press.

de la Cadena, Marisol, and Mario Blaser. 2018. *A World of Many Worlds.* Durham, NC: Duke University Press.

Deleuze, Gilles, and Félix Guattari. 1980. *A Thousand Plateaus: Capitalism and Schizophrenia.* Translated by Brian Massumi. Minneapolis: University of Minnesota Press.

Derrida, Jacques. 2009. *The Beast and the Sovereign, Volume I.* Chicago: University of Chicago Press.

Descola, Philippe. 2013. *Beyond Nature and Culture.* Chicago: University of Chicago Press.

Doig, Will. 2018. *High-Speed Empire: Chinese Expansion and the Future of Southeast Asia.* New York: Columbia Global Reports.

Du Bois, W. E. B. 1994. *The Souls of Black Folk.* New York: Gramercy.

Dugan, Patrick J., Chris Barlow, Angelo A. Agostinho, Eric Baran, Glenn F. Cada, Daqing Chen, and Ian G. Cowx et al. 2010. "Fish Migration, Dams, and Loss of Ecosystem Services in the Mekong Basin." *Ambio* 39, no. 4: 344–48.

Echaubard, Pierre, Banchob Sripa, Frank F. Mallory, and Bruce A. Wilcox. 2016. "The Role of Evolutionary Biology in Research and Control of Liver Flukes in Southeast Asia." *Infection, Genetics and Evolution* 43: 381–97.

Erickson, Amanda. 2018. "Hundreds Missing and Several Dead after Huge Dam Collapses in Laos." *Washington Post,* July 24.

Esara, Pilapa. 2009. "Imagining the Western Husband: Thai Women's Desires for Matrimony, Status and Beauty." *Ethnos: Journal of Anthropology* 74, no. 3: 403–26.

Ferguson, James. 1990. *The Anti-politics Machine: Development, Depoliticization and Bureaucratic Power in Lesotho.* Minneapolis: University of Minnesota Press.

Ferguson, Jane. 2014. "Terminally Haunted: Aviation Ghosts, Hybrid Buddhist Practices, and Disaster Aversion Strategies amongst Airport Workers in Myanmar and Thailand." *Asia Pacific Journal of Anthropology* 15, no. 1: 47–64.

Fiskesjö, Magnus. 2012. "Outlaws, Barbarians, Slaves: Critical Reflections on Agamben's Homo Sacer." *HAU: Journal of Ethnographic Theory* 2: 161–80.

Funahashi, Daena. 2012. "Wrapped in Plastic: Transformation and Alienation in the New Finnish Economy." *Cultural Anthropology* 28, no. 1: 1–21.

Funahashi, Daena. 2016. "Rule by Good People: Health Governance and the Violence of Moral Authority in Thailand." *Cultural Anthropology* 31, no. 1: 107–30.

Funahashi, Daena. 2021. *Untimely Sacrifices: Burnout and the Horror of the Social.* Ithaca, NY: Cornell University Press.

Geertz, Clifford. 1980. *Negara: The Theater State in Nineteenth-Century Bali.* Princeton, NJ: Princeton University Press.

Gilbert, Elizabeth. 2006. *Eat Pray Love: One Woman's Search for Everything across Italy, India, and Indonesia.* New York: Penguin.

Giles, F. H. 1932. "An Account of the Ceremonies and Rites Performed When Catching the Pla Buk, a Species of Catfish Inhabiting the Waters of the River Me Khong, The Northern and Eastern Frontier of Siam." *Journal of the Siam Society* 28, no. 2: 90–113.

Glenn, Cerise L. 2009. "The Power of Black Magic: The Magical Negro and White Salvation in Film." *Journal of Black Studies* 40, no. 2: 135–52.

Goldman, Michael. 2005. *Imperial Nature: The World Bank and Struggles for Social Justice in the Age of Globalization.* New Haven, CT: Yale University Press.

Graeber, David, and Marshall Sahlins. 2017. *On Kings.* Chicago: University of Chicago Press.

Gray, Christine. 1986. "Thailand: The Soteriological State in the 1970s." PhD diss., University of Chicago.

Gray, Christine. 1992. "Royal Words and Their Unroyal Consequences." *Cultural Anthropology* 7, no. 4: 448–63.

Groes-Green, Christian. 2013. "'To Put Men in a Bottle': Eroticism, Kinship, Female Power and Transactional Sex in Maputo, Mozambique." *American Ethnologist* 40, no. 1: 102–17.

Grusin, Richard, ed. 2015. *The Nonhuman Turn.* Minneapolis: University of Minnesota Press.

Han, Clara. 2011. "Symptoms of Another Life: Time, Possibility, and Domestic Relations in Chile's Credit Economy." *Cultural Anthropology* 26, no. 1: 7–32.

Handley, Paul. 2009. *The King Never Smiles: A Biography of Thailand's Bhumibol Adulyadej.* New Haven, CT: Yale University Press.

Haraway, Donna. 1988. "Situated Knowledges: The Science Question in Feminism and the Privilege of Partial Perspective." *Feminist Studies* 14, no. 3: 575–99.

Haraway, Donna J. 2016. *Staying with the Trouble: Making Kin in the Chthulucene.* Durham, NC: Duke University Press.

Harman, Graham. 2012. *Weird Realism: Lovecraft and Philosophy.* New York: John Hunt.

Harms, Erik. 2012. "Beauty as Control in the New Saigon: Eviction, New Urban Zones, and Atomized Dissent in a Southeast Asian City." *American Ethnologist* 39, no. 4: 735–50.

Harms, Erik. 2016. *Luxury and Rubble: Civility and Dispossession in the New Saigon.* Berkeley: University of California Press.

Harper, K. 2005. "'Wild Capitalism' and 'Ecocolonialism': A Tale of Two Rivers." *American Anthropologist* 107, no. 2: 221–33.

Hastrup, Kirsten, and Frida Hastrup, eds. 2016. *Waterworlds: Anthropology in Fluid Environments.* New York: Berghahn.

Heidegger, Martin. 1977. "The Question Concerning Technology." In *The Question Concerning Technology and Other Essays*, 3–35. New York: Harper.

Heidegger, Martin. 1993. "Building Dwelling Thinking." In *Basic Writings*, 343–64. New York: Harper Perennial Modern Thought.

Herbertson, Kirk. 2012. *The Xayaburi Dam: Threatening Food Security in the Mekong.* Oakland, CA: International Rivers.

Herzfeld, Michael. 2002. "The Absent Presence: Discourses of Crypto-Colonialism." *South Atlantic Quarterly* 101, no. 4: 899–926.

Herzfeld, Michael. 2005. *Cultural Intimacy: Social Poetics in the Nation-State.* 2nd ed. New York: Routledge.

Herzfeld, Michael. 2016. *Siege of the Spirits: Community and Polity in Bangkok.* Chicago: University of Chicago Press.

Hesse-Swain, Catherine. 2006. "Programming Beauty and the Absence of 'Na Lao': Popular Thai TV and Identity Formation among Youth in Northeast Thailand." *GeoJournal* 66, no. 3: 257–72.

Hogan, Zeb. 2011. *Imperiled Giant Fish and Mainstream Dams in the Lower Mekong Basin: Assessment of Current Status, Threats, and Mitigation.* Reno: University of Nevada Press.

Holbraad, Martin, and Morden Axel Pedersen. 2017. *The Ontological Turn: An Anthropological Exposition.* Cambridge: Cambridge University Press.

Holt, John Clifford. 2009. *Spirits of the Place: Buddhism and Lao Religious Culture.* Honolulu: University of Hawai'i Press.

International Rivers. 2017. *A Dangerous Trajectory for the Mekong River: Update on the Status of Mekong Mainstream Dams.* Oakland, CA: International Rivers.

Ishii, Miho. 2012. "Acting with Things: Self-Poiesis, Actuality, and Contingency in the Formation of Divine Worlds." *HAU: Journal of Ethnographic Theory* 2, no. 2: 371–88.

Ivarsson, Søren. 2008. *Creating Laos: The Making of a Lao Space between Siam and Indochina, 1860–1945.* Copenhagen: NIAS Monographs.

Jackson, Peter. 1999. "Royal Spirits, Chinese Gods, and Magic Monks: Thailand's Boom-Time Religions of Prosperity." *South East Asia Research* 7, no. 3: 245–320.

Jackson, Peter. 2009. "Markets, Media and Magic: Thailand's Monarch as a 'Virtual Divinity.'" *Inter-Asia Cultural Studies* 10, no. 3: 361–80.

Jackson, Peter. 2010. "Virtual Divinity: A 21st-Century Discourse of Thai Royal Influence." In *Saying the Unsayable: Monarchy and Democracy in Thailand,* edited by Søren Ivarsson and Lotte Isager, 29–60. Copenhagen: Nordic Institute of Asian Studies Press.

Jackson, Peter. 2016. "The Supernaturalization of Thai Political Culture: Thailand's Magical Stamps of Approval at the Nexus of Media, Market and State." *SOJOURN: Journal of Social Issues in Southeast Asia* 31, no. 3: 826–79.

Jakkrit Sangkhamanee. 2017a. "An Assemblage of Thai Water Engineering: The Royal Irrigation Department's Museum for Heavy Engineering as a Parliament of Things." *Engaging Science, Technology and Society* 3: 276–91.

Jakkrit Sangkhamanee. 2017b. "Phromdaen khong withiwhithaya: Withiwithaya thi phromdaen" [The borders of research: Research as a border]. *Wannasan Sangkhomwitthaya Manutwitthaya* 35, no. 1: 3–22.

Jakkrit Sangkhamanee. 2018. "Infrastructure in the Making: The Chao Phraya Dam and the Dance of Agency." *TRaNS: Trans-Regional and -National Studies of Southeast Asia* 6, no. 1: 47–71.

Khao Sod. 2019. "*Khamchanot keukkak lan ta di hen lek khan nam mont 3 tua ja ja rak madeua dai lun nguat ni*" [Khamchanote Is Busy! Devotees See Lucky Numbers in Three Holy Bowls, in Tree Roots]. *Khao Sod,* November 2.

Jintamas Saksornchai. 2018. "Farang Marriage Training Clinic Coming to Isaan." *Khao Sod English,* June 29.

Johnson, Andrew Alan. 2007. "Authenticity, Tourism, and Self-Discovery in Thailand: Self-Creation and the Discerning Gaze of Trekkers and Old Hands." *SOJOURN: Journal of Social Issues in Southeast Asia* 22, no. 2: 153–78.

Johnson, Andrew Alan. 2012. "Naming Chaos: Accident, Precariousness, and the Spirits of Wildness in Urban Thai Spirit Cults." *American Ethnologist* 39, no. 4: 766–78.

Johnson, Andrew Alan. 2013. "Progress and Its Ruins: Ghosts, Migrants and the Uncanny in Thailand." *Cultural Anthropology* 28, no. 2: 299–319.

Johnson, Andrew Alan. 2014. *Ghosts of the New City: Spirits, Urbanity and the Ruins of Progress in Chiang Mai.* Honolulu: University of Hawai'i Press.

Johnson, Andrew Alan. 2016a. "Dreaming about the Neighbors: Magic, Orientalism and Entrepreneurship in the Consumption of Thai Religious Goods in Singapore." *South East Asia Research* 24, no. 4: 445–61.

Johnson, Andrew Alan. 2016b. "Ghost Mothers: Kinship Relations in Thai Spirit Cults." *Social Analysis* 60, no. 2: 82–96.

Johnson, Andrew Alan. 2017. "Land and Lordship: Royal Devotion, Spirit Cults, and the Geo-body." *Kyoto Review of Southeast Asian Studies* 22.

Johnson, Andrew Alan. 2018. "Deferral and Intimacy: Long-Distance Romance and Thai Migrants Abroad." *Anthropological Quarterly* 91, no. 1: 307–24.

Jory, Patrick. 2016. *Thailand's Theory of Monarchy: The Vessantara Jataka and the Idea of the Perfect Man.* Albany: State University of New York Press.

Kamala Tiyavanich. 2003. *The Buddha in the Jungle.* Seattle: University of Washington Press.

Kamat, Vinay R. 2008. "Reconsidering the Allure of the Culturally Distant in Therapy Seeking: A Case Study from Coastal Tanzania." *Medical Anthropology* 27, no. 2: 106–35.

Kapferer, Bruce. 2003. *Beyond Rationalism: Rethinking Magic, Witchcraft and Sorcery.* New York: Berghahn.

Keyes, C. F. 1977. "Millennialism, Theravada Buddhism, and Thai Society." *Journal of Asian Studies* 36, no. 2: 283–302. https://doi.org/10.2307/2053724.

Keyes, Charles F. 2014. *Finding Their Voice: Northeastern Villagers and the Thai State.* Chiang Mai: Silkworm.

Kirksey, Eben, and Stefan Helmreich. 2010. "The Emergence of Multispecies Ethnography." *Cultural Anthropology* 25, no. 4: 545–76.

Kirsch, A. Thomas. 1977. "Complexity in the Thai Religious System." *Journal of Asian Studies* 36, no. 2: 241–66.

Kusakabe, Kyoko, and Ruth Pearson. 2012. *Thailand's Hidden Workforce: Burmese Migrant Women Factory Workers.* Chicago: University of Chicago Press.

Kwon, June Hee. 2015. "The Work of Waiting: Love and Money in Korean Chinese Transnational Migration." *Cultural Anthropology* 30, no. 3: 477–500.

Langford, Jean. 2013. *Consoling Ghosts: Stories of Medicine and Mourning from Southeast Asians in Exile.* Minneapolis: University of Minnesota Press.

Larkin, Brian. 2013. "The Politics and Poetics of Infrastructure." *Annual Review of Anthropology* 42: 327–43.

Lebel, Louis, Po Garden, and Masao Imamura. 2005. "The Politics of Scale, Position and Place in the Governance of Water Resources in the Mekong Region." *Ecology and Society* 10, no. 2: 18.

Lefebvre, Henri. 2013. *Rhythmanalysis: Space, Time and Everyday Life.* London: Bloomsbury Academic.

Le Mare, Ann, Buapun Promphaking, and Jonathan Rigg. 2015. "Returning Home: The Middle-Income Trap and Gendered Norms in Thailand." *Journal of International Development* 27, no. 2: 285–306.

Lepselter, Susan. 2016. *The Resonance of Unseen Things: Poetics, Power, Captivity and UFOs in the American Uncanny.* Ann Arbor: University of Michigan Press.

Lindquist, Johan. 2010. "Labour Recruitment, Circuits of Capital, and Gendered Mobility: Reconceptualizing the Indonesian Migration Industry." *Pacific Affairs* 83, no. 1: 115–32.

Lovecraft, Howard Phillips. 1928. "The Call of Cthulhu." *Weird Tales,* February.

Lovecraft, Howard Phillips. 1933. "The Dreams in the Witch House". *Weird Tales,* July.

Lusthaus, Dan. 2002. *Buddhist Phenomenology: A Philosophical Investigation of Yogācāra Buddhism and the Ch'eng Wei-shih Lun.* London: Psychology Press.

Lyotard, Jean-François. 1992. *The Inhuman: Reflections on Time.* Stanford, CA: Stanford University Press.

Lyttleton, Chris. 2000. *Endangered Relations: Negotiating Sex and AIDS in Thailand.* Boca Raton, FL: CRC Press.

Malinowski, Bronislaw. (1935) 1978. *Coral Gardens and Their Magic: A Study of the Methods of Tilling the Soil and Agricultural Rites in the Trobriand Islands.* Mineola, NY: Dover.

Marks, Danny. 2014. "Laos Foots the Bill for Power-Hungry Bangkok." Mekong Commons, December 11. http://www.mekongcommons.org/laos-foots-bill-power -hungry-bangkok/.

Mauss, Marcel. (1950) 2001. *A General Theory of Magic.* New York: Routledge.

Mauss, Marcel. 2004. *Seasonal Variations of the Eskimo: A Study in Social Morphology.* New York: Routledge.

McCargo, Duncan. 2005. "Network Monarchy and Legitimacy Crises in Thailand." *Pacific Review* 18, no. 4: 499–519.

McDaniel, Justin. 2011. *The Lovelorn Ghost and the Magic Monk: Practicing Buddhism in Modern Thailand.* New York: Columbia University Press.

McDaniel, Justin. 2013. "This Hindu Holy Man Is a Thai Buddhist." *South East Asia Research* 21, no. 2: 191–209.

Middleton, Carl, Jelson Garcia, and Tira Floran. 2009. "Old and New Hydropower Players in the Mekong Region: Agendas and Strategies." In *Contested Waterscapes in the Mekong Region: Hydropower, Livelihoods and Governance,* edited by Francois Molle, 23–54. London: Routledge.

Miéville, China. 2010. *The City and the City.* New York: Del Rey.

Mills, Mary Beth. 1995. "Attack of the Widow Ghosts: Gender, Death, and Modernity in Northeast Thailand." In *Bewitching Women, Pious Men: Gender and Body Politics in Southeast Asia,* edited by Aihwa Ong and Michael Peletz, 244–73. Berkeley: University of California Press.

Mills, Mary Beth. 1999. *Thai Women in the Global Labor Force: Consuming Desires, Contested Selves.* New Brunswick, NJ: Rutgers University Press.

Miyazaki, Hirokazu. 2004. *The Method of Hope: Anthropology, Philosophy and Fijian Knowledge.* Stanford, CA: Stanford University Press.

Morris, Rosalind. 2000. *In the Place of Origins: Modernity and Its Mediums in Northern Thailand*. Durham, NC: Duke University Press.

MRC. 2011. "Prior Consultation Review Report." Vientiane: Mekong River Commission Secretariat.

Muecke, Marjorie. 1992. "Mother Sold Food, Daughter Sells Her Body: The Cultural Continuity of Prostitution." *Social Science and Medicine* 35, no. 7: 891–901.

Muehlebach, Andrea. 2013. "On Precariousness and the Ethical Imagination: The Year 2012 in Sociocultural Anthropology." *American Anthropologist* 115, no. 2: 297–311.

Mukhom Wongthes. 2003. *Intellectual Might and National Myth: A Forensic Investigation of the Ram Khamhaeng Controversy*. Bangkok: Sinlapawatthanatham.

Murdoch, J. B. 1974. "The 1901–1902 'Holy Man's Rebellion.'" *Journal of the Siam Society* 62, no. 1: 47–66.

Nail, Thomas. 2016. *Theory of the Border*. New York: Oxford University Press.

Naveh, Daniel, and Nurit Bird-David. 2014. "How Persons Become Things: Shifts in Hunter-Gatherer Nayaka Relational Epistemology and Ontology with the Adoption of Agriculture and Animal Husbandry." *Journal of the Royal Anthropological Institute* 20: 74–92.

Ngaosivat, Mayoury, and Pheuiphanh Ngaosyvathn. 1998. *Paths to Conflagration: Fifty Years of Diplomacy and Warfare in Laos, Thailand and Vietnam, 1778-1828*. Ithaca, NY: Southeast Asia Program.

Nonzee Nimibutr, dir. 1999. *Nang Nak* [film]. Tai Entertainment. 100 min.

O'Connell Davidson, Julia. 1998. *Prostitution, Power and Freedom*. Cambridge: Polity.

Ong, Aihwa. 1987. *Spirits of Resistance and Capitalist Discipline: Factory Women in Malaysia*. Albany: State University of New York Press.

Ong, Aihwa. 2017. "The Chinese Silk Road: Re-territorializing Politics in Southeast Asia." Keynote Presentation at International Convention of Asia Scholars 2017. Chiang Mai, Thailand.

Osborne, Milton. 2001. *Mekong: Turbulent Past, Uncertain Future*. New York: Grove.

Pasuk Phongpaichit and Chris Baker. 2004. *Thaksin: The Business of Politics in Thailand*. Copenhagen: NIAS Press.

Patcharin Lapanun. 2013. "Social Relations and Tensions in Transnational Marriage for Rural Women in Isan, Thailand." In *The Family in Flux in Southeast Asia: Institution, Ideology, Practice*, edited by Yoko Hayami, 483–503. Seattle: University of Washington Press.

Pattana Kitiarsa. 2005. "Beyond Syncretism: Hybridization of Popular Religion in Contemporary Thailand." *Journal of Southeast Asian Studies* 36, no. 3: 461–87.

Pattana Kitiarsa. 2006a. *In Defense of the Thai-Style Democracy*. Paper presented at the Asia Research Institute, National University of Singapore, October 12.

Pattana Kitiarsa. 2006b. *Khon klai ban: Kham hai kan khong khon thai nai Singapore* [Far from home: Words from Thai people in Singapore]. Bangkok: Association for Thai Labor in Singapore.

Pattana Kitiarsa. 2007. "*Muai Thai* Cinema and the Burdens of Thai Men." *South East Asia Research* 15, no. 3: 407–24. https://doi.org/10.5367/000000007782717722.

Pattana Kitiarsa. 2009. "The Lyrics of Laborious Life: Popular Music and the Reassertion of Migrant Manhood in Northeastern Thailand." *Inter-Asia Cultural Studies* 10, no. 3: 381–98. https://doi.org/10.1080/14649370902949374.

Pattana Kitiarsa. 2014. *The "Bare Life" of Thai Migrant Workmen in Singapore*. Seattle: University of Washington Press.

Pattana Kitiarsa. 2015. "From Red to Red: An Auto-ethnography of Economic and Political Transitions in a Northeastern Thai Village." In *Bangkok, May 2010: Perspectives on a Divided Thailand*, edited by Michael Montesano, Pavin Chachavalpongpun, and Aekapol Chongvilavan, 230–47. Cambridge: Cambridge University Press.

Pearson, Ruth, and Kyoko Kusakabe. 2012. *Thailand's Hidden Workforce: Burmese Migrant Women Factory Workers*. London: Zed.

Peleggi, Maruizio. 2002. *Lords of Things: The Fashioning of the Siamese Monarchy's Modern Image*. Honolulu: University of Hawai'i Press.

Povinelli, Elizabeth. 2002. *The Cunning of Recognition: Indigenous Alterities and the Making of Australian Multiculturalism*. Durham, NC: Duke University Press.

Povinelli, Elizabeth. 2016. *Geontologies: A Requiem to Late Liberalism*. Durham, NC: Duke University Press.

Pratchatai. 2017. "Academics, Students Accused of Violating Junta's Ban on Gatherings." *Pratchatai English*, August 15.

Raffles, Hugh. 2002. *In Amazonia: A Natural History*. Princeton, NJ: Princeton University Press.

Rainboth, Walter. 1996. *Fishes of the Cambodian Mekong*. Rome: Food and Agriculture Organization of the United Nations.

Redfield, Robert. 1956. *Peasant Society and Culture: An Anthropological Approach to Civilization*. Chicago: University of Chicago Press.

Rhum, Michael. 1994. *The Ancestral Lords: Gender, Descent and Spirits in a Northern Thai Village*. Monograph Series on Southeast Asia. De Kalb: Northern Illinois Center for Southeast Asian Studies.

Richter, Brian D., Sandra Postel, Carmen Revenga, Thayer Scudder, Bernhard Lehner, Allegra Churchill, and Morgan Chow. 2010. "Lost in Development's Shadow: The Downstream Human Consequences of Dams." *Water Alternatives* 3, no. 2: 14–42.

Robbins, Joel. 2013. "Beyond the Suffering Subject: Toward an Anthropology of the Good." *Journal of the Royal Anthropological Institute* 19, no. 3: 447–62.

Rod-Ari, Melody. 2009. "Thailand: The Symbolic Center of the Theravada Buddhist World." *Explorations* 9: 55–64.

Rojas, David. n.d. "Disjointed Times in Amazonia's 'Climate Smart' Landscapes." Unpublished manuscript.

Samak Kosem. 2017. "Khwampenchaykhop kap Kanrapru Chaidaen: Withiwithaya Wa Duai Phromdaen Satsana lae Chathiphan khong Muslim nai Khai Phu Li Phai" [Marginality and border perception: Religious and ethnic boundaries among the Muslims in a refugee camp]. *Wannasan Sangkhomwitthaya Manutwitthaya* 35, no. 1: 1233–45.

Saowanee Alexander. 2016. "Ubon Ratchathani Red Shirt Prisoners and the Holy Man Rebels: Some Notes on Inferences." *Isaan Record*, March 22.

Saowanee Alexander. 2019. "On Thailand's 2019 Election: The Isaan Red Shirts Have Returned, but Where Is Godot?" *The Isaan Record*, January 24. https://isaanrecord .com/2019/01/24/on-thailands-2019-election-the-isaan-red-shirts-have-returned/.

Sarasawadee Ongsakul. 1982. "Kan patirup kansueksa nai lanna: Kan sang ekaphap haeng chat" [Lanna studies: Building an image of the nation]. *Sueksasat* 10, no. 2: 31–38.

Sarasawadee Ongsakul. 2005. *A History of Lan Na*. Chiang Mai: Silkworm.

Schein, Louisa. 1997. "Gender and Internal Orientalism in China." *Modern China* 23, no. 1: 69–98.

Schwenkel, Christina. 2017. "Haunted Infrastructure: Religious Ruins and Urban Obstruction in Vietnam." *City and Society* 29, no. 3: 413–34. https://doi.org/10.1111/ciso.12142.

Scott, James. 2005. *Weapons of the Weak: Everyday Forms of Peasant Resistance*. New Haven, CT: Yale University Press.

Scott, James. 2009. *The Art of Not Being Governed: An Anarchist History of Upland Southeast Asia*. New Haven, CT: Yale University Press.

Shalardchai Ramitanon. 1984. *Phi Chao Nai*. Chiang Mai: Chiang Mai University.

Sharp, Lauriston, and Lucien Hanks. (1978) 2018. *Bang Chan: Social History of a Rural Community in Thailand*. Ithaca, NY: Cornell University Press

Shoemaker, Bruce, and William Robichaud. 2018. *Dead in the Water: Global Lessons from the World Bank's Model Hydropower Project in Laos*. Seattle: University of Washington Press.

Siegel, James. 1969. *The Rope of God*. Ann Arbor: University of Michigan Press. https:// doi.org/10.3998/mpub.9092.

Siegel, James. 2005. *Naming the Witch*. Stanford, CA: Stanford University Press.

Siegel, James. 2011. "The Hypnotist." In *Objects and Objections of Ethnography*, 97–115. New York: Fordham University Press.

Sinnott, Megan. 2004. *Toms and Dees: Female Same-Sex Sexuality and Transgender Identity in Thailand*. Honolulu: University of Hawai'i Press.

Sinnott, Megan. 2014. "Baby Ghosts: Child Spirits and Contemporary Conceptions of Childhood in Thailand." *TRaNS: Trans-Regional and -National Studies of Southeast Asia* 2, no. 2: 293–317.

Sit But-in. 1980. *The Worldview of Thai Lanna People* [Lokkathat chao Thai Lanna]. Chiang Mai: Book Center.

Skeldon, Ronald. 2012. "Going Round in Circles: Circular Migration, Poverty Alleviation and Marginality." *International Migration* 50, no. 3: 43–60.

Soimart Rungmanee. 2015. "Unravelling the Dynamics of Border Crossing and Rural-to-Rural-to-Urban Mobility in the Northeastern Thai-Lao Borderlands." *Population, Space and Place*, October 2. http://onlinelibrary.wiley.com/doi/10.1002/psp.1989/abstract.

Soimart Rungmanee. 2017. "Tamnaeng haeng thi: nai thana khreuang meu kan khao theung khomun bot sathon jak kanthamngan phak sanam nai pheun thi chaidaen Isan-Lao" [Positionality as research method: Reflections from field research along the Thai-Lao border]. *Wannasan Sangkhomwitthaya Manutwitthaya* 35, no. 1: 25–46.

Sopranzetti, Claudio. 2012. *Red Journeys: Inside the Thai Red-Shirt Movement*. Chiang Mai: Silkworm.

Sopranzetti, Claudio. 2014. "The Owners of the Map: Mobility and Mobilization among Motorcycle Taxi Drivers in Bangkok." *City and Society* 26, no. 1: 120–43.

Sopranzetti, Claudio. 2017a. "Framed by Freedom: Emancipation and Oppression in Post-Fordist Thailand." *Cultural Anthropology* 32, no. 1: 68–92. https://doi.org/10.14506/ca32.1.07.

Sopranzetti, Claudio. 2017b. *Owners of the Map: Motorcycle Taxi Drivers, Mobility, and Politics in Bangkok*. Berkeley: University of California Press.

Spiro, Melford. 1996. *Burmese Supernaturalism*. Expanded ed. New York: Transaction.

Sprenger, Guido. 2015. "Dimensions of Animism in Southeast Asia." In *Animism in Southeast Asia*, edited by Guido Sprenger and Kaj Århem, 31–54. New York: Routledge.

Sprenger, Guido. 2018. "Buddhism and Coffee: The Transformation of Locality and Non-human Personhood in Southern Laos." *SOJOURN: Journal of Social Issues in Southeast Asia* 33, no. 2: 265–90.

Sprenger, Guido, and Kaj Århem, eds. 2015. *Animism in Southest Asia*. New York: Routledge.

Ssorin-Chaikov, Nikolai. 2017. *Two Lenins: A Brief Anthropology of Time*. Chicago: HAU Books.

Steedly, Mary. 1993. *Hanging without a Rope: Narrative Experience in Colonial and Postcolonial Karoland*. Princeton, NJ: Princeton University Press.

Stengers, Isabelle. 2005. "The Cosmopolitical Proposal." In *Making Things Public: Atmospheres of Democracy*, edited by Bruno Latour and Peter Weibel, 994–1003. Cambridge, MA: MIT Press.

Stengs, Irene. 2009. *Worshipping the Great Moderniser: King Chulalongkorn, Patron Saint of the Thai Middle Class*. Singapore: NUS Press.

Stevenson, Lisa. 2014. *Life beside Itself: Imagining Care in the Canadian Arctic*. Berkeley: University of California Press.

Stoker, Bram. 1897. *Dracula*. London: Archibald Constable.

Stoler, Anne. 1996. "Race and the Education of Desire: Foucault's History of Sexuality and the Colonial Order of Things." *Journal of Asian Studies* 55, no. 4. https://doi.org/10.2307/2646611.

Strang, Veronica. 2016. "Reflecting Nature: Water Beings in History and Imagination." In *Waterworlds: Anthropology in Fluid Environments*, edited by Kirsten Hastrup and Frida Hastrup, 247–78. New York: Berghahn.

Strangio, Sebastian. 2015. "The Strongman of Siam." *Foreign Policy*, May 21.

Strate, Shane. 2015. *The Lost Territories: Thailand's History of National Humiliation*. Honolulu: University of Hawai'i Press.

Streckfuss, David. 2010. *Truth on Trial in Thailand: Defamation, Treason, and Lèse-Majesté*. New York: Routledge.

Sujane Kanparit. 2012. *Tam roi Jao Anouvong: Khli pom prawatisat Thai-Lao* [In the footsteps of King Anuvong: Untangling the knot of Thai-Lao history]. Bangkok: Sarakadee Press.

Sujit Wongthes. 2016. *Khon Thai ma jak nai* [Where do Thai people come from?]. Bangkok: Sinlapa Watthanatham.

Sulak Sivaraksa. 2009. *Rediscovering Spiritual Value: Alternatives to Consumerism from a Siamese Buddhist Perspective*. Bangkok: Sathirakoses-Nagapradipa Foundation.

Tambiah, Stanley J. 1970. *Buddhism and the Spirit Cults in Northeast Thailand*. Cambridge: Cambridge University Press.

Tambiah, Stanley. 1977. *World Conqueror and World Renouncer: A Study of Buddhism and Polity in Thailand against a Historical Background*. Cambridge: Cambridge University Press.

Tej Bunnag. 1987. *Kabot R.S. 121* [Uprisings of 1902]. Bangkok: Thai Watthanapanit.

Terwiel, Barend J. 2012. *Monks and Magic: Revisiting a Classic Study of Religious Ceremonies in Thailand*. Copenhagen: NIAS Press.

Thanet Aphornsuvan. 1998. "Slavery and Modernity: Freedom in the Making of Modern Siam." In *Asian Freedoms: The Idea of Freedom in East and Southeast Asia*, edited by David Kelly and Anthony Reid, 161–86. Cambridge Asia-Pacific Studies. Cambridge: Cambridge University Press.

Thompson, Eric C. 2015. "Circular Migration and Theatres of Accumulation." Paper presented at American Anthropological Association annual meeting, Denver, CO, November 15. https://aaa.confex.com/aaa/2015/webprogram/Paper45256.html.

Thompson, Eric C., Pattana Kitiarsa, and Suriya Smutkupt. 2016. "From Sex Tourist to Son-in-Law: Emergent Masculinities and Transient Subjectivities of *Farang* Men in Thailand." *Current Anthropology* 57, no. 1: 53–71.

Thongchai Winichakul. 1994. *Siam Mapped: A History of the Geo-body of a Nation*. Honolulu: University of Hawai'i Press.

Thongchai Winichakul. 2000. "The Others Within: Travel and the Ethno-spatial Differentiation of Siamese Subjects 1885–1910." In *Civility and Savagery: Social Identity in Tai States*, edited by Andrew Turton, 38–62. Surrey: Curzon.

Todorov, Tzvetan. 1975. *The Fantastic: A Structural Approach to a Literary Genre*. Ithaca, NY: Cornell University Press.

Toem Wiphakphotchanakit. 1987. *Prawattisat Isan* [History of Isan]. Bangkok: Thammasat Press.

Trandem, Ame. 2011. "Fatally Flawed Xayaburi EIA Fails to Uphold International Standards: A Preliminary Review of the Environmental Impact Assessment (EIA) Report for the Xayaburi Hydropower Dam on the Mekong River Mainstream in Northern Lao PDR." International Rivers, March 14. https://www.internationalrivers.org/sites/default/files/attached-files/preliminary_review_of_xayaburi_eia_14.03.11_final.pdf.

Tsing, Anna L. 2005. *Friction: An Ethnography of Global Connection*. Princeton, NJ: Princeton University Press.

Tsing, Anna L. 2015. *The Mushroom at the End of the World: On the Possibility of Life in Capitalist Ruins*. Princeton, NJ: Princeton University Press.

Tsing, Anna L., Heather Anne Swanson, Elaine Gan, and Nils Bubandt, eds. 2017. *Arts of Living on a Damaged Planet*. Minneapolis: University of Minnesota Press.

TWC2. 2017. "HOME and TWC2 Submit Joint Report on the Exploitation of Migrant Domestic Workers." Transient Workers Count Too, October 3. http://twc2.org.sg/2017/10/03/home-and-twc2-submit-joint-report-on-the-exploitation-of-migrant-domestic-workers/.

Tylor, E. B. (1871) 2016. *Primitive Culture*, vol. 1. Dover Books on Anthropology and Folklore. New York: Dover.

Ünaldi, Serhat. 2013. "Working Towards the Monarchy and Its Discontents: Anti-Royal Graffiti in Downtown Bangkok." *Journal of Contemporary Asia* 44, no. 3: 377–403.

Vail, Peter. 1998. "Violence and Control: Social and Cultural Dimensions of Muay Thai Boxing." PhD diss., Cornell University.

Van Esterik, Penny. 2000. *Materializing Thailand*. New York: Berg.

Visisya Pinthongvijayakul. 2015. "Performing the Isan Subject: Spirit Mediums and Ritual Embodiment in a Transitional Agrarian Society." PhD diss., Australia National University.

Visisya Pinthongvijayakul. 2018. "Personhood and Political Subjectivity through Ritual Enactment in Isan (Northeast Thailand)." *Journal of Southeast Asian Studies* 49, no. 1: 63–83.

Viveiros de Castro, Eduardo. 2015. *The Relative Native: Essays on Indigenous Conceptual Worlds*. Translated by Martin Holbraad, David Rodgers, and Julia Sauma. HAU Special Collections in Ethnographic Theory. Chicago: University of Chicago Press.

Wakin, Eric. 1998. *Anthropology Goes to War: Professional Ethics and Counterinsurgency in Thailand*. Madison: University of Wisconsin Center for Southeast Asian Studies.

Walker, Andrew. 2000. "Regional Trade in Northwestern Laos: An Initial Assessment of the Economic Quadrangle." In *Where China Meets Southeast Asia*, 122–44. New York: Palgrave Macmillan.

Walker, Andrew. 2008. "Andrew Walker: Sufficiency Economy, Sufficiency Democracy, and Rural Constitution." *Pratchatai*, August 9. https://prachatai.com/english/node/746.

Walker, Andrew. 2011. "Thailand's Latest Lèse-Majesté Disgrace." *New Mandala*, November 23. http://www.newmandala.org/thailands-latest-lese-majeste-disgrace/.

Walker, Andrew. 2014. *Thailand's Political Peasants: Power in the Modern Rural Economy*. Madison: University of Wisconsin Press.

Wassana Nanuam. 2009. *Lap Luang Phrang*. Bangkok: Post Books.

Whitington, Jerome. 2018. *Anthropogenic Rivers: The Production of Uncertainty in Lao Hydropower*. Ithaca, NY: Cornell University Press.

Wiener, Margaret. 1995. *Visible and Invisible Realms: Power, Magic and Colonial Conquest in Bali*. Chicago: University of Chicago Press.

Willerslev, Rane. 2007. *Soul Hunters: Hunting, Animism, and Personhood among the Siberian Yukaghirs*. Berkeley: University of California Press.

Willerslev, Rane. 2012. "Laughing at the Spirits in North Siberia: Is Animism Being Taken Too Seriously?" *E-flux* 36. https://www.e-flux.com/journal/36/61261/laughing-at-the-spirits-in-north-siberia-is-animism-being-taken-too-seriously/.

Wilson, Ara. 2004. *The Intimate Economies of Bangkok: Tomboys, Tycoons and Avon Ladies in the Global City*. Berkeley: University of California Press.

Wolters, O. W. 1999. *History, Culture and Religion in Southeast Asian Perspectives*. Ithaca, NY: Cornell Southeast Asia Program Press.

Xu Zheng, dir. 2012. *Lost in Thailand* [film]. Beijing Enlight Pictures. 105 minutes.

Yos Santasombat. 2012. *The River of Life: Changing Ecosystems of the Mekong Region*. Chiang Mai: Silkworm.

Zhou Daguan. 2007. *A Record of Cambodia: Its Land and Its People*. Translated by Peter Harris. Seattle: University of Washington Press.

foreigners, 6, 9–11, 17–18, 67, 73, 96, 105–9, 116–24, 127, 156, 164

Freud, 9, 13, 163–64

gall bladder cancer. *See* fish: gall bladder flukes

Geertz, Clifford, 32

gender, 56–57, 67, 108–9, 111, 117–18, 155, 175n3

globalization, 40, 48, 50

Gray, Christine, 132, 139

Greater Mekong Subregion, 2

Haraway, Donna, 18

Harman, Graham, 16–19

hauntology, 19, 160

Heidegger, Martin, 2, 7, 17, 143; and dwelling, 7, 101–3, 117, 129, 162; and techné, 7

hermit 65, 140, 165

Herzfeld, Michael, 34, 59–60; and crypto-colonialism, 34

hierarchy, 30, 37, 119–20, 136, 139, 141

Holy Man revolts, 26, 35–37, 67, 173n10. *See also* revolution: Phu Mi Bun

hydropower, 1, 5, 7, 8, 11, 24, 27, 39–42, 44–48, 98–103, 158; collapse of, 39; as provider of electricity, 44, 49–51; and environmental collapse, 44, 78, 94, 100; Jinghong, 11, 24, 42, 98–103; Sayaburi, 24, 45–49, 94, 156, 174n14

impermanence, 127–29

infrastructure, 2, 10, 23, 27, 165; houses, 120

inhuman, 7, 9, 28, 145, 167

Jakkrit Sangkhamanee, 20, 41, 68, 84

kinship, 11, 25, 35, 65–66, 118–19, 122, 128, 151

kingship, 26, 31, 33, 38–39, 59–60, 65, 94, 131–33, 138–42, 160; as Buddhas, 132; and democracy, 49, 57–66, 95; potency of kings, 131; and sufficiency, 94

landscape, 141; of the river, 74–81, 155, 160, 167

local knowledge, 89, 93–98, 172n13

logging, 47, 60

lordship, 32, 131–33, 140–44, 160

lottery 3, 105, 124–27, 156, 163

Lovecraft, H. P., 16–19, 163, 172n15

magic, 12, 93, 97, 105

materiality, 2, 8–9, 71–98, 159, 167; river features (*see* landscape)

maybe, 10, 13–14, 107, 124, 161

Mekong giant catfish. *See* fish: beuk; *Pangasianodon gigas*

Mekong River Commission, 46, 98

migration, 6, 20–21, 25, 27, 104–30, 158–59; circular migration 116, 120–21; marriage migration, 119–24; and sex work, 60, 108–9, 116–19

military, 23, 52–54, 57, 65, 145; junta, 22, 49, 57, 62, 65, 95

mimesis, 139

mining, 49, 65, 77, 131

monarchy. *See* kingship

monsoon. *See* floods

naga, 7–9, 13, 15, 18, 23, 26, 28–31, 41, 72, 77, 84, 100, 109, 131–32, 140, 144–45, 149–50, 152–54, 158, 160–61, 164–67; spitting fireballs, 72, 100–1, 153; Lord of Nagas, 84

nationalism, 129, 173n6, 174n16

nature, 71, 102–3

networks, 14

nongovernmental organizations (NGOs), 47–49, 58

nonhuman, 8, 9, 11, 14, 18, 28, 71, 103, 135, 145, 165

numina, 13–14

occult, 5, 12, 15, 166; occult economies, 12, 19

ontology, 13–16, 18–19, 36, 135, 141–44, 150–54, 167–68, 171n3

opacity, 11, 13–14, 20, 28, 50, 55, 67–68, 107, 162. *See also* Bubandt, Nils
orientalism, 12, 67

Pangasianodon gigas (Mekong giant catfish), 44, 70, 74–75, 83–84,
phenomenology, 14–15, 18, 172n10
Phu Mi Bun. *See* revolution: Phu Mi Bun
police, 60–62, 96
politics. *See* democracy; kingship; Red Shirts
potency, 6, 7, 9–10, 19, 28, 57, 70, 87, 122–124, 130–131, 143, 146, 164
power, 10, 19, 57–60, 141; barami 10, 31, 58–60. *See also*: kingship; lordship
precarity, 12, 51, 77, 104, 117
psychoanalysis, 9, 71, 124, 127

race, 12, 17, 37–38, 51, 67, 109, 151, 176n13, 177n23
rapids, 44, 72–75, 155
Red Shirts, 58–60, 64, 168; and Yellow Shirts, 22, 58, 59, 65
religion, 145. *See also* animism; Buddhism
revolution, 26; Phu Mi Bun, 26, 35–37, 67, 138, 173n10, 173n12. *See also* communism; Red Shirts

Scott, James, 36, 42
sex work. *See* migration
Siegel, James, 19, 68, 166, 168
Special Economic Zones, 6, 14, 117; Economic Quadrangle, 42–44; Greater Mekong Subregion, 2
spirits, 3, 7, 11–12, 142–60, 164, 172n9; and ghosts, 13, 15, 73, 125–27, 142–43, 150,

174nn2–3; jao, 130–33, 136–38, 143, 152, 156–60; jao don, 3–4, 6, 8–9, 161–69; Lord of the Fish, 69–70, 85, 109, 160; takhian tree, 3, 124–27, 163, 168. *See also* naga
Sprenger, Guido, 6, 136, 138, 142, 166

Tambiah, Stanley, 131, 140, 144–46, 151–53, 177n5
technology, 90, 92–93. *See also* fishing; Heidegger, Martin
Thai-ness, 38, 68
Thaksin Shinawatra, 48–49, 58–59, 62, 64, 114, 173n4
Thongchai Winichakul, 31, 37–38
time, 70, 98–103, 117
Todorov, Tzvetan, 16–19, 163
tourism, 22, 23, 42, 44, 50, 52, 54, 63, 64, 67, 74, 75, 113, 114, 117–121, 176n16
transformation, 115–18
Tsing, Anna, 27, 71, 86, 89, 97, 167, 173n1

unassimilable, 19, 166
uncanny, 17, 144, 163–64
uncertainty, 8, 14, 84–90, 111–13, 117, 130, 142–43, 159
unconscious, 9, 127, 155, 161, 163
utopia, 6, 43, 67

Vientiane, 21, 33–37, 67–68
violence, 55, 73, 96, 110, 122, 139

waiting, 78, 121
weird, 14–18, 163
Whitington, Jerome, 8, 40–41, 48, 167

Yellow Shirts. *See* Red Shirts